11 **Decade of Crisis**

1938   1939   1940

Newsweek Books New York

Editor Roger Morgan

1940

1941

1941

1942

Milestones of History

11 Decade of Crisis

1942   1942   1944   1945

ISBN: Clothbound edition   o 88225 078 7
        Deluxe edition   o 88225 079 5
Library of Congress Catalog Card No. 73 86877

© George Weidenfeld and Nicolson Ltd, 1970 and 1975
First published 1970. Revised and expanded edition 1975

Printed and bound in Italy
by Arnoldo Mondadori Editore—Verona

1945   1945   1946   1947

1948

1948

1948

1949

Contents

Introduction

During the decade from the late 1930s to the late 1940s, the political shape of the world changed more profoundly than in any other period this century. In 1938 the political leaders of Britain, France, Germany and Italy met at the Munich Conference to settle the fate of Czechoslovakia—and indirectly the fate of the world—without taking any account of the policies of the United States and the Soviet Union. By 1949, London, Paris, Berlin and Rome were reduced virtually to impotence—Berlin, in fact, to rubble—while Washington and Moscow held the fate of the world in their hands. The proud Third Reich of Hitler and the new Roman Empire of Mussolini had both vanished, and the European powers who had sought to appease them—France and even Britain—had lost much of their prewar power.

By 1949 the balance of power had not only shifted in such a way that Europe was dwarfed by the two superpowers. In the colonial empires of the European powers, the war had also stimulated forces of nationalism so strong that European rule could never be reestablished there. The Japanese conquest of Singapore in 1942 was only part of a larger process by which the foundations of British, French and Dutch rule in Asia were shattered. After 1945 Britain had no choice but to grant independence to India; Dutch rule over Indonesia was also, after a struggle, abandoned; and even though France was still fighting in 1949 to reestablish French power over Indochina, independence of this region, too, was not to be long delayed. The forces of nationalism made themselves felt, also, in areas that had not been directly under European colonial rule, including the Middle East.

One reason why the political effects of World War II were so far-reaching was, of course, that the war itself was literally worldwide in terms of actual armed combat. Unlike the fighting in 1914–18, which had been essentially limited to Europe and the Middle East, the military conflicts that raged in 1939–45 included among their theaters almost every continent of the globe. The conflicts in the Far East, for instance—which began with Japan in virtual control of the Chinese mainland and finished with Japan eclipsed, Russian power enhanced and the Communists well placed to win the Chinese Civil War—had no precedent in World War I.

If the war was universal it was also a total war, in the sense that the "home front" was an integral part of the battlefield. The frightful destruction of European and Asian cities and the appalling slaughter of civilians formed part of this story; so too did the mobilization of the working populations of the world —men, women and children—for war production.

The impact of the war on the structures of society was correspondingly profound: in order to inspire their peoples with the will to victory, the political leaders of the world promised better conditions in the years ahead, and the results of these wartime promises and expectations can be seen in such diverse manifestations as the "welfare state" in Britain, votes for women in France and the reforming legislation of President Harry S Truman.

The war years not only accelerated social change: they also led to significant advances in science and technology. As in earlier periods of history, the demands of war led to scientific developments of which some at least had a contribution to make in peace. The development of the jet engine, of radar and of atomic energy would have been very much slower without the pressures imposed by the war and the consequent governmental decisions to allocate funds for research.

Perhaps the idea that best summarizes the impact of World War II on society is what Adlai Stevenson was later to call "the revolution of rising expectations." Whereas the bitter Depression years of the 1930s had left men with a sense that those who had a job—any kind of job—were the lucky ones, the experiences of the war years insured that their expectations in the postwar world would be higher. Unemployment had disappeared during the war: people counted on their governments to maintain full employment once it was over. Industrial production during the war had reached record levels in aid of the military effort: it was expected that production for civilian purposes would be just as high when peace came. During the war, the public authorities in many countries assumed responsibility for guaranteeing adequate rations of food, health services and social security payments to those in need: it was expected that the "welfare state," in one form or another, would continue to provide these benefits in peacetime. During the war, many millions of people became aware of the problems of foreign countries through traveling abroad on war service (14.5 million Americans served in the armed forces, compared with under 5 million in World War 1): they could not withdraw into an isolationist mentality when the war was over. The "United Nations" was a fair description of the wartime alliance—the "Grand Alliance," as Churchill also called it—which was ultimately victorious: people throughout the world expected—wrongly, in the event—that this unity would be maintained in peacetime by the United Nations Organization. Again, people whose horizons had been broadened by the war demanded new ideas and new experiences in every aspect of life, whether in politics, social relationships or entertainment. World War ii, more than any war in history, acted as the catalyst and stimulator of innovation and change.

Although such technical innovations as jet travel and the widespread availability of television were probably the developments that most affected men's everyday lives, the most far-reaching effect of World War ii was probably the change wrought in the world balance of power. The Czechoslovak crisis of 1938, as we have noted, was an episode in the process of power politics among a group of European nations; the next major crisis in Czechoslovakia, the Communist takeover in 1948, was a move in an essentially "bipolar" contest between two powers centered outside Europe, the United States and the Soviet Union.

The old balance or power had been destroyed and replaced by a new one, but in the meanwhile, in China, the forces were gaining strength that were to set up the Chinese People's Republic in 1949 and then to swing the global balance once more in a new direction.

ROGER MORGAN

IM BEDARFSFALLE WERDEN WIR ALLE SOLDATEN

Appeasement at Munich 1938

Czechoslovakia had been established by the Treaty of Versailles as a French ally, a state of affairs repugnant to Adolf Hitler, who seized on discontent among German-speaking Czechs to demand annexation of the Czech territory in which they lived. Hitler seemed ready to go to war over the issue, and Europeans debated whether war was inevitable or whether granting him such grievances as seemed just might "appease" him. The final decision fell on Britain's Prime Minister, Neville Chamberlain. An authority on the domestic economy, not foreign affairs, Chamberlain nonetheless knew that he could count on no help either from the Commonwealth or the United States in the event of war. At a meeting in Munich with Hitler, Chamberlain agreed to the dismemberment of Czechoslovakia and this act of appeasement brought not the "peace with honor" he sought but the beginnings of history's most terrible war.

The Munich Agreement, signed on September 30, 1938, by the leaders of Germany, Britain, France and Italy, handed over to Germany a large part of the territory of Czechoslovakia, up to then an independent state. This was the crowning moment of "appeasement," the policy by which Britain and France tried to satisfy the demands of the German dictator Adolf Hitler; it was also the moment when this policy no longer seemed a means to peace in Europe, but rather an encouragement to Hitler to make further demands in a way that could only end in war.

In order to understand how the Munich crisis marked the last hope of "appeasing" Hitler, and why it failed to do so, it is necessary to look both at Czechoslovakia's problems after 1918 and at Hitler's foreign policy since 1933.

The new state of Czechoslovakia, set up in 1918 by the victorious Allies of World War I, had inherited the most valuable industrial areas of the Austro-Hungarian Empire. In addition to its economic wealth the Czechoslovak Republic was led by two outstanding statesmen, Thomas Masaryk and Eduard Beneš. However, the Republic had one fundamental weakness—mixed racial composition. In a population of under fifteen million, a million were Hungarians who clamored for reunion with Hungary, and nearly three-and-a-half million were German-speaking, the inhabitants of the area called the Sudetenland. This part of the country, located around the western fringe of Czechoslovakia, commanded the gateways to the capital Prague, situated in the center of Bohemia, the country's western province. Any foreign power to take control of the Sudetenland would have a stranglehold on the whole of Czechoslovakia.

Although the Sudetenland had never been part of Germany, there was some demand from the Sudeten Germans in the 1920s to be allowed to join the German Reich, and German governments had lent a sympathetic ear. However, the strength of the demand should not be exaggerated; unlike the population of Austria, who felt a burning desire to join the German Reich in 1918–19 and was only restrained by the ban imposed by France and her allies, the Sudeten Germans felt some degree of loyalty to the Czechoslovak state of which they were citizens. As long as the economic prosperity of the 1920s lasted, the discontent of the Sudeten Germans could be kept within manageable limits. The Sudeten Germans had always had at least one representative in the cabinet of Czechoslovakia, and the idea of changing their allegiance from Prague to Berlin was, for most of them, only a passing fancy. In 1919 Herbert Henry Asquith, the former British Prime Minister, had said ". . . some of the new boundaries in Europe must be regarded as provisional. There must be an opportunity for deliberate review and revision." However, the statesmen of Europe normally saw such arguments as applying to the new frontier between Germany and Poland, the subject of constant complaints by every German government from 1919 onward, and not to Germany's frontier with Czechoslovakia.

The Great Depression of the early 1930s changed the picture. As the prosperity of the Sudetenland ebbed and unemployment rose, grievances that had been bearable ceased to be so. The Sudeten Germans now found it intolerable that Czechs should hold jobs as civil servants or village postmasters in the Sudetenland, or that the German language should not be given equal status with Czech. Their grievances were voiced with increasing bitterness by the Sudeten German Nationalist Party, led by Konrad Henlein.

By leaving more than six million unemployed in Germany, the Great Depression had also brought to power Adolf Hitler, who was to lend

A Czech woman weeping in despair while forced to salute German troops crossing the frontier. At Munich Britain and France agreed to sacrifice Czechoslovakia for the sake of world peace.

Opposite A German language poster, probably issued by the Czech government, asserting Czechoslovakia's independence: *We'll all become soldiers if necessary.*

The partitioning of Czechoslovakia, 1938

Territory ceded to Germany at Munich, September 30, 1938 ○

Territory given to Hungary by Germany and Italy at Vienna, October 2, 1938 ○

Territory seized by Poland in September, 1938, and formally annexed on November 1, 1938 ◑

Occupied by Hungary on March 14, 1939 ◔

GERMANY

SUDETENLAND

Asch
Eger
Prague

SILESIA

BOHEMIA

MORAVIA
Brno

Teschen
Cracow

POLAND

SLOVAKIA

RUTHENIA
(Carpatho-Ukraine)

BAVARIA

Danube River   Vienna

Bratislava

RUMANIA

AUSTRIA

HUNGARY

Budapest

Protest demonstration in Prague against the Munich Agreement at the end of September, 1938. The agreement ceded the Sudetenland to Germany and recognized the territorial claims of Poland and Hungary.

achievement of these aims. He withdrew Germany from the League of Nations and its disarmament conference in 1933, announced a vast program of rearmament in 1935, and in 1936 marched his army into the demilitarized Rhineland Zone, to the dismay of France. He then sent military help to General Francisco Franco, the right-wing general who had provoked the Spanish Civil War by rebelling against the Spanish government, and in March, 1938, he brought the independent state of Austria into the German Reich by a mixture of armed threats, skillful diplomatic exploitation of divisions between his opponents and emphasis on the fact that the great majority of Austria's six million inhabitants wished for unity with Germany.

The union with Austria—the so-called *Anschluss*—extended Germany's power to the southern as well as the northern and western flanks of Czechoslovakia. This gave Hitler new opportunities to help and encourage Henlein's extremist forces in the Sudetenland, and on April 24 Henlein put forward demands that were rejected by the Prague government. In May, 1938, after violent incidents during a local election campaign in the Sudetenland, accompanied by rumors that Germany was moving troops toward the frontier, the Czechoslovak government mobilized its army and received declarations of support from its foreign allies, France and Russia. The agitation in the Sudetenland then subsided, and Henlein, who had been consulting with Hitler in Berlin, was ordered to return to Czechoslovakia and continue pressing his demands on the Prague government. Hitler also decided, before the end of May, that he would take action against Czechoslovakia by autumn.

The simmering situation in the Sudetenland, and Hitler's evident determination to exploit it, meant the other governments of Europe were faced with the decision of how far they would go in resisting Hitler's designs. Czechoslovakia's main ally was France, who had backed her against Germany since 1918, and was bound by treaty to help her in case of attack. More recently, in 1935, Czechoslovakia had signed a similar treaty with the Soviet Union, but in order to prevent a situation of one-sided dependence on Soviet protection (for reasons that were to become clearer after 1945), the Czech government had insisted that Soviet military support would only be called in if help from France were already on the way. A great deal thus depended on Paris, but the French Republic in 1938 was in a state of internal weakness and strife, with weak governments succeeding each other every few months, and it was clear that France would only come to the help of Czechoslovakia if Britain did.

The critical element in the whole situation was therefore the attitude Britain would adopt, and the eyes of Europe turned toward her Prime Minister, Neville Chamberlain. The seventy-year-old statesman had never concerned himself much with foreign affairs. As Chancellor of the Exchequer in the early 1930s, he had concentrated on trying to revive the British economy after the

Henlein powerful support in detaching the Sudetenland from the rule of Prague. When Hitler became Chancellor of Germany in January, 1933, the world could have known, had it chosen, how he saw the long-term aims of his foreign policy. In his book *Mein Kampf* (*My Struggle*), published in 1924, Hitler had declared that his aim was to destroy the Versailles Treaty imposed on Germany in 1919 ("using force, if necessary"), to unite all the German race in one *Reich*, liberating the German minorities abroad from Polish or Czech rule, and to conquer "living space" (*Lebensraum*) for Germany in the east by overrunning Soviet Russia which, he claimed, was "ready to collapse."

In the years after 1933, encouraged by weakness and division among the states that might have opposed him, Hitler took several steps toward the

German troops entering Czech territory are welcomed by the inhabitants.

Great Depression, and his earlier experience had been in the municipal politics of Birmingham. Chamberlain knew little of European problems and had no confidence in either the French or the Russians, but he could see that the pacification or appeasement of Europe was essential if a new European war was to be avoided. He also realized that, as British Prime Minister, he must take the initiative. "Appeasement," in Chamberlain's mind, meant the removal of the grievances that might lead to war. In itself it was a noble aim, and it was only when Chamberlain attempted to appease the unappeasable Hitler that "appeasement" fell into disrepute.

Chamberlain, like all British—and French— political leaders of his generation was haunted by the memory of World War I, and was prepared to go to considerable lengths to avoid any such catastrophe occurring again. He was also deeply influenced by British public opinion which appeared to be clearly against war (the evidence for this had been provided by several opinion polls and election results) and by the conviction that Germany had suffered a degree of injustice after 1918. The idea that Germany's eastern frontiers were unjust, and should be revised, had been expressed by British statesmen ever since Asquith's remark in 1919; and although Britain had pledged herself in the 1920s to insure that Germany's western frontier remained unchanged, she had firmly refused to recognize Germany's eastern frontier as final in the same way; and in the 1930s, despite the concern of successive British governments at the rising strength of Hitler, the statesmen remained hopeful that the removal of Germany's legitimate grievances, as they seemed to be, would reconcile Europe and remove the danger of war.

In any case, Chamberlain knew that Britain could not count on overseas support for a policy of resistance to Hitler. The Commonwealth governments—particularly that of Australia, a country that had suffered heavy losses in Europe during World War I—warned that they would not be drawn into a European war again. As for the the United States, there was clear evidence of the strength of isolationism. As international tension over Czechoslovakia rose, the American Ambassador to Paris, William Bullitt, publicly mentioned the possibility of the United States adding her strength to the Anglo-French side in any new European war, but this idea was promptly and firmly disavowed by President Roosevelt.

These were the pressures that made Chamberlain approach the German-Czechoslovak conflict in the spirit of a conciliator, hoping to get both sides to accept a compromise solution. His first step was to press Czechoslovakia to accept an unofficial British mediator, an elderly ex-minister, Lord Runciman, who was sent to survey the state of affairs in the Sudetenland in August. Runciman in fact sided with Henlein and the Sudeten Germans, and urged the Czechoslovak leader Beneš to accept a number of their demands on such questions as their right to civil service positions and the status of the German language.

By early September Beneš had gone a long way toward accepting Henlein's demands—he resisted only the demand that Czechoslovakia align her foreign policy with Germany's—but this unexpectedly conciliatory attitude disconcerted Henlein, who had in fact counted on Beneš rejecting his demands thus preparing the way for a total secession by the Sudetenland. Henlein therefore broke off his talks with the Czech government on September 9, and the stage was set for the next phase of the crisis.

Events now developed quickly. Hitler, after ordering his armed forces to be ready to invade Czechoslovakia by the end of September—an order that made some of his generals consider using the tense situation to remove him from power and certify him as insane—made a violent speech in Nuremberg on September 12. He accused the Czech government of inflicting intolerable oppression on the Sudeten German minority, and issued a warning that Germany would soon be forced to intervene. Words were quickly followed by action. On September 13–14, Henlein, operating from Berlin, gave orders for a general uprising of the Sudeten Germans against the Czech government. The uprising was easily suppressed by the government and a state of emergency declared in the Sudeten areas.

The next move was made by Chamberlain, who sent the following telegram to Hitler: "In view of increasingly critical situation, I propose to come over at once to see you with view to trying to find peaceful solution." Hitler accepted the proposal, and Chamberlain flew off to meet him in his mountain retreat at Berchtesgaden, near the German-Austrian border, on September 15. The Sudeten Germans were encouraged by Chamberlain's move to step up their demands for union with the Reich; the Czech government was dismayed and despondent; and the British press joyfully welcomed the hope of a compromise that would save the peace.

Against this background, Neville Chamberlain and his close adviser, Sir Horace Wilson, set off to meet Hitler, in the words of the British diplomat and writer, Harold Nicolson, "with the bright faithfulness of two curates entering a pub for the first time." They confronted a Hitler who insisted on Germany's right to annex the Sudetenland in the name of the principle of national self-determination, and who totally rejected Chamberlain's plea that he issue an appeal for moderation by both sides in the dispute. The talk ended with Chamberlain accepting the principle of self-determination for the Sudetenland, but adding that he must consult the British cabinet about the means of execution.

Chamberlain then consulted not only the British cabinet but also the French government, with the result that Britain and France put strong pressure on Czechoslovakia to accept a settlement in which Germany would take over large parts of the Sudetenland, and then would join with Britain and France in guaranteeing Czechoslovakia's new frontiers.

The position of Czechoslovakia seemed hopeless —especially as her neighbors Poland and Hungary made it clear that they would join Germany in demanding territory from her—and the Czech government had no choice but to give way to French and British pressure. Chamberlain returned to Germany on September 22; this time he met Hitler in Bad Godesberg on the Rhine, where the violent behavior of the German dictator came as a great shock to him. Hitler, raging and storming, now insisted that the Sudetenland be handed over by October 1, "free of Czechs." The Czech minority was to leave quickly and each person was to take only one suitcaseful of belongings. Hitler also insisted that a plebiscite be held in large areas of Czechoslovakia, to decide whether these areas, with a considerable German population, should join Germany. (After the way Hitler had used plebiscites in Germany and Austria even Chamberlain realized the dangers of letting the Nazis employ this device in Czechoslovakia too.) The Godesberg meeting ended with Hitler insisting on marching into the Sudetenland within a few days, and also strongly backing the claims of Hungary and Poland to Czechoslovak territory.

After returning to London, Chamberlain met the French Prime Minister and Foreign Minister Edouard Daladier and Georges Bonnet. The British and French governments agreed that even though they would press Czechoslovakia to give Hitler most of what he wanted, they would warn him that he must not take it by too obvious a display of force, and that he must agree to an international conference to settle the matter.

Hitler, however, was by now determined to make

Below right One of the last pictures of Hitler in civilian clothes. Architect of the Czechoslovak crisis, the German leader followed up the concessions of Munich by annexing the remainder of Czechoslovakia.

Prior to the agreement at Munich. Left to right: British Ambassador Henderson, Göring, Chamberlain, Mussolini, Dolmetscher, Hitler, Daladier. The Czech representatives were kept outside the conference room to hear their country's fate.

it clear to the world that he was imposing his will on Czechoslovakia by the threat of superior force, as well as meeting the just claim of the Sudeten Germans to self-determination. On the evening of September 26 he spoke at a mass rally of Nazi supporters in the Sport Palast stadium in Berlin, accusing Beneš in savage terms of terrorizing the Sudeten minority and acting as a "warmonger" in resisting Germany's demands. By October 1, Hitler proclaimed, Beneš must hand the Sudetenland over to Germany. He repeated a promise he had given Chamberlain, that after this he would make no further territorial claims, and in particular would guarantee not to molest the Czechoslovak state within its new diminished frontiers.

Later that night, after the world had heard Hitler's threats on the radio, the British Foreign Office put out a statement that if Hitler insisted on taking over the Sudetenland by military attack rather than peaceful negotiation, he must face the likelihood of war with France, Britain and the Soviet Union. It now seemed that Hitler had gone too far, as all the main governments of Europe issued warnings that he would be opposed unless he acted, as Chamberlain put it, "by discussion and not by force."

There were in fact many reasons why Britain, France and the Soviet Union found it almost impossible to cooperate in opposing Hitler's plans: there was a long history of mistrust between Soviet Russia and the Western powers, and they had not worked out any plans for coordinated military action against Germany.

But in Britain, as in France, war seemed a distinct possibility. The Royal Navy was mobilized, a state of emergency was declared, school children were evacuated from London, and trenches intended as emergency air-raid shelters were dug in Hyde Park. Chamberlain's broadcast on the evening of September 27 sounded the mingled notes of despair and a faint hope that war might still be averted:

How horrible, fantastic, incredible it is that we should be digging trenches and trying on gas masks here because of a quarrel in a faraway country between people of whom we know nothing.

Chamberlain went on to stress that the dispute had already been "settled in principle"; he suggested that only the method of transferring the Sudetenland to Germany was now at stake, and declared himself willing to go to Germany a third time.

The next day Chamberlain followed up this hint by proposing an international conference, in which Britain, Germany, France, Italy and Czechoslovakia would jointly decide the method of transferring the Sudetenland. Even when Hitler insisted that the conference be limited to the four powers—Czechoslovakia not being consulted on her own fate—Chamberlain still agreed to attend, and thus a meeting was arranged in Munich on September 29.

Backed by the near-hysterical support of

British and French public opinion and parliaments, Chamberlain and Daladier set off for Munich. The conference resulted, in the early hours of September 30, in an agreement that gave Hitler almost all he wanted. German troops were to march into the Sudetenland at the beginning of October, plebiscites would be held in areas under dispute, and Germany and Italy would only be expected to guarantee the frontiers of Czechoslovakia *after* the territorial claims of Poland and Hungary had been met.

By this outright sacrifice of Czechoslovakia, whose representatives at Munich waited outside the conference-room to hear their country's fate, Chamberlain and Daladier thought they had "appeased" Hitler. Chamberlain flew back to England with a declaration signed by Hitler and himself, pledging their two countries never to go to war again, and told a delirious crowd in Downing Street that he had brought back "peace with honor." It did not take long for events to show that this had been a vain hope, and that Chamberlain's attempt to prevent war by giving way to Hitler's demands had been an attempt to appease the unappeasable.   ROGER MORGAN

Germany brings peace to the world, a pro-Nazi cartoon, 1936.

When Hitler finally shows his hand

Spain

The Munich Conference forced Britain and France to concentrate on Central European affairs and to reinterpret the future in the light of the threat posed by Hitler. Germany became the main subject of European political interest.

Between 1936 and 1938, European political interest had focused almost exclusively on the Spanish Civil War. The official postures European powers adopted toward the Spanish conflict symbolize the attitudes that exploded into World War II: Britain and France banned supplies to the legally elected Second Republic while Hitler and Mussolini boldly intervened on the side of a fellow fascist, the insurgent Francisco Franco. Russia, the only major power to intervene officially on the side of the Spanish government, seemed more concerned with the destruction of anarchists and Trotskyites than with winning the war.

This pattern of international relations after 1936 merely etched earlier patterns more clearly as the fascist states sought to expand their power. In 1935, for example, Mussolini had attacked Ethiopia. The League of Nations was prevented from issuing effective sanctions against Italy by the French, who feared another major European catastrophe if they interfered. These fears had soon spread to the British and resulted in the Hoare-Laval Pact, which suggested the partitioning of Ethiopia. Neither Mussolini nor Hitler failed to identify safe targets of opportunity: when England and France abandoned Spain and Ethiopia, the fascists moved in.

Right-wing elements in both England and France regarded General Franco as the savior of Christian society, while the left supported the Republic. This division in itself precluded a decisive policy, particularly when coupled with the fear of general war that infected both sides of the Channel. The two countries therefore set up the Nonintervention Committee (which would prove ineffective in preventing fascist aid to Franco as well as Soviet aid to the Republic).

Ironically, Soviet policy toward the Spanish Civil War could not have been less revolutionary. Russia had already abandoned both the German and the Chinese Communists in favor of Hitler and Chiang Kai-shek, thus demonstrating the basically conservative nature of Stalinist foreign policy. Stalin was interested mainly in Russia's security—a fact made abundantly clear when he signed a nonaggression pact with Hitler in 1939, although Stalin hoped to gain from the pact.

In 1936 Stalin was still trying to court the Western Allies, largely because Hitler was casting covetous eyes on the Ukraine. He therefore could not permit the Spanish Republic to collapse— not out of revolutionary zeal, but because the alternative, a fascist regime in Spain, would increase France's growing timidity. Yet Stalin did not want to risk fostering an all-out civil war to keep the Republic alive, lest it alienate the conservative British and French. Consequently, Soviet policy in Spain seemed contradictory: on the one hand Russia supplied enough arms to keep the Republic alive; on the other it ruthlessly purged Republican revolutionary elements. By prolonging the conflict, Stalin hoped to trap Hitler in a war of attrition, one that would prevent an attack in the east before Russia was ready. The Russians saw the Nonintervention Committee established in London as a hypocritical sham, and both Hitler and Mussolini cheerfully took advantage of its ineffectiveness. For Hitler, limited intervention meant keeping France preoccupied with the threat of a fascist state to the south, embarrassing the Russians and keeping the international diplomatic situation unbalanced. There was also the possibility of solid economic advantage in the capture of Spain's mineral resources, and the valuable combat experience to be gained by the Condor Legion— Germany's "volunteers" who fought for Franco. Mussolini gained much less. The League of Nations' failure to cope with the Ethiopian crisis had encouraged Mussolini's tendency to use force and had made him eager to expose the decadence of the democracies. He saw Spain as a battleground in his much-vaunted crusade against Marxism, and, like Hitler, he saw the war as an opportunity for his army to gain practical experience. Italy's entry into the Spanish Civil War was designed to throw international affairs into a state of uncertainty, which the Italian leader could then exploit. It seemed an opportunity to assert ideological solidarity with a disciple of fascism, but it proved to be a huge miscalculation. Italy's large-scale intervention won little prestige, ruled out rapprochement with Britain and France and threw Mussolini firmly into Hitler's camp.

The war itself was marked by atrocities on both sides. Anarchistic assassinations by the Republicans were matched by the insurgent Nationalists, whose Moorish troops spread terror wherever they went. The actual rising in July, 1936, soon crystallized into a physical division of Spain. The crucial issue was the siege of Madrid, which dragged on until 1939. A huge Nationalist assault was repelled by the courage and determination of Madrid's defenders (with the help of Russian arms), but Franco's better armed and better trained troops gradually conquered more and more of the Republicans' territory. The greatest triumph of the Nationalists came in February of 1939 when Catalonia fell. In that action the Nationalists benefited from a Communist-inspired strategy to prevent arms from reaching the anarchists of the Catalan militias. In the last analysis, however, foreign arms and aid were probably the crucial factors in deciding the victory. The intensive bombing of civilians, which had already occurred in Ethiopia and would later take place in Poland, was practiced widely in Spain. The terrible climax to these raids came on April 26, 1937, when the Basque town of Guernica was bombed by German aircraft. In the raid, 1,600 unarmed, undefended civilians lost their lives. By 1939 it was obvious that the Republican government had been defeated and Europe began to look elsewhere.

"Volunteers" of the German army embarking for home at Gijo harbor in Spain after fighting for General Franco in the Spanish Civil War as the Condor Legion.

Czechoslovakia

Important though the Munich Agreement had been, it did little to satisfy Hitler's ambitions. He now saw the possibility of achieving all the various aims that he had outlined in *Mein Kampf*. The rearmament of the Rhineland, the seizure of Austria and the occupation of the Sudetenland had merely whetted Hitler's appetite. After Munich it became clear to Britain—the French had already been convinced—that Hitler could not be trusted. Believing the democracies would allow anything in their desire to appease him, Hitler took the rest of Czechoslovakia in March, 1939. This was his first miscalculation, for it forced the

The German invasion of Prague, 1939, signaled the end of Czechoslovakia.

Britain and France prepare for war

British to realize that Hitler could not be relied upon unless he was faced by serious threats of war.

Tension in the Orient

That realization brought war in Europe nearer—but war in the Far East was also brewing at this time, and for this Hitler was only indirectly responsible.

German ambitions in Europe were matched by Japanese ambitions in the Pacific. The preoccupation of the Western powers with the Spanish Civil War and the threats posed by Hitler and

The Japanese flag raised over Mukden, the ancient capital of Manchuria, 1931.

Mussolini both encouraged and facilitated Japanese aggression, which was directed against all countries with interests in the Far East. This became clear with the Japanese invasion of Manchuria in 1931, and was further emphasized by the Amau Declaration of April, 1934, which made China a protectorate of Japan and proclaimed that Japan had the exclusive right to maintain peace and order in East Asia.

In July of 1934, Japan provoked China into open war. The Sino-Japanese conflict that followed is sometimes regarded as the first stage of World War II. China's two main political and military groupings, Mao Tse-tung's Communists and Chiang Kai-shek's Kuomintang, formed a shaky coalition to combat the Japanese onslaught. At Mao's insistence, the coalition inaugurated a policy of giving up land to gain time. The Chinese encouraged the Japanese to take more territory than they could handle, to overextend their lines of communication, and to penetrate so deeply into hostile

territory that it would be relatively easy to surround them. This design was in accord with the theory of guerrilla warfare that Mao had evolved, a theory that has been recognized as one of his most original concepts. The theory is summed up in one of Mao's famous quotations: "The enemy advances, we retreat; the enemy halts, we harass; the enemy retreats, we pursue." During the late 1930s, Mao perfected this policy and simultaneously strengthened the Communist Party by creating strong links between the army and the peasants.

For a brief time, the Japanese benefited enormously from Mao's scheme. By the beginning of 1939, they had made huge advances inland and had secured most of the major coastal cities. The Japanese instituted harsh measures in an effort to break the Chinese people's will to fight, but these outrages merely served further to arouse the nation against them. (It also gained support for the Communists, who emerged as the only resolute fighters against Japan.)

Despite attacks on their Chinese holdings, the Western powers were as inept in the face of Japanese aggression as they were before Hitler. The British concession at Tientsin was blockaded; British and American shipping was attacked; and the American gunboat *Panay* was sunk. Yet all that the American and British governments did was to register protests. Meanwhile, the richest, most populous and most developed provinces in China fell to the Japanese, whose success served as a warning to the rest of the world of their determination to dominate the Pacific.

War in Europe

In Europe, Hitler was as unhesitating as the Japanese about taking what he wanted. The destruction of independent Czechoslovakia had been a great Nazi victory, for it meant that the one army in Eastern Europe that might have halted Germany's eastward advance had been eliminated. As Czechoslovakia was stripped of its fortifications, arms and munitions works, Hitler's dreams became even more ambitious.

Machine guns for the Polish army bought from the armament fund, to which Polish people donated rings, savings and family jewels.

The next step was the acquisition of the Polish Corridor. Hitler began making demands for Danzig. But the Poles, who refused, had learned the lesson of Czechoslovakia and began to prepare for war. When the Germans became more threatening, the British and the French—who had also learned a vital diplomatic lesson at Czechoslovakia's expense

—pledged themselves to support the Poles. Undaunted by the Anglo-French pledge, convinced of Germany's invincibility and enraged by the British, Hitler tore up the Anglo-German Naval Agreement and the Polish Non-aggression Pact. In May of 1939, he signed the Pact of Steel with Mussolini, which emboldened him to risk war over Poland. At the same time Hitler temporarily shelved his crusade against what Nazis termed the "Jewish-Bolshevik world conspiracy" and signed a nonaggression pact with Stalin. This pact safeguarded Hitler's

eastern flank at a time when war was imminent.

When the Stalin-Hitler pact was announced, Britain reaffirmed her guarantees to Poland. Hitler reiterated his demands to the Poles, and when they were not met at 6:30 A.M. on September 1, 1939, Germany invaded Poland. On September 3, Britain and France declared war.

Hitler declaring war on Poland, September 1, 1939, and receiving an ovation. Behind him, seated, is Hermann Göring.

Germany Invades Poland 1939

In the wake of Germany's invasion of Czechoslovakia, British Premier Neville Chamberlain formally abandoned the policy of appeasement, announcing that Britain and France would aid Poland if her independence were threatened. However, the guarantors moved too late and for the fourth time in little more than a hundred and fifty years Poland would be overrun by more powerful neighbors. Two days after Hitler's attack, Britain and France declared war on Germany, but sent no troops to Poland.

When Adolf Hitler annexed the remainder of Czechoslovakia in March, 1939, he dropped the last veil concealing his intention to go to war. From that moment the world knew that the German dictator was bent upon conquest by any means at his disposal. On March 31, the British Prime Minister, Neville Chamberlain, publicly abandoned his policy of appeasement while, by temporary mobilization and strong words, the Poles made it plain that they would not concede Germany's territorial demands upon their nation. However, by March 25, Hitler had instructed his military chiefs to settle the "Polish problem" by force, and by April 3, the operational plan of *Oberkommando der Wehrmacht* was ready. Plan Weiss epitomized the full aggressive vigor of modern German methods. Its stated intention was to "destroy the Polish military strength" and to achieve that aim, what was more, without a formal declaration of war. Nevertheless it had a qualifying clause, inserted, presumably, to mollify the many doubters in the German hierarchy; it was hoped to "limit the war to Poland only." The target date was September 1.

Hitler realized that to achieve his ends he must act quickly because Germany's economic strength was relatively weak. He was prepared, therefore, to generate war by propaganda—regardless of whether the excuses were plausible or not. Throughout the summer the German political and war machines concentrated on these aims: the armed forces training hard, while reequipping as fast as German industry could supply them; the diplomats and propagandists creating pressure against Poland; and the underground agencies and Nazi minorities in Poland and the free city of Danzig stirring up disorders. When Hitler abrogated the Polish-German Nonaggression Pact of 1934 in April, tension increased and mounted steadily as, with every passing week, violence and the threat of war was intensified. By mid-August, along the

German-Polish frontier, a virtual state of guerrilla warfare prevailed. On the diplomatic front a battle of bid and counterbid for allies went on. The French and the British were attempting, without much encouragement, to commit the Russians to their side as a deterrent to German ambitions in the east; the Poles sought support wherever they could find it. But it was the Germans who stole the thunder. In April, Russia had indicated her desire for better relations with Germany—Hitler seized on this and, on August 23, after some lightning diplomacy, could announce the signing of a German-Russian nonaggression pact—nonaggression, that is, between the two signatories but steeped in belligerence toward others. For, in a secret clause, the subdivision of Poland along the line of the Narew, Vistula and San rivers was agreed upon, while Russia was granted a free hand in Finland, Estonia and Latvia and Germany assumed rights over Lithuania. Not only did Hitler believe that the pact would neutralize Russia, he also thought it would so frighten France and Britain that they would withdraw their support from Poland. In effect it did precisely the reverse. Chamberlain immediately restated guarantees, on behalf of Britain and France, to Poland; Benito Mussolini took fright and decided to stand back from conflict—for the moment; while the third member of the Axis, Japan, took umbrage at an alliance between Germany and a Communist power. Nevertheless, Hitler set August 26 as the day for Plan Weiss' commencement.

In the opening stages of the coming war sheer numbers were to be of far less account than had been the case during the closing stages of World War 1. When fully mobilized, the Polish army could raise some forty-five infantry divisions, eleven cavalry brigades and a single tank brigade, but of modern equipment it was exceedingly short—particularly of tanks and antitank guns.

Ignace Moscicki, President of Poland. He went into exile in Switzerland when Poland fell to Germany in 1939.

Opposite Free Europe! A triumph of German arms! German propaganda poster for occupied Poland, 1939.

At the beginning of the Polish campaign advancing German troops destroy border posts to mark the extension of the rule of National Socialism.

Nevertheless, against the forty-four German infantry divisions and single cavalry brigade, the Polish army might well have resisted for a prolonged period even though there was no possibility of its receiving direct aid from France and Britain. However, the balance swung hopelessly against the Poles because of their technical inadequacy. The German forces had eleven armored (Panzer) or partially armored divisions with a combined strength of 3,195 tanks; the Poles had only 225 modern tanks. The Germans could put 850 modern bombers and 400 fighters into the air whereas the Poles had only 210 bombers and 150 fighters, not all of them up-to-date. German combat techniques were also far in advance of those practiced by the Poles. In the past the former had always striven to fight battles of highly mobile encirclement, a strategy that they still embraced and that was enhanced by the introduction of mechanized forces supplemented by air power; the latter were compelled to adopt linear defense to shield the length of the frontier because of their poor mobility. Thus, while the Germans, with the choice of launching their attacks in a wide arc from East Prussia in the north to Slovakia in the south, could choose their axes of attack by concentrated masses, the Poles had to wait for the German advance, at a disadvantage in all respects.

At sea the Polish navy, a mere four destroyers, sixteen river gunboats and five submarines, was of no account; either it would be sunk at the outset or make its escape to Britain. Everything would be settled on land. The Germans began the concentration of their forces in June; the Poles deferred the start of mobilization until August 30, although they had adopted full defensive positions with their peacetime army long before that date.

The Germans planned a massive drive by their Eighth and Tenth Armies toward Warsaw from Silesia, with a subsidiary thrust by the Fourteenth Army from Slovakia toward Cracow and Lvov on its right. In the north the Fourth Army was to strike from Pomerania, cut the Polish Corridor and then join hands with the Third Army operating southward from East Prussia. The Polish forces were to be destroyed to the east of the Vistula and Narew rivers. Everything on the German side was ready for August 26 and the troops were moving to their assault positions when, suddenly, Hitler called a halt. Some troops actually crossed the frontier and had to be brought back.

It was a British guarantee to the Poles on August 24 that made Hitler hesitate and resort once more to diplomacy in an effort to shake this attitude of belligerence. Göring, among others in the Nazi hierarchy, counseled moderation. The military leaders were scared. Hitler offered an alliance to Britain and guarantees as to her Empire—providing Germany's colonial claims were met—but it was only a gesture. On August 30 he reverted to his original plan and demanded the immediate return of the Polish Corridor and Danzig to Germany. When no answer was forthcoming from the Poles the final decision to attack on September 1 was made.

At 8 P.M. on August 31 men in Polish uniform took possession of the radio station at Gleiwitz near Cracow and broadcast that an attack upon Germany had begun. The attack was repulsed, as it was bound to be, for the affair was engineered. The assailants were German, dressed for a role, and the part they played was the simulation of Hitler's final propaganda provocation for his attack next day. At 4 P.M. on September 1 German bombs fell on Polish air and naval bases as naval forces moved into action at Gdynia. Then came the German ground attack. The invasion had begun. So, also had World War II, for contrary to Hitler's hopeful expectation and the advice he had received from Ribbentrop, his Foreign Minister, the British and French were no longer prepared to stand aside. On September 3 both nations were to declare war; by then it was plain that Germany would not cancel her aggression.

There was no question of Germany turning back in any sense. September 3 was the last day of resistance by the Polish air force: it had either been destroyed on the ground or shot down in aerial combat. The Polish Corridor had been cut and massive forces were flooding toward Warsaw and Lvov. Polish resistance was furious, though ill coordinated, and already beginning to fall into disorder. Mobilization, which had begun far too late to be completed before the surprise attack, was in confusion. An army that moved mainly by rail or horse-drawn transport was utterly disrupted by widespread attacks upon communication centers and thrown into deeper distress when, after September 3, the air attacks began to shift from the Polish air bases to army targets.

However, where the Poles stood and fought, particularly in the fortified zones of the Polish Corridor, the Germans suffered heavily. The bomber attacks in support of the army were sometimes misdirected due to poor liaison and control. Where Polish antitank guns remained in action, German tanks were held at bay, and when the tanks found it difficult to operate, the infantry at times showed unwillingness to assert themselves. After the campaign the commander of Army Group North, General von Bock, was to criticize the over-caution of the infantry. This was quite understandable, however, when it is recalled that these infantry divisions, whose artillery and transport was horse-drawn and vulnerable, were also deprived of armored support. Failures in leadership were commented upon by General Guderian, whose XIX Corps attacked across the Corridor. Following modern German command practice he commanded from an armored vehicle at the point of the advance and in person witnessed inertia when danger prevailed.

Nevertheless, the German offensive enjoyed an almost universal run of success. Within five days the frontier defenses had disintegrated and a massive haul of prisoners had been taken. Cracow fell and the southern spearhead was half way to Warsaw and gathering pace behind the Panzer division spearhead. Those Polish formations which had not been broken in the initial attacks fell back upon the Vistula, making for Modlin, northwest of Warsaw where the only intact reserve existed. In the capital the garrison and population prepared for the worst under threat of air raids.

Now a new threat appeared, as strong German forces, transferred from Pomerania to East Prussia, regrouped and prepared for their next intrusion into Poland. Such anxieties as those the German military command may have felt at the outset were dispelled. Clearly the Polish forces were incapable of prolonged resistance. Equally obviously, there was no likelihood of a large-scale diversionary offensive by the French into Germany

from the west. There was barely a mutter of gunfire between the opposing Maginot and Siegfried lines, and such air activity as took place was limited to attacks by the British RAF against the German fleet in port and to routine reconnaissance flights. Not a bomb fell either on French or German soil.

Yet the Poles had not given up. The German Fourth Panzer Division arrived at the outskirts of Warsaw on September 9 and, upon trying to break in, was very roughly handled, losing 57 out of 120 tanks. At the same moment it suddenly appeared to the Germans that a large Polish concentration—some twelve infantry divisions plus three cavalry brigades—was moving against the northern flank of General von Rundstedt's Army Group South. Led by three infantry divisions and flanked by cavalry, the Poles, under General Kutrzeba, drove back a German division, which was dangerously strung out, and threatened a breakthrough. At first the Germans were slow to

Hitler's myrmidons marching off captured Poles. Thousands were rounded up and executed and many more deported as part of Germany's policy of racial subjugation.

Top Warsaw occupied, 1939. The antiquated Polish army was no match for the technologically sophisticated German war machine.

23

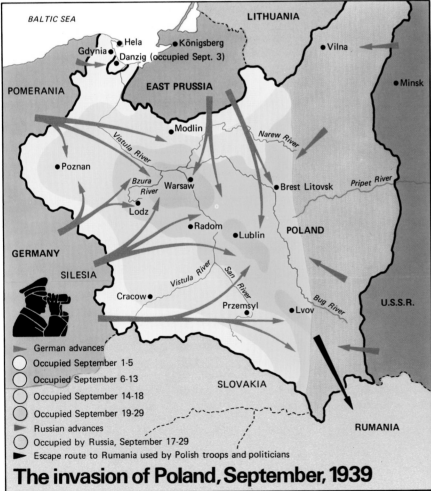

Map legend

▸ German advances
◯ Occupied September 1-5
◯ Occupied September 6-13
◯ Occupied September 14-18
◯ Occupied September 19-29
▸ Russian advances
◯ Occupied by Russia, September 17-29
▸ Escape route to Rumania used by Polish troops and politicians

The invasion of Poland, September, 1939

realize their peril, but at last took alarm and called loudly for reinforcement. Von Rundstedt, however, recognized this as a marvelous opportunity for a grand encirclement. Withholding further attacks upon Warsaw, he swung every available formation into an embrace of the Polish forces between the Vistula and Bzura. The fighting became heavy but the outcome was inevitable. Pummeled by almost endless waves of dive-bombing attacks, as well as intensifying artillery fire, the Polish attacks were first smashed by a cordon of German infantry and then driven into a cul-de-sac by a gathering swarm of armored and infantry formations. Apart from scattered elements that escaped to Modlin or Warsaw, the last major Polish reserve was annihilated.

To the south, the German Fourteenth Army made an almost uninterrupted sweep toward Lvov, crossing the San River and laying siege to Przemsyl. Lvov was to hold out until September 21, after a week's siege; its resistance was courageous but to no avail. It was even easier for Guderian's XIX Corps when it launched its drive from East Prussia and made haste for Brest Litovsk. In this operation Guderian made no attempt to destroy scattered pockets of resistance but, instead, bypassed them in order to achieve the maximum incursion into the Polish forces from the rear as a means of crushing the enemy by an assault upon the command and communications of the Polish nation. He succeeded in full. The encirclement of Brest Litovsk was completed on September 15, though its capture was delayed until September 17 after fierce fighting in which the Germans suffered heavy losses.

September 17 was, indeed, crucial. That day a French offensive was expected to begin against the Siegfried Line, but was put off. To the Poles it no longer mattered. Not only was their army destroyed by the Germans, but the Russian army suddenly began rolling in from the east, enjoying an easy run against the few Polish units remaining there. This was the first example of the meaning of the German-Russian nonaggression pact.

All that survived of coherent Polish resistance was to be found in besieged cities: Gdynia, which fell after a concentrated bombardment and assault on September 19; at Hela, on the peninsula opposite Danzig, until it surrendered on October 1; at Modlin, which capitulated on September 29; at Lvov, which surrendered eight days before; and, above all, at Warsaw. It would have been easy enough for the Germans to leave these places to fall of their own accord, but external factors compelled Hitler to accelerate matters. It was desirable to have absolute domination over the German slice of Poland in order to forestall any extra incursion by the Russians. It was also vital to withdraw the mechanized and air forces for maintenance and to send them as quickly as possible, along with the rest of the army, to the Western front in case the French and British should attack in earnest.

Norwegians evacuated from their home in Oslo in order to billet German troops.

cluded an armistice with Germany.

It had been the most traumatic defeat of the century. Poland had not been expected to resist the German army, but France had had the foremost army in Europe. Bad strategic planning and poor leadership had brought it to defeat in six weeks. Now France was divided into two zones, one occupied by the Germans, one administered by Pétain from Vichy. Her colonies were at the mercy of her conquerors and, as a final insult, her fleet was shelled and captured by the British.

Britain and her Empire now stood totally alone. At home Britain had a new leader who had caught the mood of the people and who would never surrender. But against the most successful

army in Europe she had only the wreck of her expeditionary force, a small air force and her navy. It was known that the Germans were planning a cross-Channel invasion. In the Atlantic the u-boats were imperiling the trade routes. It was imperative that the French fleet should not fall into German hands to tip the balance against the British Mediterranean fleet. So at Oran, Alexandria, Mes-el-kebir and Dakar, the French fleet was disarmed or reduced by gunfire as the final scene in the tragic first act of World War II.

The British had not been defeated yet, and as the Battle of Britain was to show in the summer of 1940, the Germans had to fight an enemy more determined than France.

mans captured the fortress of Eben Emael with glider-borne troops and secured the vital river crossings. In the south the main German thrust met little opposition. Brilliant staff work had moved General Rommel's tanks through the Ardennes, which the French had thought impassable. By May 14 German troops had crossed the Meuse and created a fifty-mile gap between the two main French armies. General Maurice Gamelin, French Commander in Chief, now disclosed that he had no reserves, and by May 20 German armor had reached the Channel coast.

Dunkirk

The French and British forces, instead of facing the main enemy in Belgium, were cut in two. Gamelin was replaced by the aged General Weygand, but an attack against the German line from both north and south miscarried. Even the Germans had been slightly startled by their success; their tanks had far outrun the infantry and there were still supposedly powerful French forces south of the Somme. Göring, commanding

the Luftwaffe, assured Hitler that his planes could reduce the forces trapped around Dunkirk. So, with the Panzers halted, 350,000 British and French soldiers were evacuated across the Channel between May 27 and June 4. On June 5 the Germans attacked southward across the Somme. Militarily there was little that France could do. Her armies were still fighting an uncoordinated series of battles but defeat was inevitable. Churchill was urging the French government under Paul Reynaud to fight on: France still had a fleet and an empire. But Reynaud's cabinet was suspicious of Britain and was already resigned to defeat. Reynaud, emboldened by an overenthusiastic American ambassador, appealed to the United States for help. But President Roosevelt, although he was sympathetic and in 1939 had amended the Neutrality Act to allow Britain and France to buy arms on a "cash and carry" basis, was unable to act. On June 10 Italy declared war: "I only need a few thousand dead for a seat at the conference table," said Mussolini. On June 22 the French government, under Marshal Henri Philippe Pétain (1856–1951), con-

French refugees fleeing from aerial bombardment in June, 1940.

British pilots training at the flying school at Market Drayton in 1940.

The evacuation of British troops from Dunkirk.

Battle of Britain

Winston Churchill's stirring observation about the six-week air battle over Britain—"Never in the field of human conflict was so much owed by so many to so few"—was quite literally true. Great Britain, whose population numbered some 47 million in the late summer of 1940, was saved from imminent invasion by the skill and valor of slightly more than one thousand Royal Air Force pilots—one-third of whom were killed during the battle. At short odds that occasionally approached thirty to one, the battered RAF exacted a heavy—and increasingly telling—toll on Hitler's Luftwaffe. As the Germans' numerical superiority dwindled, so did their optimism. In early August, Air Marshal Göring had promised to smash the RAF within two weeks; by mid-September it was obvious that he had failed. England was saved.

Winston Churchill in a characteristic pose, from the portrait by Sickert.

Opposite A German pilot bales out of his Messerschmitt 109 fighter.

The Battle of Britain was fought over the English Channel and southeastern England during six weeks in August and September, 1940. The struggle waged by the British and German air forces was the most momentous air battle in world history. In previous wars, and in the Polish, Norwegian and French campaigns of World War II, military aircraft had been used like artillery—to provide close support for invading armies and to damage the enemy's communications. In the Battle of Britain, the fighting was solely in the air, and the armies and navies of both sides remained in reserve to await the outcome. The air battle was a preliminary to Hitler's planned invasion of Britain, but it was so essential that when Hitler lost it, he abandoned the invasion.

The Royal Air Force's victory did not win the war, nor was German power crippled by it. Hitler conquered the Balkans and embarked on his greatest campaign—the one against Russia—within a few months of his failure to smash England. In that sense the Battle of Britain was not decisive, like the battles of Salamis or Waterloo. But it saved Britain from defeat at the moment when defeat seemed probable. It gained time for the British to strengthen their home defenses against a renewal of the threat of invasion and to extend the war to the Atlantic and the Mediterranean, where their strategic advantages outmatched those of the Germans. It imposed a check upon unbroken German successes, and although it left Hitler still with many options, he chose the wrong one by invading Russia. Above all, the air battle preserved the British Isles as a base from which the Continent of Europe was eventually reconquered.

After the defeat of France in June, 1940, Hitler had only one enemy left: Great Britain and the Empire. He held the shores of the Atlantic and the North Sea from northern Norway to the Spanish frontier, and the Continent in depth from Brittany to central Poland. With Italy now his active ally, and with Russia, Japan, Spain and the United States in their very different ways at least neutralized,

the balance of power in his favor was overwhelming. On the European mainland only the fortress of Gibraltar remained in hostile hands. The German armed forces were elated and intact.

Although this situation had been foreseen and indeed planned, Hitler had given no thought to the strategy that should flow from it. He did not know what to do with his triumph. Nurtured on the mentality of World War I, he was nonplussed when his continental army reached the limits of the Continent. To defeat Britain by cutting its imperial communications and occupying the French provinces of North Africa was a concept alien to him. He hesitated, toying first with the idea of starving Britain into submission by unrestricted u-boat warfare and air attacks on its ports, and then, intermittently, with the idea of invading the country. He still hoped that political methods might render military methods unnecessary. Britain might be induced to make peace if its leaders were convinced of the impossibility of victory. Hitler could offer peace on terms so generous that even Churchill would find them preferable to annihilation.

The British position was not quite so hopeless as Hitler allowed himself to assume. The majority of Britain's best-trained troops had returned safely from Dunkirk and central France and were now being rapidly reequipped from reserve stores and new production. The fleet had scarcely been affected by the campaign in the west and only marginally by the Norwegian disaster, and it was still greatly superior to the German. The RAF, thanks to the difficult refusal to involve more than a small part of it in the later phases of the campaign in France, still had sixty fighter squadrons left intact. The spirits of the people, the armed forces, factory workers and the government were exhilarated by the prospect of single combat, and Churchill enhanced their optimism by expressing it so nobly. Several of the defeated Allied governments had taken sanctuary in Britain and had added ships and men to British reserves. In default of a French government-in-exile, de Gaulle

The London Blitz: St. Paul's Cathedral surrounded by smoke and flame. Miraculously, the cathedral survived.

Lord Dowding, commander of Fighter Command during the Battle of Britain.

rallied to his illegal standard thousands of young Frenchmen. The untouched Empire and the Mediterranean bases still existed. Britain could survive on 60 percent of its prewar imports, and Germany could neither stop them at their sources nor seriously interfere with their passage.

By such arguments the British reached the conclusion that surrender was not only unthinkable but unnecessary. They could survive. But how could they win? Their answer was a little more tentative: by the counterblockade of Germany; by air bombing; by the revolt of the European peoples under German occupation. Nobody spoke yet of the liberation of Europe by invasion. But in the closing words of Churchill's great speech of June 4, 1940, the significance of which was obscured by their splendor, he pointed to the ultimate, the only real solution: "... until in God's good time the new world with all its power and might steps forth to the rescue and liberation of the old."

The United States did what it could to help England "by all steps short of war," but Britain had to face the immediate dangers alone. Both Britain and Germany soon reached the same conclusion— the British in June, the Germans in July—that the war could be ended in 1940 only by a successful invasion of England; that invasion would have no chance of success unless Germany could put ashore some thirty well-equipped divisions; and that such an operation was impossible unless British naval superiority in the English Channel could be matched by German air superiority over it. The key to the Channel and its northern shoreline was the airspace above, and this could not be won as part of the invasion battle itself. It must be won beforehand in a preliminary contest between the air forces of each side in order to prevent British reconnaissance of German preparations, to protect the German ships and barges from air attack while still at sea and the troops when they landed, and to give German bombers every opportunity to harass British defenses and prevent the movement of British reserves.

This, in essence, was why the Battle of Britain was fought.

The Germans were convinced that they could smash the southern defenses of the RAF within one or two weeks. Air Marshal Göring had promised it. The Luftwaffe had 1,050 first-line fighters at the end of July, and some 500 in reserve; the RAF (having lost 430 aircraft during the fighting in France) had 625 in the first line and 230 in reserve. Because the Germans could bomb any part of Great Britain from their long continental coastline, Air Chief Marshal Sir Hugh Dowding, Commander in Chief of RAF Fighter Command, could not concentrate all his squadrons on the most vulnerable sector in the southeast; he was obliged to hold back half his force to defend the factories of the Midlands and the north against a threat that never materialized.

Thus the superior strength of the Luftwaffe was magnified by its possession of the initiative. The Germans could mass their squadrons against any point they chose, and London, the largest and most vulnerable target of all, lay within their fighter range. Against all this the British held certain advantages. They were fighting over their own country and nearby coastal waters, and their pilots would at least be safe from capture if shot down. They had, in the Spitfire and the Hurricane, two fighter planes that were superior in turning speed—but not in height ceiling—to the German Messerschmitt 109. They had a chain of radar stations that could give them adequate warning of the size, direction and height of approaching raids in time to send up home squadrons to meet the German planes on more level terms. Still, the RAF was outnumbered by two to one generally, and by as much as thirty to one in individual engagements, and their enemies had the advantages of concentration and surprise. The struggle could be won by the RAF only if British pilots could shoot down at least three German planes for every two they lost themselves; if the production of new aircraft could keep pace with British losses; if fresh pilots could be trained in time to take the place of the dead and wounded; and if the enemy made errors of strategy that would ease the strain.

All these things occurred. The greatest cause for anxiety on the British side was the problem of pilot replacement. Other commands were skimmed of young pilots to fill the gaps in Fighter Command. As the novices began to fill the cockpits of the veterans, the quality—although not the mettle—of the fighter pilots inevitably declined. The Germans had no equivalent worries, having started with greater reserves and having recovered from captivity the four hundred pilots shot down during the battle for France. The loss rate of fighter aircraft was also of critical concern to the British. Their losses so greatly exceeded replacements during the crux of the air battle (from August 24 to September 6) that, in the words of the Air Ministry's report, "in three weeks more of activity on the same scale, the fighter reserves would have been completely exhausted." But from September 7 on, the losses fell below the output of new machines, and at the end of the air battle the reserves were in fact greater than at the beginning.

By German reckoning the air battle proper began on August 7. During the preceding month the Luftwaffe had carried out a series of test raids on Channel merchant shipping. The Germans had sunk 30,000 tons, but the proportion of their losses to British aircraft shot down foreshadowed later averages: at least 286 German aircraft were destroyed, while only 148 British planes were lost.

In mid-August the main attack began with an assault on the radar installations and southern airfields of Fighter Command. This was clearly the right tactic for the Luftwaffe. By sending over large bomber fleets escorted by clouds of fighters, Göring hoped to draw the defenders into the air and defeat them by attrition (while simultaneously making further resistance impossible by destroying RAF bases and the warning system). Two things went wrong with this plan. First, German losses of both fighters and bombers rapidly whittled down the numerical superiority with which they had started. Secondly, German pilots failed to press home their initial advantage and abandoned too soon the tactics by which they might have won. They attached so little importance to the radar system that, although five stations were temporarily damaged and one (in the Isle of Wight) was destroyed, the system was allowed to continue to operate efficiently throughout the air battle. Similarly, in early September, at the critical moment when five forward airfields and six of the seven sector stations had suffered extensive damage, Göring switched his main effort further inland to attack factories and oil installations. "Had the enemy continued his heavy attacks on the airfields," wrote Air Vice-Marshal K. R. Park, who was in command of the southeastern group of Fighter Command, "the fighter defenses of London would have been put in a perilous state."

This was the turning point. Göring was persuaded to divert the Luftwaffe to the outskirts of London by the optimistic reports of his pilots that the RAF was on the verge of collapse. At the same time, Hitler was sufficiently stung by the British bombing of Berlin to insist that the Luftwaffe retaliate on London. On September 7, the day on which the British prematurely issued the codeword Cromwell to warn that invasion was imminent, three hundred German bombers escorted by six hundred fighters attacked the docks and oil depots on the lower Thames. On the fifteenth, the day still celebrated as Battle of Britain Day, German bombers attacked London itself, losing sixty aircraft to twenty-six British. As soon as the Luftwaffe turned against London, RAF Fighter Command, which had been perceptibly weakening, began to recover strength. Pressure was taken off the vital sector stations. (Because the strength of the British defenses made daylight raids too costly, much of the German bombing was by night, when at that stage of the war the fighter aircraft had almost no role to play.)

In mid-September the Germans admitted to themselves that the attack had failed. The RAF was as active as ever. Civilian morale was unaffected by the bombing. The British still dominated the Channel by sea and continued to fight in the air. The weather was beginning to worsen. On September 14, Admiral Erich Raeder advised Hitler that "the present air situation does not provide conditions for carrying out the invasion, as the risk is still too great." Hitler agreed. On the nineteenth he postponed the invasion, and on the twenty-third he gave orders for the dispersal of the invasion fleet. The British and German armies were allowed to believe that the plan might be revived in the spring of 1941, but Hitler himself had very different ideas. He was already preparing to switch the weight of his attack against the Soviet Union.

In retrospect, the British air victory can be attributed to four factors. First, in the mid-1930s the British had had the foresight to design and construct a fleet of superb fighter aircraft and to exploit the discovery of radar. They had kept their fleet intact by denying the French the twenty fighter squadrons that could have made little difference to the battle

A radar tower on the south coast of England. Stations like this one allowed RAF planes to get airborne in time to intercept the Luftwaffe. Also of considerable importance was the invention of Ultra, a primitive computer that enabled the British to unscramble German coded messages.

Spitfire pilots run to their planes—a common event during the Battle of Britain.

A Supermarine Spitfire. These fighters were clearly superior to their Luftwaffe opponents.

Messerschmitt 109s flying up the English Channel past the white cliffs of Dover.

in France after it had passed the point of no recovery, but that were enough to decide the issue in Britain two months later.

Second, Churchill knew that he could count on high civilian morale. He could take for granted his countrymen's support when he rejected Hitler's offer of peace. He was confident that they would endure air attack by day and night. He and Lord Beaverbrook, the Minister for Aircraft Production,

could demand from the aircraft factories unparalleled efforts to replace the broken weapons of air defense.

Third, the Germans failed to appreciate the effort needed to knock out a well-trained and scientifically superior defense, or to allow for its recuperative powers.

Finally—and this will be remembered when the details of the air battle are forgotten—the spirit of dedication, adventurousness and rivalry among the fighter pilots of both sides stimulated them to deeds of unexampled valor. The difference was that Dowding's men were fighting for survival, while Göring's were fighting to finish a war that they considered already won. During the air struggle, 414 British and Allied pilots were killed. That seems a small number for so great a victory. But it was a high proportion—about one-third of those engaged. It was this very slenderness of the fighting force, added to the greatness of the issue, that has given the Battle of Britain the quality of a crusade. "Never in the field of human conflict was so much owed by so many to so few." Churchill's famous words were spoken on August 20, before the air battle had reached its climax. They were a prophesy, but they lived to become a verdict.

How much, in fact, was owed to these men? Perhaps it is best summed up by Churchill's remark to de Gaulle in August of that year: "Sooner or later the Americans will come in, but on condition that we here won't flinch. That's why I can't think of anything but the fighter air force." What was at stake was the only base from which a counterattack on Germany could one day be launched. No one will ever know whether the invasion of Britain would have succeeded, or would even have been attempted, if the RAF had been defeated. The British navy and army might have succeeded if the air force had failed. For the Germans it would still have been a very perilous operation. They would

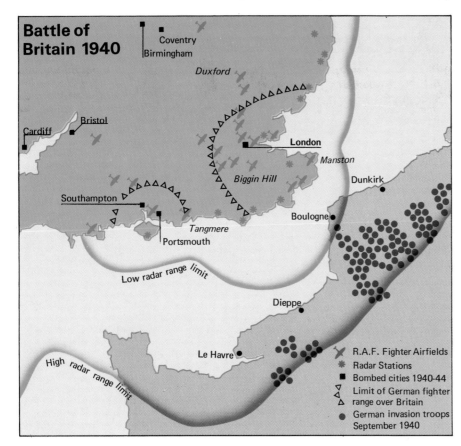

Battle of Britain 1940

Coventry
Birmingham
Duxford
Bristol
Cardiff
London
Manston
Biggin Hill
Dunkirk
Southampton
Boulogne
Tangmere
Portsmouth
Low radar range limit
Dieppe
High radar range limit
Le Havre

✗ R.A.F. Fighter Airfields
✳ Radar Stations
■ Bombed cities 1940-44
▽ Limit of German fighter range over Britain
△
● German invasion troops September 1940

have been obliged to organize and protect a sea crossing for an initial force of more than twenty divisions, and would afterward have had to maintain them in face of an undefeated navy.

But while invasion would still have been a gamble, it is probable that Hitler would have risked it if the Luftwaffe had won the first round. In 1945 Field Marshal Karl Rudolf von Rundstedt, who was to command the expedition, told his interrogators: "We looked on the invasion as a sort of game." At the time, however, it was not a game to the Luftwaffe, nor to Hitler. Otherwise he would never have retrained and deployed so great an army on the French coast, nor damaged the economy of Europe by withdrawing from its ports and canals so great an armada of shipping and barges, nor foregone adventures elsewhere when his fortunes were at their peak. From what historians have discovered about his secret intentions, he thought of the attack on Russia as an alternative, not a substitute, for the decisive struggle with Britain. Although victory in the air would certainly have led to the continuance of the war with Britain as a first priority, Hitler would first have considered the use of his bomber force alone. The bomber, not the fighter, was the true instrument of air power. The cities of England would have been defenseless if Fighter Command had failed; the ports would have been unusable, the factories wrecked. How long could the British people have withstood the barrage?

The air battle saved Britain from invasion or unendurable air attack. It probably saved the nation from defeat. It provided the British people with clear proof that defiance had not been foolhardy. It created in the free world—and above all in the United States—a wave of admiration and hope that resulted in immediate practical help (such as the arming of the Home Guard with American rifles and the exchange of fifty American destroyers for British bases in the Western Atlantic). The United States could not enter the war unless Germany or its allies challenged a vital American interest. But after the Battle of Britain, the British became for the United States what France had been to Britain, with the difference that Britain was undefeated. The longer the British kept their islands intact, the more honorable and viable seemed their cause, the more essential their survival. The United States did not enter the war to save Britain. But Britain was the United States' base in Europe and became its closest ally. The defeat of Germany assumed in President Franklin Roosevelt's mind equal importance with the defeat of Japan. None of this would have happened if Britain had been defeated in the summer of 1940. By far the greater part of the American war effort would have been deployed in the Far East, and Russia might have overrun the whole of Europe and much of the Middle East and North Africa. Speculation on what might have been is unprofitable beyond a certain point, but it is legitimate to call the Battle of Britain a milestone not only of World War II, but of the history of the entire century and the entire world.   NIGEL NICOLSON

German Dornier bombers over the East End of London at the height of the Blitz.

A German ground crew rearms a Messerschmitt before sending it back into the battle.

A reconstructed Luftwaffe fighter base.

The First Jet Airplane

By 1940 the piston-engine aircraft was nearing its peak efficiency. Ten years before, however, an English aeronautical engineer, Frank Whittle, had taken out a patent on a gas-turbine engine that would provide a jet and eliminate the propeller, thus overcoming the limitations imposed by size, component complexity and altitude on the conventional piston engine. In 1937 tests were begun on Whittle's new engine, and in 1940 Britain's Air Ministry took up the project, placing a contract for an experimental fighter using a test engine, the "WI." Increasingly improved upon, Whittle's jet engine thus began the mainstream development in aviation in Britain and the U.S.A., a development that has revolutionized world transport, with far-reaching consequences for a "shrinking world."

In the development of aviation in the twentieth century, two major events stand out. The first is the successful flight of a piston-engined airplane by the Wright brothers in 1903; the second is the development of the jet engine in 1941.

By 1940 the piston engine was nearing its peak efficiency. Altitude was restricted by the need to supply air for combustion and by the fall-off in propeller efficiencies in thin air. The jet engine overcame most of these problems. It has the advantage of relatively light weight and simplicity, having approximately one-third the number of components of a piston engine. It has few moving parts and is thus simple to construct and service, and because it has no metal-to-metal surfaces, frictional losses and lubrication problems are reduced. It is easy to install and remove for servicing and requires fewer instruments than a piston engine. It is self-cooled and therefore needs no radiator. The rotating parts are in perfect balance, torque is uniform, and vibration minimal, which allows greater flexibility of airframe design. The jet engine is ideally suited to aviation use as it has a low frontal area that gives unobstructed pilot vision and eases the problem of armament location. It can use a low grade of fuel, and, in contrast to a piston engine, there is virtually no limit to its maximum size. As a result it has been possible to build aircraft such as the 366-ton Boeing 747 and fighters capable of over 2,200 mph and altitudes of twenty miles or more. World transport has been revolutionized by increased payloads and speeds, and the social consequences of the "shrinking world" that this change implies have been far reaching.

Although the jet airplane is such a recent development in modern life, the natural law under which it operates has been understood for three hundred years and used in simple machines since early times. The "aelopile" described by Hero of Alexandria over two thousand years ago consisted of a sphere containing water which, when heated, boiled and forced steam through two nozzles set at right angles from the body of the sphere. The reaction caused by the action of the jets set the machine in motion around a lateral spindle. A model of 1629 ascribed to Giovanni Branca, an Italian engineer, also utilized a steam jet—in this case it was made to rotate a fan wheel mounted on a vertical shaft that could be connected to, and thereby drive, other machines. In 1687, Sir Isaac Newton explained the principle by which such devices worked as his third law of motion: "To every action there is an equal and opposite reaction." Jet reaction was considered as a way to drive boats at the end of the eighteenth century in the United States when James Rumsey tested a vessel driven by a steam pump that forced water through jets at the stern.

Although never built, the French engineer, Charles de Louvrié, produced an advanced design in his *Aéronave* of 1865, which included an essential feature of the modern jet—the burning of "a hydrocarbon, or better, vaporised petroleum oil," which was to be expelled through two pipes. Similar ideas were pursued, though not put into practice, by J. W. Butler and E. Edwards who in 1867 patented a delta-wing monoplane driven by jets of steam, compressed air or a gas and air mixture. A machine of the same kind was proposed, also in 1867, by the Russian Nicholas de Teleicheff. Of course, it must be appreciated that all these machines, although sometimes sound in principle, predate the first flight of a practical airplane—that of the Wright brothers in 1903—and their inventors thus lacked the essential knowledge of aerodynamics and control and the advanced engineering principles necessary for the construction of an efficient jet engine. However, within a few years of the Wrights'

Frank Whittle, the young officer and pilot in the RAF who pioneered the development of the turbojet engine.

Opposite Lockheed P–80 interceptors (the T–33 Shooting Star). The prototype of this aircraft, begun in 1943, used a British De Havilland H.1. turbojet engine; the followup used an American General Electric J 33—Ge–9 (or Ge–11) engine and was operational in 1944.

Meteor IV

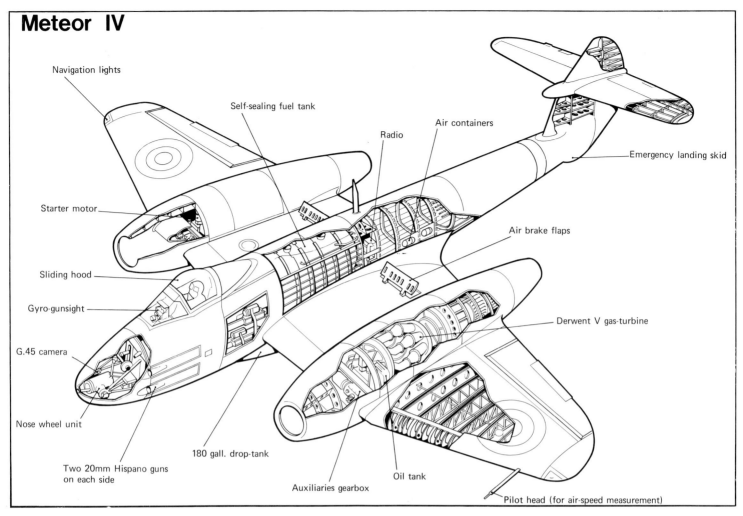

Navigation lights

Self-sealing fuel tank

Radio

Air containers

Air brake flaps

Emergency landing skid

Starter motor

Sliding hood

Gyro-gunsight

G.45 camera

Nose wheel unit

Derwent V gas-turbine

180 gall. drop-tank

Two 20mm Hispano guns on each side

Auxiliaries gearbox

Oil tank

Pilot head (for air-speed measurement)

breakthrough, several almost feasible projects were envisaged. In France in 1908, René Lorin proposed an engine working on the principle of the ejection of exhaust gases from a gasoline engine, and two years later the first full-sized—though unsuccessful—jet airplane (powered by a conventional engine driving ducted fans) was exhibited in Paris. A "thrust augmentor" of similar operat on was examined by French military authorities during World War I and later in the U.S.A. with results that were promising but not sufficiently so to warrant further research.

Dr. A. A. Griffith (who later undertook important research on axial-flow jets) presented a paper to the British Royal Aeronautical Establishment in 1926 on *The Aerodynamic Theory of Turbine Design*. His conclusions indicated the feasibility of using the gas turbine as a means of aircraft propulsion, perhaps by replacing the piston engine with a turbine—as was later to take place, giving rise to the turbo-prop type of aircraft. In 1928, a rocket-powered glider was flown successfully at Wasserkuppe, Germany, and in the following year a similar machine attained one hundred mph and flew for ten minutes. (The distinction, however, must be drawn between the rocket and the jet. While both operate on the action/reaction principle, the rocket carries its own fuel and a combustant, such as liquid oxygen, while the true jet, though carrying its fuel, draws

air from the atmosphere in which to burn it. The rocket is thus of necessity much heavier, and although the only possible method of propulsion in airless space, it is impractical over long distances in the Earth's atmosphere.

By the late 1920s and early 1930s several engineers were considering the possibilities of using gas turbines in place of piston engines in airplanes, and a small number were also examining such radical alternatives to conventional propeller power as jet reaction. Among these pioneers was a young man called Frank Whittle.

Whittle was born in Coventry, England, on June 1, 1907, the son of a mechanic who later bought a one-man valve and piston-ring factory in Leamington, where Frank was educated. After initial rejection on medical grounds (he was considered undersized), he was eventually accepted as a boy apprentice by the RAF, which enabled him to pursue his interests in airplanes and engineering. He was selected for a cadetship at the RAF College, Cranwell, in 1926, and became a skilled pilot. In his last term at Cranwell, in 1928, he was required to write a thesis. He chose as his subject *Future Developments in Aircraft Design* in which he examined some of the problems that were beginning to confront aeronautical engineers. At the time of writing the top speed of airplanes was under three hundred mph. Whittle envisaged speeds of five hundred mph or more, but recognized that in order to overcome wind resistance at these speeds, airplanes of the future would be compelled to fly at great heights. At these heights, however, although resistance is reduced, the efficiency of the propeller in the thinner air would also be reduced, and the lower air density would necessitate the use of some form of supercharger to supply sufficient oxygen for satisfactory combustion by compressing the available air. Whittle speculated on alternatives to the conventional piston engine and wrote:

It seems that as the turbine is the most efficient prime mover known, it is possible that it will be developed for aircraft, especially if some means of driving a turbine by petrol could be devised.

Whittle's idea was that the turbine, in which a fan-like wheel is rotated by the action of a stream of air or gas on its blades, should take the place of an internal-combustion engine, but should still be used to turn a propeller. Although in his thesis he referred to the possible future use of rockets, he did not at this time consider the turbine as a means of creating thrust by jet reaction.

Whittle was posted to the Central Flying School to train as an instructor. Meanwhile, he continued his interest in the theoretical questions posed by high-speed and high-altitude flight. He examined the possibility of using a gasoline engine to force the products of its combustion process through a jet, but discovered that this system had been already patented in 1917 by H. S. Harris. As it did not appear that a jet of this type would have any real advantage over existing engines, Whittle abandoned this line of investigation. (In fact, this principle was adopted, with limited success, in the Italian Caproni Camprini airplane of 1940.)

Late in 1929, Whittle revised his ideas and began to consider the use of a gas turbine, not to replace the piston engine in driving a propeller, but actually to provide a jet and thereby eliminate the propeller altogether. The principle appeared sound, but the research and development necessary to put it into practice would require considerable time and financial backing. Whittle approached the Air Ministry with his proposals, but their experts were convinced that the high temperatures and stresses on the turbine blades of an engine of this type represented problems that at the time were technically insoluble, and his plans were rejected as impracticable.

Whittle, though discouraged, was urged to apply for a patent on his preliminary work, which was filed on January 16, 1930. He then attempted, at length but fruitlessly, to persuade various manufacturers to build a workable engine. At the same time, he was undertaking tests of catapult launching systems and, in such spare time as he could find, was able to devise several military inventions. After this interlude, the RAF sent him to Cambridge University to study engineering.

In January, 1935, the renewal of his patent was due, but hard-up financially and pessimistic about the likelihood of any further developments,

The Gloster E 28/39, Britain's experimental single-seat jet fighter using the W.1. test engine. The first flight on May 15, 1941, proved that the jet was a feasible alternative to the piston-engined airplane.

Whittle declined to pay the $13 renewal fee and the patent was allowed to lapse. Shortly afterward Whittle's friend and associate, R. Dudley Williams, and his partner, J.C.B. Tinling, impressed by his plans, managed to interest the bankers O.T. Falk and Partners in the project. Backed by the encouraging technical report of the bank's consulting engineer, M.L. Branson, a company, Power Jets Ltd., was established in March, 1936, and research and development of a workable jet engine began in earnest.

Whittle became Honorary Chief Engineer and Technical Consultant to Power Jets Ltd., under certain conditions stipulated by the Air Ministry, since he was still a serving RAF officer. After his graduation from Cambridge with a first-class degree, he was granted time for postgraduate work, which he utilized in jet engine research.

The initial problems confronting the company were considerable. Funds were inadequate for testing individual components, and so it was necessary to build the revolutionary engine as a complete unit. Essentially, it was to consist of a compressor, combustion chamber, turbine, exhaust pipe and jet nozzle.

During its cycle of operation, air is drawn in the front intake and compressed. Fuel and air mixture is burned in the combustion chamber; compressed and heated exhaust gases are then passed through the turbine which rotates, thereby providing power to the compressor to which it is connected by a shaft. The gases then pass at great velocity through the exhaust duct and emerge from the jet nozzle in the form of a propelling jet.

In order to achieve this end, calculations showed that a powerful compressor providing a compression ratio of 4:1 would be required, although a ratio in excess of 2.5:1 (in an aerosupercharger) had never previously been attained. Whittle was also aiming at a mechanical efficiency

The F 9/40 Meteor, powered by the W.1.'s successor, the W.2., which held the world speed record in 1946 of 616 mph.

of eighty percent, compared with the previous record of sixty-five percent. The problem of combustion was also great—a capacity of two hundred gallons of fuel an hour in a six-cubic-foot combustion chamber was called for—perhaps twenty times greater than any earlier combustion intensity. There were innumerable other problems, not least among them the requirement for strong heat-resistant metals for the combustion chamber and turbine blades. Since no widespread demand for such metals had existed previously, metallurgists were only now becoming involved in their production, and had just created an alloy known as "stayblade" for the turbine wheel and blades and another, "RR56," for the compressor impeller and casing.

In June, 1936, an order was placed with the British Thomson-Houston Company, a leading turbine manufacturer, for an engine according to Whittle's specifications. They were to make the entire engine, with the exception of certain combustion components, instruments and accessories. Laidlaw, Drew & Company received the contract for the combustion chamber. The total cost of this prototype was about $8,000. Tests on the complete engine were begun on April 12, 1937, but the results were disappointing. However, the Air Ministry was sufficiently impressed with Power Jets' progress to place a contract with them for further experimental work. The engine was reconstructed and tested again in April and May, 1938, when turbine-blade failure halted work. Tests indicated that many basic design concepts, especially those relating to turbine blades, were at fault, and Whittle was compelled to reappraise many existing assumptions in order to achieve the necessary level of efficiency.

The third engine was first tested in October, 1938, and continued to operate until February, 1941, by which time it had provided a wealth of valuable technical data on which subsequent design modifications were made.

By the summer of 1939, after ten months' tests, the Air Ministry placed a contract for an engine suitable for flight with Power Jets, and a contract with the Gloster Aircraft Company for an experimental single-seat jet fighter. Gloster's specification number for this aircraft (known popularly as "the squirt") was "G. 40," but it became more widely known by the government designation, "E28/39." This was a low wing monoplane, twenty-five feet three inches long with a twenty-nine foot wingspan, weighing 3,440 pounds. It had an all metal monocoque fuselage and all metal wings, with fabric-covered control surfaces (which were larger than those of a conventional piston-engined aircraft, owing to the lack of a propeller-induced slipstream). The absence of a propeller also meant that a lower tricycle landing gear could be fitted. The engine was to be located in the fuselage behind the cockpit, fed by air from an intake in the nose. The air passed round the pilot via bifurcated trunking into the compressor intakes. The propulsion jet from the engine passed through pipes in the rear fuselage and from a nozzle at the rear of the tailplane.

The test engine was to be called the "W.1." It consisted of a centrifugal compressor and ten interconnected combustion chambers into which the fuel (kerosene) was pumped under pressure and burned continuously (as in a blowtorch). In action, the work of the compressor is augmented by the forward motion of the aircraft. The heat released in combustion expands the air and the products of combustion that pass at high velocity into the turbine, causing the blades to rotate at eight to sixteen thousand rpm. The turbine is connected by a shaft to the compressor and all its energy is thus expended in this way, while the exhaust gases create thrust by jet reaction.

While the W.1. engine was under construction during 1940, a second engine the "w.1.x." was being tested and the results of these experiments used to make certain modifications to the w.1. In April, 1941, the E28/39 was ground tested with the w.1.x. engine. During these tests, the aircraft actually left the ground for a few seconds, but did not make a sustained flight. The w.1.x. was removed and the w.1. installed, and on May 14, Gloster's chief test pilot, Flight Lieutenant Philip E. G. Sayer, undertook taxiing trials at Cranwell, Lincolnshire. The first flight took place the next day (May 15, 1941) and lasted seventeen minutes, during which speed runs were made at two thousand five hundred and four thousand feet.

The success of the flight program in the next few weeks, during which speeds of 366 mph were attained, showed that the jet was an entirely feasible alternative to the piston-engined airplane. In October, 1941, the w.1.x. engine was sent to the U.S.A. where, despite advanced work on turbo-superchargers for piston-engined aircraft, little research had been undertaken on pure jets. Development was begun immediately by General Electric of Lynn, Mass., and American-built Whittle w.2.B. engines were used in the Bell XP-59A Airacomet, the first jet flown in the United States, in October, 1942.

Development in Great Britain continued with the F9/40 Meteor, designed as an RAF fighter and powered by the w.1's successor, the w.2. Rolls-Royce and De Havilland also entered the jet aircraft industry, although no official announcement of the success of the new type of airplane was made until January, 1944. During the same year, jets were used to intercept German V-1 rockets. Whittle was awarded a CBE and numerous other honors. He resigned from Power Jets Ltd., which was nationalized. In 1948 he was awarded £100,000 for his work, and received a knighthood.

Since then he has been concerned with matters relating to aviation and social questions.

After the war, it was discovered that parallel developments had been undertaken in Germany. Jet research had been begun about 1930 by Professor Prandtl of Junkers at Dessau, and the importance of Whittle's work was recognized. The aircraft designer, Ernst Heinkel, became interested in jets at about this time, and especially after 1935 when Dr. von Ohain patented his designs. In the mid 1930s, BMW of Munich was also involved in jet research. Ohain's He5-3B turbojet engine actually flew briefly, but effectively, in a Heinkel 178 at Marienehe on August 27, 1939 (just four days before the Wehrmacht invasion of Poland) piloted by Flight Captain Erich Warsitz. This engine operated on somewhat different principles from Whittle's.

During the war, the twin-jet Messerschmitt Me 262 first flew in 1942 and was in production as a successful operational fighter by 1944, and subsequently as a light bomber. It had two axial-flow Jumo engines, a maximum speed of 525 mph, and a ceiling of forty thousand feet, and was more than a match for any Allied fighter of the time— but certain technical defects are believed to have made it so dangerous that it resulted in the accidental loss of twenty-three pilots in three months of operation. The Heinkel He 162 Salamander flew in 1945, and the prototype of the first heavy jet bomber, the Junkers Ju 287, was complete when the war ended.

Whittle's jet engine was not the first to power an airplane, but it was the beginning of the mainstream of all subsequent developments in Great Britain and the U.S.A. In overcoming the technical problems posed by the jet engine Whittle established himself as one of the foremost engineers of the century and the founder of a new age in aviation.

RUSSELL ASH

The Heinkel 162, in service by 1945. Parallel advances in aeronautics had taken place in Germany but were not influential in postwar development.

Above left The Whittle W.1. jet turbine, progenitor of a long line of successful centrifugal compressor turbojets, and a Gloster E 28/39.

39

The war in the south

Hitler did not seem to have been very disappointed by the failure of the Luftwaffe over Great Britain. With some reason he regarded Britain as a spent force, and already his thoughts were turning toward the coming campaign in Russia. But some of his generals argued that the attention of the Wehrmacht should more properly be directed southward. Britain still had a Mediterranean and Middle Eastern empire and the events of the next ten months were largely centered on the Balkans and North Africa.

raid turned into a rout. In January, 1941, the Italians surrendered the strategic town of Bardia. At the same time British, Indian and South African troops were clearing East Africa and by February Benghazi had been taken and the Italian threat to the Mediterranean and Indian Ocean neutralized.

But this success had serious consequences. Hitler had ignored his generals' advice to strike southward. On racial grounds he considered the Russians to be *Untermenschen* (or subhuman); he loathed their economic teachings and regarded their western lands as the proper territory for the expansion of the German people.

The desert railroad extended by the British to link Alexandria and Tobruk.

German troops in the main square of Tobruk after its capture by Rommel.

In a general way Hitler was prepared to allow Italy a Mediterranean empire. He had failed to gain control of Gibraltar, since Franco was too cautious to become a full belligerent, but he had looked with distinct favor on Britain's expulsion from Somaliland and in September, 1940, Italian forces under General Rodolfo Graziani (1882–1955) had moved ponderously out of Tunisia to Sidi Barrani in Egypt. With only two reinforced divisions at his disposal, General Archibald Wavell (1883–1950) was responsible for the entire Middle East Command. In addition to facing Graziani's 215,000-man army, he had to maintain the security of Palestine, Suez, the Iraqi and Iranian oilfields as well as fighting a war in East Africa. In November the Italian fleet at Taranto had been crippled and on December 9 Wavell's Eighth Army made a raid in force on Sidi Barrani. The

It was the Russians who were the main enemy. Now the failure of his ally's army was rendering his southern flank unstable. In October, 1940, Mussolini had invaded Greece through Albania. His ill-trained army of three divisions had been repulsed by the Greeks, and an adventure that was to have emulated German victories became an embarrassment. Now the Italians were in trouble in North Africa and in February, 1941, General Rommel was dispatched to help them with the leading units of the *Afrika Korps*. In March the Yugoslavs rejected the pro-German policies of the Regent Paul. It is probable that their new government merely wished to avoid all entanglements, but Hitler was worried. In April Yugoslavia fell to the German armies and was dismembered by Germany, Italy, Hungary and Bulgaria, Serbia remaining a vassal state and Croatia achieving

nominal independence. At the same time Greece was invaded. Britain had halted her North African attacks in order to send 60,000 men to Greece, although the Greek government was doubtful of their usefulness. Although the British political advisers were wildly overoptimistic, it is probable that the troops would have been sent anyway; how could Britain fail to help any ally in arms against Germany? By the end of the month all the British troops had been evacuated, mainly to Crete, which by the end of May, and in spite of a 32,000-man garrison, had fallen to a German airborne attack.

Meanwhile in Egypt, Rommel had outwitted the British forces and had advanced past Tobruk, though that vital supply port had not fallen. General Wavell had counterattacked inconclusively in May, but the already overburdened Middle East Command had also

to find troops for a nationalist rising in Iraq, which was crushed, for the invasion of Vichy-French Syria, which had refused to give guarantees against German collaboration, and for the overthrow of the suspiciously pro-German Shah of Iran. On June 22, 1941, as the Wehrmacht crossed into Russia, General Wavell was relieved of his command.

It had been a disastrous year for Britain. She was fighting desperately to defend the strategic Suez Canal. She was overstretched in the oil-rich states of the Middle East and her hopes of a Balkan front against Germany had ended in ignominy. The British Treasury had already warned the government that at the current rate reserves of gold, foreign currency and overseas assets would be exhausted by 1942. On the other hand, Hitler had successfully reinforced his forces, demonstrating yet again the power of the German

Convoy crossing Iran, the main route for lend-lease supplies to Russia.

Japanese policy challenges the West

army, and was ready to strike at Russia. It has been argued that the Balkan campaigns fatally delayed the attack on Russia, or, conversely, that Hitler should have reinforced the Mediterranean theater to capture North Africa and the Middle East. In fact, weather and training would anyway have delayed Barbarossa and Hitler regarded the Middle East as a prize that would fall into his hands after the successful completion of the Russian war. There was little consolation, real or imagined, for Britain in Europe and ominous signs that she would soon have to defend her Empire in the East were appearing.

The Far East

In appearance Britain was the greatest power in the Far East. She held India, Ceylon, Burma, Malaya and Hong Kong. She was responsible for the defense of Australia and New Zealand. Beside her stood French Indochina and the Dutch East Indies. But in reality Britain no longer had the power, and was slowly losing the will, to defend her possessions. It was a cardinal policy of the Royal Navy that she would not fight both an Atlantic and a Far Eastern war. But since 1914 a new power had been growing. Japan, fast industrializing and victorious in World War I, was expanding. She sought markets for her goods, room for her inhabitants and secure sources of new materials. Since 1931 and her attack on Manchuria, she had been conducting a slow and expensive war against China, which, although militarily inept, seemed unconquerable as a whole. This policy had brought Japan into conflict with Russia, who had blocked her in 1939; with Britain, who rightly suspected her of casting covetous eyes on her colonies; and with the only other Pacific power, America. The United States, although unwilling to engage in war, was most hostile to both the European and Far Eastern dictatorships. By March, 1941, Roosevelt had brought forward the Lend-Lease Act, by which Britain could lease war matériel from America, which would be either returned or paid for after the war. It was a lifeline to a country that had for too long neglected her industries and was

fast spending her money, although, until the u-boats were cleared from the Atlantic by more efficient escort vessels and a greatly expanded ship-building program, it would not be fully effective. At the same time America was hardening her attitude toward Japan. In 1940 and 1941 Japan had used Britain and France's difficulties to demand a presence in Indochina and the closing of the Burma Road, convinced that, cut off from Western sympathy and help, China would eventually wither and die. The United States, believing Chiang Kai-shek to be a force for peace in China, had, in 1940, placed an embargo on the sale of iron or war matériel to Japan. In 1941 she froze Japanese assets and embargoed her oil. All this was done with at least the concurrence of Britain. After all Britain was desperate for American help; Churchill and Roosevelt had corresponded regularly; and the Atlantic Charter of August, 1941, was a signal that America might enter the war. It also seems that Churchill never took the Japanese threat very seriously. But Japan saw her choices being limited. Increasingly she began to look south and west for the new materials she needed and began to believe that China and Southeast

General Hideki Tojo, who replaced Prince Konoye as Premier of Japan and initiated a regime of narrow-minded militarism.

Asia under "The Greater East Asia Co-Prosperity Sphere" could banish American and Western influence. In October, 1941, the interminable talks between the United States and Japan were interrupted by the fall in Tokyo of the relatively moderate Konoye government and its replacement by the narrow-minded militarism of General Hideki Tojo. America made one more attempt to negotiate terms: in return for

Japanese abandonment of Indochina, Manchuria, and all of China, the United States would abandon its oil embargo. Not surprisingly the Japanese refused.

Lebensraum

In the European theater, meanwhile, Hitler was poised to implement his policy of conquest and Eastern colonization.

President Roosevelt and Winston Churchill at an informal gathering during the Atlantic talks.

Operation Barbarossa

Germany's lust for Lebensraum *led her into the greatest land battle the world has ever seen—a battle that would take Hitler's armies to the gates of Moscow and Leningrad and end with their final defeat among the ruins of Berlin. Although Germany's armies were the better trained and equipped they could not match Russia's inexhaustible manpower and her traditional ally—the Russian winter. With the German armies on the defensive the downfall of Hitler's empire was inevitable.*

British propaganda pamphlet dropped in Germany to draw attention to German losses during the invasion of Russia.

Opposite Russian cartoon of 1941 showing the defeat of the Axis powers by the Allied powers.

The bombardment began at 3:15 A.M. On a nine-hundred mile front from the Baltic to the Black Sea more than six thousand German guns began destroying the Russian frontier fortifications. At the same moment assault troops dashed across to seize the bridges over the Bug River, and engineers began cutting gaps in the wire. At daybreak on June 22, 1941, the Panzers were pouring through the disorganized defenses to begin their headlong race deep into Russia. Operation Barbarossa, the greatest land battle the world has ever seen, had begun; it was a battle that was to take Hitler's armies to the gates of Moscow and Leningrad, and end with their final defeat among the ruins of Berlin.

It was inevitable that Hitler would eventually attack Russia. Long before he had come to power he had written of Germany's need for *Lebensraum*— living space to be hacked out of the vast plains of Russia—and now that he was master of Western Europe his rule could not allow the existence of any rival. His superb army had proved its worth in two lightning campaigns in Poland and France, and as the Führer himself had written: "Armies do not exist for the preparation of peace. They exist for triumphant exertion in war." Although Britain was still undefeated, she was helpless and could no longer be considered a real threat. Everything encouraged Hitler to turn and unleash his triumphant army on his last serious rival on the Continent of Europe.

Even before France had been defeated Hitler had told Colonel General Jodl, chief of staff of the Wehrmacht's high command, that his pact with the Soviet Union had been designed solely to win time, and that Russia must be destroyed as soon as possible. On July 29, 1940, after a series of meetings with the Führer, Jodl instructed a select group of planners to begin studies for an invasion of Russia. In November, OKH (*Ober-*

kommando des Heeres or Army High Command) submitted draft proposals to Hitler and on December 18 the Führer issued Directive No. 21 setting out the strategic objectives of Operation Barbarossa, and detailed planning began.

It was proposed that the German army would use the same methods of armored warfare that had served it so well in the past:

The bulk of the Russian army in western Russia is to be annihilated in bold operations by deeply penetrating Panzer wedges, and the withdrawal of combat-capable units into the wide-open spaces of Russia is to be prevented.

The directive was emphatic that the main objective must be the destruction of Russia's armies in the field; the capture of cities—even Leningrad and Moscow—was incidental to this.

Russia's western territories are divided in two by the Pripet marshes. This vast and almost impassable area forces both attacker and defender to fight completely separate battles both north and south of it. The main weight of the German attack was to be in the north with two army groups heading for Leningrad and Smolensk while only one was allotted in the south aiming at Kiev. The main encirclement battles would be fought by a particularly powerful central group and once this had crushed the armies facing it, it would wheel north from the area of Smolensk to help destroy the Russian armies in the Baltic states and eliminate Leningrad. Only when this had been done would the seizure of Moscow be undertaken.

However, as the detailed planning proceeded, both Field Marshal Heinrich von Brauchitsch, the commander in chief of the army, and his chief of staff, Colonel General Franz Halder, became convinced that the central group should not wheel north, but strike immediately for Moscow. This was

December, 1941 : German infantrymen advance through the snow in a temperature of minus 40°.

not discussed with Hitler, probably because it was felt that the overall plan could be altered once the first battles were over, but out of this difference of approach was to come the first crisis of Operation Barbarossa.

The German army, which was to carry out the massive task that had defeated Napoleon's *Grande Armée,* was at the height of its powers. The armored and mechanized divisions that had spearheaded the earlier victories had been doubled in number from seventeen to thirty-five and were grouped in powerful independent forces led by men who had shown themselves to be masters of the new art of the *blitzkrieg.* In retrospect one can see the standard of equipment did not match the men who would use it, for German industry had been unable to meet the demands of the new divisions and the number of tanks in each had been reduced from 258 to 196. Also, the standard tank was still the fifteen-ton Pzkw III with a fifty-mm gun; the twenty-ton Pzkw IV with a seventy-five-mm gun had only just come into service and only 439 were available. In contrast, the Russians had two tanks with a seventy-five-mm gun, the superb twenty-six-ton T-34 and the forty-three-ton infantry support KV-1, and both were already available in larger numbers than was the Pzkw IV, although they had not yet reached combat units. But, however important these deficiencies were to become, there can be no doubt that in June, 1941, the German army was superbly trained, combat tested and supremely confident that it could take on and beat any opponent.

In contrast, the Red Army was in a state of transition. It was a huge force with much good equipment, more than four million men under arms, and more tanks and aircraft than the rest of the world put together. But its leadership had been shattered by the purges begun in 1937. All but two of its marshals, all military district commanders, thirteen out of fifteen army commanders, and 110 out of 195 divisional commanders had been disgraced or executed. At every level its ranks had been decimated, and from being a vigorous body in tune with all the latest military theories, the Red Army had become a vast, hesitant and badly led mass. Its large armored forces—the equivalent of at least thirty-nine divisions were in existence—had been split up to provide infantry support, and although desperate attempts were being made to reorganize it after the successes of the German Panzers in 1939 and 1940, this process had only just begun.

The main weight of the Russian defense was south of the Pripet marshes guarding the industry and agricultural areas of the Ukraine and the Donbas regions. In the north the occupation of the Baltic states and part of Poland had had the fatal effect of pulling the Red Army forward so that most of its strength was lying close to the border. This was particularly bad in the central sector where the forces of the western military district were in a salient around Bialystock, positively

44

inviting the sort of mobile encirclement battle that the Germans were preparing to fight.

In this vital sector the Russians were also outnumbered, for the western military district with forty-five infantry divisions and fifteen armored brigades was faced by Army Group Center, commanded by Field Marshal Fedor von Bock with forty-nine divisions including nine armored and six motorized which were organized into two groups, *Panzergruppe* II commanded by General Guderian and III by General Hoth. In the north, the German army group commanded by Field Marshal Ritter von Leeb with twenty-nine divisions—including three armored and two mechanized in *Panzergruppe* IV under General Hoeppner—faced the Leningrad and Baltic fronts that had thirty divisions and eight armored brigades. Only in the south did the Russians have a clear numerical superiority; the Kiev and Odessa districts with sixty-four divisions and fourteen armored brigades faced Field Marshal Gerd von Rundstedt's army group of forty-two divisions, including five armored divisions and three motorized in *Panzergruppe* I under General Kleist.

But the Russians had one great advantage that might have helped to redress the balance—they knew the exact time of the German attack. The Sorge spy ring in Tokyo and the "Lucy" rin in Switzerland had both sent information of the impending invasion and specified when it would come. But Stalin, determined not to give Hitler any excuse for aggression, chose to treat the warnings with suspicion and did not alert his forces. When the attacks did begin on June 22, the Red Army was still on a peacetime footing and totally unprepared for the holocaust.

By the evening of June 22 the Panzers of Army Groups North and Center had penetrated more than fifty miles. Everywhere Russian resistance was spasmodic and uncoordinated, but everywhere the Russians were showing that they would fight to the death rather than surrender easily. The Luftwaffe had virtually eliminated the Russian air force—most of it on the ground. Only in the south was Russian resistance stiffer and the Panzers unable to break through.

During the next week the headlong advance continued. By June 27 the Panzers of Guderian and Hoth had met at Slonim and Minsk, forming two huge pockets around the forces of the western military district; and these were swiftly eliminated by the infantry while the Panzers turned east again. In the north, Russian counterattacks on June 23 and 24 were destroyed and by June 26 Hoeppner's Panzers had reached the Dvina River and seized bridgeheads across it.

Guderian and Hoth's tanks were now racing in two massive thrusts north and south of Smolensk, and by July 16 their advance units met east of the city. During the next three weeks the Russian forces that they had surrounded struggled to break out and Marshal Timoshenko, who was now commanding the forces of the western front,

Left German officers consulting a map on the road to Moscow.

Antiaircraft gunners protecting Moscow during a German air raid.

The German invasion of Russia, 1941

WHITE SEA

Frontiers of August, 1939 ----
Russo-German frontier, October, 1939 ■ ■

German gains in 1941:
from June 22 to July ○
August ○
September ○
October ◐
November ◑
December ●
Front line at the end of 1941 ━

Archangel

FINLAND

Lake Onega

Lake Lagoda

Helsinki

Leningrad supply and escape route

Gulf of Finland

Narva

Leningrad

Vologda

Kazan

Staraya Russa

Kalinin

Yaroslavl

Gorki

Pskov

Ostrov

Moscow

RUSSIA

Riga

Dvina River

Vyazma

Volga River

Memel

Smolensk

Tula

GERMANY

Vilna

Yelnya

Saratov

Roslavl

Orel

Minsk

Bryansk

Voronezh

Slonim

Kursk

Bialystock

Pripet Marshes

RUSSIA

Pinsk

Bug River

Brest Litovsk

Kharkov

POLAND

Kiev

Lokhvitsa

Stalingrad

Zhitomir

Dnieper River

Lvov

Berdichev

Dnepropetrovsk

Dniester River

Uman

Rostov

Pervomaysk

Cernauti

Pruth River

HUNGARY

Odessa

RUMANIA

Novorossiisk

Sevastopol

BLACK SEA

Constanza

Batum

Right above Poster attacking Hitler's hypocrisy in breaking the Russo-German non-aggression treaty.

Right below A Panzer division taking part in the attack on Terek. During the summer months of 1942 the Germans made enormous advances.

sought to gather some sort of force around Roslavl for a major counterattack while harassing the Germans by throwing in continual local attacks with hastily gathered reserves.

In the north, the Panzers had been halted at the Dvina for several days while the infantry caught up, but on July 2 they set off again and breached the Stalin line defenses on the Russo-Latvian border at Ostrov on July 8. The Panzer forces were now divided, part heading toward Staraya Russa and part toward Narva. This dispersal of effort and increasing Russian resistance inevitably slowed down the rate of advance. In the south, von Rundstedt's forces continued to grind their way forward, capturing Lvov on June 30 and closing up to the fortifications on the Russo-Polish border.

Already, despite their massive gains, some German officers were becoming disturbed by the apparent inexhaustibility of Russian manpower. No matter how many men were captured or units

БЕСПОЩАДНО РАЗГРОМИМ И УНИЧТОЖИМ ВРАГА!

ДОГОВОР о ненападении между СССР и Германией

КУКРЫНИКСЫ-4

destroyed there always seemed to be more. Faced with increasing resistance, the disagreements latent in the planning of Barbarossa began to come out into the open. Army Group Center had fought its encirclement battles and was now liquidating the resistance around Smolensk; should it now turn north as directed by Hitler or continue east to Moscow? The speed of its advance had meant that it formed a huge salient with its tip near Yelnya, and the Russian Fifth Army lying along its southern flank seemed to threaten its communications.

At Hitler's headquarters it was felt that the Army Group should halt to recuperate, destroy the threat to the south, and give help as directed to the other army groups before pushing on toward Moscow and running the risk of becoming even more isolated. On July 19 Hitler confirmed that this should be done, and that the remaining Russian strength should be destroyed in further encirclement battles. Immediately Guderian, Bock and OKH began scheming to alter the decision and be allowed to press on. For more than a month, while the Panzers could have been refitting and operating effectively in other areas, little was done. Guderian did use his instructions to strike southeast at the Russian Fifth Army as an excuse for moving south on August 1 toward Roslavl and destroying Timoshenko's troops gathering there; but having done so he continued his campaign hoping to be allowed to push on.

On August 3 Hitler turned down OKH's proposal for a new offensive toward Moscow and on August 18 he repeated his instructions that battles must first be fought in the north and south. It was not until the last week of August, with Hoth's *Panzergruppe* already helping Army Group North, that Guderian accepted the inevitable and turned his group south.

For here there had been a transformation. The fortifications of the Russo-Polish frontier had been breached on July 15 between Zhitomir and Berdi-chev and Kleist's Panzers had poured through south of Kiev and along the southern bank of the Dnieper. At the same time the German Eleventh Army had crossed the Dniester south of Uman. Marshal Budenny, who was now commanding the Russian forces in the south, failed to appreciate the danger and pull back his forces around Uman. On August 2 the two German forces linked up at Pervomaysk taking 103,000 prisoners. The Panzers continued on down the Dnieper to Dnepropetrovsk, which was reached on August 25, while other forces fanned out toward the Black Sea.

By the beginning of September German forces were more than one hundred miles east of Kiev both to north and south. Yet, even as Guderian began to move into the gap between his armies around Kiev and the next large Russian force near Kharkov, Budenny did nothing to guard his rear. On September 12 Kleist broke out of the bridgeheads he had been pushing across the Dnieper and struck north to link up with Guderian. On September 16 their tanks met at Lokhvitsa to form the largest pocket of the war in which at least half a million Russians were captured.

The reinforcements which had been sent from the center had enabled Army Group North to speed up its advance and by September 5 its forces were within sight of Leningrad. The next day it was decided that the city should not be attacked but surrounded and blockaded. By September 15 the siege of Leningrad, which was to last until January, 1943, had begun.

Now at last, with summer ending and the temperature beginning to drop ominously, the Germans were able to prepare for Operation Typhoon, the assault on Moscow. More than three-quarters of the army on the Eastern front was to take part, spearheaded once again by the Panzers. Hoeppner's group was to break through in the center with Guderian and Hoth on the flanks curving in to form two huge pockets around Vyazma and Bryansk. Once these had been

German machine guns on the Terek front in November, 1942. The German advance was halted by the onset of winter.

Запруда трымае

A German propaganda poster claiming to have halted the spread of Bolshevism.

Right Russian soldiers leaving Moscow for the front. Russia's huge reserves of manpower made up for the poor quality of her matériel.

eliminated it was hoped that the way to Moscow would lie open.

To the massive German array the Russians could only oppose fifteen understrength and under-equipped armies. But on September 14 Stalin had received the vital news from the Sorge spy ring that the Japanese had no intention of attacking Russia in the east. This meant that the only fresh and properly trained troops available, the twenty to twenty-five Siberian divisions in the Far East, could be brought westward to form a last reserve for the defense of Moscow.

The German assault opened brilliantly on October 2 with the Panzers lancing through the Russian front. By October 7 the two pockets had been formed as planned and the tanks turned back toward Moscow. But on that same day came the first light snow and rain that was to turn the unpaved Russian roads into quagmires and fatally slow the German advance.

After the disasters at Vyazma and Bryansk, panic had gripped the Russian capital and a massive evacuation to the east took place. But Stalin stayed in the Kremlin and Marshal Zhukov was appointed to command all the armies defending Moscow. He began the desperate task of delaying the German advance while building up his reserves and waiting for the onset of the ferocious winter—Russia's traditional ally.

By the end of October a combination of mud and desperate Russian counterattacks had brought the Germans to a standstill. For two weeks they regrouped, waiting until the ground froze solid enough for the Panzers to become fully mobile

again. Finally on November 15–16 the last great assault to seize Moscow before winter really set in began. Zhukov had been expecting the attack and once again tried to use his shattered armies to slow down the German advance while hoarding the Siberian divisions for a counterattack and putting them into action only when a break-through seemed to be inevitable.

As the temperature dropped steadily below the freezing point the Germans edged forward. The troops lacked any winter equipment and frostbite began to incapacitate the Germans more easily than their enemy. Rifles and guns froze solid, the engines of the tanks had to be kept running continuously to keep them operating, and all the time the Russians harassed and counter-attacked the advance units while partisans attacked the long, tenuous supply lines.

At the end of November, most German units were physically incapable of moving forward, and a last despairing attack on December 2, which got one unit within sight of the Kremlin, could not be supported. By December 4, almost without any official order being given, the German offensive had come to an end.

That same night Zhukov launched his counter-offensive. Seventeen armies spearheaded by the Siberian divisions, which were fully equipped and trained for winter fighting, tore into Army Group Center from north and south. Well-equipped Russian troops swirled through the blizzards around the frozen and desperate Germans, scattering units and cutting communications. Amid general demands for a retreat only Hitler stood

Russian war photograph of German dead on the road to Moscow.

firm—every unit must fight to the last where it stood. This order, although extensively criticized subsequently, probably saved the German army, for its men were in no condition to fall back through the Russian winter. By standing and fighting they blunted the momentum of the Russian attacks. Zhukov's offensive had been a masterpiece of improvization but the Red Army could not sustain it. When, after three months of confused mauling, the situation clarified the Germans were left within forty miles of Moscow.

The Red Army had savaged but not destroyed its opponent, but the very fact that it had been able to react at all meant that Hitler's gamble in Operation Barbarossa had failed. The enemy was still in existence and fighting bravely; the German armies had been lured deep into Russia and suffered irreplaceable losses. Germany would see fresh triumphs in the following year, but the Reich could never match the vast resources that Russia could call on. Once these could be brought into action and the German armies forced onto the defensive the downfall of Hitler's empire was inevitable. The process might take years, but eventually the Reich would be ground away.

JONATHAN MARTIN

"Tora! Tora! Tora!" 1941

On the morning of December 7, 1941, Japanese carrier-based planes unexpectedly swooped down upon Pearl Habor, the huge American naval base in Hawaii, destroying half the American fleet. It was a heavy blow, both physically and psychologically, but as Japan's Admiral Isoroku Yamamoto realized, all Japan had done was to awaken a sleeping giant and fill him with terrible resolve. President Roosevelt labeled December 7 "a date which will live in infamy." The consequence of Japan's attack was the immediate entry of the world's strongest industrial nation into the war againt the Axis powers.

At precisely three minutes before 8 A.M. (Pacific time) on Sunday, December 7, 1941, Commander Mitsuo Fuchida trained his binoculars on the airfield at Barber's Point, Oahu—the main island of the Hawaiian group. He focused on American planes, parked in neat rows, glinting in the sunlight that lanced down through the broken, scudding clouds, then swung on to antiaircraft batteries, barracks, the control tower. Nothing stirred. Fuchida yelled above the deep drone of the "Kate" bomber's engine, "We've done it! They're still asleep down there!" In front of him the pilot, Lieutenant Matsuzaki, had been scanning the sky—"Nothing in the air either, sir!" Fuchida shouted over his shoulder to the third crewman seated behind him, Warrant Officer Mizuki, "Signal the flagship!" Mizuki's Morse key began to click out an historic message— *"Tora! Tora! Tora!"* ("Tiger! Tiger! Tiger!"). The prearranged code-word told the commander of the Japanese fleet, Admiral Chuichi Nagumo, waiting tensely with his staff on the bridge of the carrier *Akagi*, two hundred miles north of the island, that after all the months of planning, experimenting, special training and unprecedented security precautions the great gamble had paid off—they had completely surprised the enemy.

To Nagumo it had seemed an impossibility that he could bring this armada of six carriers, two battleships, two heavy cruisers, with destroyers and supply ships, and three submarines scouting ahead—thirty-two vessels in all—across more than 3,500 miles of open ocean without being detected. Even now that the feat had been accomplished he felt no surge of relief, no lift of confidence that the final phase of the operation would attain its objective—the destruction of the American fleet in Hawaii's Pearl Harbor.

The Admiral had been given command of the First Air Fleet because of his stern courage and proven seamanship in handling unwieldy formations of ships, keeping them safely on station in all kinds of weather and through complex maneuvers; but he set a low value on the airplane as a weapon in naval warfare—he was by nature "a battleship man" who, his aviation officers often complained, "can't see beyond the range of his own big guns."

The audacious plan had been conceived by the Imperial Navy's Commander in Chief, Admiral Isoroku Yamamoto, at least a year earlier, when U.S.-Japanese relations suddenly had tautened to near-crisis pitch. Working in the most stringent secrecy with progressive-thinking young air officers, engineering and ordnance experts, Yamamoto painstakingly and obdurately had evolved his strategy for delivering a crippling, long-range blow at the heart of American power in the Pacific "immediately after the declaration of war."

Yamamoto had faced, and overcome, political opposition, obstruction from the General Staff, and innumerable technical snags. Tucked under the bellies of the low-level torpedo planes now winging in on Pearl's "Battleship Row" were strange, cumbersome missiles with large wooden fins. Pearl Harbor, his intelligence network had warned, was only forty feet deep and a conventional aerial torpedo needed at least eighty feet to level out after entry, settle down and run straight and true. "Taranto Bay in Italy is even shallower," Yamamoto had replied. "And yet the British torpedo bombers sank three of Mussolini's battleships there. Find out how *they* managed it." And a few weeks later a coded report from the air attaché in Rome gave him the answer, complete with sketches of the wooden extensions that more than doubled the missiles' buoyancy.

The odd, the ironic thing about Yamamoto, architect and driving force of what President Franklin D. Roosevelt afterward was to call "the

Admiral Isoroku Yamamoto, Commander in Chief of the Japanese navy, who planned the attack on Pearl Harbor.

Opposite The *West Virginia* ablaze during the Japanese attack on Pearl Harbor.

Zero fighters on the flight deck of the Japanese aircraft carrier *Akagi*.

Day of Infamy," was that he was widely regarded by his own people as pro-American, and a pacifist. In this convulsive time of Japanese militarism and expansion, his life had been threatened more than once by political and religious extremist groups.

Certainly he knew, and admired, the United States—and said so, often. On one memorable occasion, when the Prime Minister, General Hideki Tojo, and his army commanders boasted that their troops, battle-hardened in the Manchuria campaigns, would swiftly crush the "soft-bellied Yankees," he roared at them: "If we fight, it won't be enough for us to take Guam and the Philippines, nor even Hawaii and San Francisco. To defeat them we should have to march into Washington and dictate the peace terms in the White House! Have you thought about *that*?"

And again, addressing the officers of the attack force before they sailed for Hawaii, he said, "I want to caution all of those who believe that America is a nation divided and weak. They may appear to exist in a spiritual vacuum, with a taste for luxurious living, in a society full of corruption. This simply isn't true. I've lived among them, and I can tell you they are a people filled with the spirit of justice, fight and adventure. Japan has faced many powerful enemies, but none more formidable than the United States of America."

But the words that portray Yamamoto most clearly as a prisoner of history were spoken to two of his most trusted aides, Captain Kamohito Kuroshima and Commander Yasuji Watanabe, while they were working with him on the draft attack plan: "Gentlemen, you know I'm against war with the United States. But I am an officer of the Imperial Navy, and a subject of His Majesty the Emperor. Recent international events, and developments here at home, make such a war seem almost inevitable, and it is my duty as Commander in Chief to be ready."

Yamamoto always had intended to lead the attack himself, but the Emperor, the cabinet and the General Staff had refused to let him leave Japan at this crucial stage when other, simultaneous operations were about to be launched against Malaya, the Aleutians and Hong Kong. Confined to his flagship, the battleship *Nagato*, at the navy's inland sea base, at this moment he would be pacing the deck, awaiting Nagumo's first report.

07:59 hours—Fuchida spotted a solitary destroyer, patrolling off the mouth of the narrow channel that linked the harbor with the sea, and wondered how many of the tiny, two-man submarines had got through. The advance squadron of "midgets" had left Japan weeks ahead of the main force, carried "piggy-back" by large mother-subs, to be released a few miles from the island. Their almost suicidal task was to sneak into the harbor, lie on the bottom until the air onslaught began, and then attack the American capital ships from beneath.

The level bombers began swinging left. Fuchida's heart lurched as just over a mile ahead the clouds parted like a theater curtain and he got his first view of "Battleship Row." He counted eight great ships of war, instantly identifying the nearest of them: *West Virginia, Tennessee, Arizona, California, Oklahoma.* The Japanese airmen had spent months studying mast structures and silhouettes, using models, sketches—and blowups of picture postcards bought by Japanese "tourists" in Honolulu shops, and mailed to Tokyo.

As yet he could not see the American carriers. They must be moored deeper in the harbor, still cloaked by tattered clouds. The only activity was on *Nevada*'s afterdeck. He trained the binoculars: rigid ranks of white-clad sailors and marines, the sunlight flashing on metal—brass band instruments. The color party, standing by to play the—national anthem and run up the flag at exactly

8 A.M. Then on the right fringe of his field of vision he glimpsed the first of Lt. Murata's forty torpedo planes, sweeping in from the Kolekole Pass, east of the harbor, to begin their run on the battleships, just sixty feet above the water. Slowest and most vulnerable of the Japanese aircraft, they were to strike the first blow and then return to their carriers, leaving the target clear for the forty-nine level bombers, fifty-one dive bombers and forty-three escorting Zero fighters. One hundred and eighty-three machines in all—and already the second wave would be on the way.

08:00 hours—Admiral Husband E. Kimmel, Commander in Chief United States Pacific Fleet, paced the palm-fringed lawn outside his official residence on the slopes above the harbor, listening to the mounting drone of planes and scanning the hazed and cloud-broken sky with increasing uneasiness. He knew that a flight of twelve B-17 ("Flying Fortress") bombers was due in from Hamilton Field, California, at about this time, to refuel and fly on to Midway Island; but his trained ear recognized the sound of single-engined aircraft.

A great many—too many for a Sunday morning.

Some thirty minutes earlier the telephone had interrupted breakfast to inform him that the destroyer *Ward*, patrolling off the harbor entrance, had signaled Fourteenth Naval District Headquarters shortly after 7 A.M., reporting that she had "attacked, fired at and dropped depth charges upon a submarine operating in the defensive sea area." Headquarters had asked for confirmation but so far no further signal had been received. The Admiral was aware that the *Ward's* skipper, Lieutenant William Outerbridge, was a very young officer—on his first patrol, with his first command, in fact. Nevertheless, Kimmel had decided to cancel a golf date with his army counterpart, Lieutenant General Walter C. Short.

A tall, serious Kentuckian, "Ed" Kimmel had been in command of the "Pineapple" Fleet for ten months. Since the summer, when President Roosevelt imposed an embargo on exports of strategic materials to Japan, all forces in Hawaii had, on several occasions, been placed on various conditions of alert. But intelligence reports from

Japanese aerial photograph of Pearl Harbor taken during the attack.

53

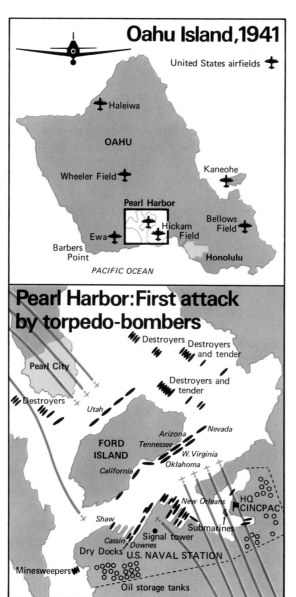

Oahu Island, 1941

United States airfields ✈

Haleiwa

OAHU

Wheeler Field

Kaneohe

Pearl Harbor

Ewa
Barbers Point

Hickam Field

Bellows Field

Honolulu

PACIFIC OCEAN

Pearl Harbor: First attack by torpedo-bombers

Pearl City

Destroyers
Destroyers and tender

Destroyers

Destroyers and tender

Utah

FORD ISLAND

Arizona
Tennessee
Nevada
W. Virginia
Oklahoma

California

New Orleans

HQ CINCPAC

Shaw

Submarines

Cassin
Downes

Signal tower

Dry Docks
U.S. NAVAL STATION

Minesweepers

Oil storage tanks

Washington were sparse and ambiguous, even contradictory sometimes, and the Admiral, two thousand miles from home, felt he was being left out of the international relations picture, and denied essential facts on which he could have formed his own judgment. His frequent requests and complaints to the Chief of Naval Operations, Admiral H. R. Stark, had gone unanswered.

Now, as he waited impatiently for his car, his strained and troubled mind recalled yet again grim phrases from the joint staff study which Hawaii's two air commanders, General Frederick Martin and Rear Admiral "Buck" Bellinger, had presented to him a few weeks after his arrival: "Japan has never preceded hostile action by a declaration of war," they had stated. "It is therefore possible that a fast-raiding Japanese carrier force might arrive in Hawaiian waters with no prior warning. . . . The enemy probably would employ a maximum of six carriers, and strike on a weekend . . ."

These nightmare thoughts haunted him each day, but with insufficient planes to maintain search

patrols in any effective depth, there was little he could do. Only ten days before Washington had ordered him to send fifty army pursuit planes—half Hawaii's effective fighter strength—to reinforce Midway and Wake. His two carriers, *Enterprise* and *Lexington*, with escorting task forces, had delivered the aircraft and now were on their way back.

Less than twenty-four hours before, at his Saturday morning conference, Kimmel had analyzed Washington's latest "war warning," which reported "a huge Japanese fleet" moving down the coast of Malaya, and predicted possible attacks on "the Philippines, Thai, the Kra Peninsula, Borneo. . . ." All distant areas, and Hawaii was not even mentioned. The conference had concluded that the message was aimed primarily at Admiral Hart and the Asian Fleet. Everyone agreed that with the two carriers not yet back from their missions, it would be foolhardy to send out the battleships without air cover.

The American Admiral had no way of knowing that at this moment, some five thousand miles away in Washington, two dedicated intelligence men, Lieutenant Commander Alvin D. Kramer and Colonel Rufus S. Bratton, had finally seen General George C. Marshall, Chief of General Staff, and shown him a series of intercepted messages from Tokyo to the Japanese embassy. Many months before, a cipher machine known as "Purple" had cracked the Japanese diplomatic code, enabling the Americans to eavesdrop on all traffic between the Japanese Foreign Ministry and their ambassadors all over the world. But so obsessed with secrecy were the U.S. military chiefs, that only a dozen names had been cleared to read

A model of Pearl Harbor used by the Japanese to help plan their attack.

Left The USS *Enterprise* with TBDs overhead.

the intercepts—indeed, only recently had the President, and the Secretary of State, been added to the list. Admiral Kimmel was not one of "the twelve apostles."

The latest "Purple" intercepts included instructions for the two Japanese ambassadors in Washington, Kichisaburo Nomura and Saburo Kurusu, to present a "final statement" to the United States government "at precisely 1 P.M. on the seventh, your time" (07:00 Hawaiian time); and orders to destroy all secret papers in the embassy. Marshall read through them once, immediately dictated a "Full Alert" signal, to be radioed to four commands: San Francisco, Canal Zone, Philippines—and Hawaii.

08:00 hours—From the harbour below came a deep, rumbling explosion. Kimmel wheeled, shaded his eyes against the sunlight. Incredulous, horrified, he saw flames and oil-black smoke spouting. Tiny, silvery shapes flitted across the water. A second blast, then another, and another, and now the smoke reared up in mighty towers. He stood immobile on his lawn, the wind plucking at his uniform, watching his fleet being destroyed.

08:01 hours—The marine band on *Nevada*'s

afterdeck was still playing the anthem, and the flag was still going up, as the first section of three torpedo planes howled close overhead, climbing away. Moments later the deck heaved, the men lurched and staggered as spray lashed over them, and the music faltered—but no one attempted to break ranks until the ceremony was over. Then came the cry: "General quarters!" All ran to their battle stations, the bandsmen still clutching their instruments.

Nevada and *West Virginia*, two berths away to the south, had both taken torpedoes. Now bullets stitched along the decks, and the first of the dive bombers came screeching down. From the hatches the rest of the crew came scrambling, some dressed for Sunday morning baseball, others in their underclothes. Thus did the United States of America enter World War II.

The first wave of Japanese planes wrought havoc among the unprepared Americans. Within minutes *Arizona*'s magazine blew up and "Battleship Row" swiftly became a shambles, engulfed in a raging fire storm. Other formations struck at the island's airfields—Hickam, Wheeler, Bellows, Ewa, Kaneohe—and destroyed the bulk of the American air strength on the ground. Only two planes, P-40 fighters piloted by Air Corps Lieutenants Welch and Taylor, got off to challenge the raiders, but they fought with great gallantry and took a remarkable toll. Miraculously, both survived, although Taylor lost an arm.

Some of *Enterprise*'s planes, coming in ahead of the returning carrier, flew into the thick of the battle, and so did the flight of twelve B-17s arriving, unarmed and short of fuel, from California. The bombers' commander, Major Landon, finding

The battleship *California* sinking at Pearl Harbor.

himself under fire from both sides, ordered his pilots to break formation and get down wherever they could. One crash-landed on a golf course.

Admiral Kimmel's car delivered him to his headquarters at the height of the first onslaught. Ignoring pleas to take shelter he went to his office window and watched the attack, questioning his staff, receiving first reports and assessments and giving orders in a calm tone. A pane shattered, something struck his chest and tinkled harmlessly to the floor. His communications chief, Captain Curts, picked it up. "Spent bullet, sir." The Admiral stared at it, his shoulders slumped, he spoke quietly: "It would've been merciful if it *hadn't* been." Then he straightened, and continued organizing the defense of his command.

By the time the Japanese second wave swooped in, the Americans were ready. The attackers met spirited resistance from antiaircraft guns on ships and shore, from machine guns, and even rifles. On board the maimed cruiser *New Orleans*, Navy Chaplain Forgy joined gun-loaders with the cry: "No Sunday service today, boys! So praise the Lord and pass the ammunition!" His words were to inspire a famous wartime song.

The Japanese air leader, Fuchida, remained over the target area until he had barely enough fuel left to get back to his carrier. Reaching *Akagi* he was startled to find the third-wave planes had not taken off. He ran from his cockpit to the bridge. Admiral Nagumo listened politely to his report and then said, "It's clear that the enemy carriers have not been found. That means they are at sea, no doubt with task forces. They will come looking for us now." He would not risk being caught with some of his aircraft away, others being rearmed and refueled. Fuchida, and the

other air officer, Commander Minoru Genda, pleaded with him, but he remained adamant. "The six carriers of the fleet are irreplaceable fighting units of the Imperial Navy, and I intend to take them home intact. All ships will retire. Set course for Japan!"

At Pearl Harbor the battered defenders watched the second wave retire, tended their wounded, then checked their weapons—ready for the next onslaught. But the minutes dragged by and no more planes appeared. They began to take stock. Four battleships were lost, another grounded, two more severely damaged. The target ship *Utah* was capsized and sinking, with many of her crew still trapped below. Destroyers *Cassin*, *Downes* and *Shaw* were destroyed, three cruisers crippled, and nearly two hundred aircraft totally wrecked. Almost three thousand military and civilian personnel were killed—over one thousand in the *Arizona* alone—and over nine hundred wounded. On the credit side, at least thirty Japanese planes had been shot down, three midget submarines sunk—and one prisoner, a sub survivor, taken. Above all, the two American carriers were unharmed—and at this moment hunting for the enemy fleet.

It was while Kimmel and his staff were assessing these results that an RCA messenger boy—ironically a Japanese-Hawaiian, or "Nisei," Tadao Fuchikami—arrived on his motorcycle, with a telegram for the Admiral. Kimmel read it aloud:

The Japanese are presenting at one P.M. eastern standard time today what amounts to an ultimatum. Just what significance the hour set may have, we do not know, but be on alert accordingly. Signed George C. Marshall, Chief of Staff.

There was silence as the Admiral crumpled the message, raised his smarting eyes to survey once more the burning wreckage of his fleet. Marshall's warning should have been radioed from Washington and delivered in about forty-five minutes—at least an hour before the first bombs fell. But the operator at the War Department's message center, after transmitting it to the other three commands, had found the direct channel to Hawaii blocked by static, and the colonel in charge had ordered: "Send it as an ordinary telegram—Western Union." Here was yet another compounded coincidence in the long and complex chain of misfortunes that led to the greatest defeat in American history.

It was little wonder that in later years, embittered by interrogations and accusations at innumerable inquiries, Kimmel was to convince himself that President Roosevelt and certain political and military leaders in Washington had conspired against him, deliberately withholding information so that Japan could strike the first blow, shocking the isolationists into silence and bringing a united and angry America into the war. Again and again he begged to be court-martialed, tried by his peers, but no charge was ever made. Instead the navy retired him on half-pension, to

The dock at Pearl Harbor after the attack, showing sunk and sinking warships.

live out the war in obscurity and inaction. "I asked them to let me serve my country, in any capacity," he said in a rare interview years later, "but they wouldn't even give me a stores job."

Oddly, one of the few voices that seemed to support Kimmel's claim that he was a scapegoat, in no respect guilty of negligence, and that the full responsibility for the disaster lay with "the over-secretive, conspiratorial, and muddle-minded hier-archy" in Washington, was that of his enemy, the designer of his downfall, Yamamoto. The Japan-ese Commander in Chief, fearlessly frank as ever, told his staff, and later a number of neutral ob-servers in Japan, that he was "profoundly dis-appointed" in the results of the Pearl Habor operation. In the first place, he declared, it had never been intended as a "sneak attack." When the Emperor was asked to approve the plan he had insisted that although Japan was not a signatory of the Geneva Convention, "due notification" should be given to the United States government. Yamamoto himself had suggested that the ultima-tum be presented eight hours before hostilities began, but Prime Minister Tojo and the General Staff had argued that this was too much warning, and eventually the period was cut to one hour.

The ambassadors in Washington had been in-structed to deliver the ultimatum "at precisely I P.M." (7 A.M. Hawaiian time). But the embassy's secretarial staff had gone off duty for the weekend, only one cryptologist could be found to decode the lengthy messages, and an under-secretary, a "two-finger typist," was pressed into service to prepare the English transcript. Because of this slow pro-cessing the ambassadors did not arrive at the office of the Secretary of State, Cordell Hull, until 2:20 P.M.—twenty minutes after the start of the attack. The two ambassadors, Yamamoto in-sisted, had known nothing about the plan. "For obvious security reasons they were kept completely in the dark. We simply could not have men walking about in the American capital with such knowledge in their heads. One of them could have panicked, had a nervous breakdown, or been knocked down in the street, and inadvertently betrayed us while in delirium or under drugs."

Second, in the Admiral's opinion the blow struck against United States naval power "was not mortal." The Americans had recovered quickly and fought back effectively, and Nagumo's force had failed to find the two most vital targets, the two great aircraft carriers. Moreover, the raiders had not sunk a single American submarine, nor damaged any of the important shore installations—machine-shops, storage tanks and dumps. "Pearl Harbor," Yamamoto had predicted, correctly, "will be fully operational again within a few months." And with equal accuracy he concluded: "I fear all we have done is to awaken a sleeping giant, and fill him with a terrible resolve."

Nevertheless, Premier Tojo's elated militarist regime pushed on with their ambitious strategy for the Pacific—to overrun Southeast Asia and then build "an impregnable defense perimeter" around their conquests. At first success followed success, while America licked her wounds and her allies suffered appalling losses and humiliations.

Almost six months were to pass before the awakened giant emerged from his lair to return the surprise, not only on Admiral Nagumo, but on Yamamoto himself, who this time had been permitted to put to sea. It was to be a very different battle, one that was to turn the tide—the Battle of Midway.

LARRY FORRESTER

57

The new alliance

From the middle of 1941, the situation for Britain became much more hopeful. Hitler's two mistakes—in invading Russia and declaring war on America on December 11—and Japan's attack on Pearl Harbor had brought into being an Anglo-American-Soviet alliance of herculean strength. Victory was now inevitable, although there would still be disasters to be faced.

Germany, Japan and their allies had not calculated the grave consequences that the immense economic and military strength of the United States would have on their plans. Although it had been probable that the Soviet Union and the United States would ultimately enter the war, the Axis powers now found themselves facing the two most powerful states in the world. Russia and America had both retreated into isolationist policies after the end of World War I and both had suffered from serious economic problems during the interwar period, but both had emerged strengthened by the outbreak of World War II. While France fell and Germany and Britain exhausted themselves in a death struggle, Russia and America looked on. December, 1941, saw an extension of the war that turned the conflict into a true world war rather than a predominantly European struggle such as World War I had been.

The war at sea

At first the main effect of the entry of Russia into the war was to hold down German troops in Eastern Europe and this had little immediate impact on the fighting elsewhere. American involvement was felt in the Far East and the Atlantic. For the hard-pressed British, American assistance in the Atlantic came at a crucial moment. As early as 1940, Roosevelt provided Britain with fifty somewhat antiquated destroyers in return for long leases of air bases in Canada and some of Britain's Caribbean colonies. The Lend-Lease Act of 1941 had made it possible to provide the Allies with arms, munitions and equipment. Even before the United States had entered the war she occupied Greenland and took over Iceland's defense, relieving Britain.

At sea, American navy ships had already begun to assist the British in convoying merchant ships to Europe, and the U.S. naval escorts had been ordered to "shoot first," rather than await an attack by German warships. German naval weakness assisted the Allies; even the fall of France, which had the world's fourth largest navy, did not benefit the Germans as the French fleet was sunk in Toulon harbor. Allied shipping was, however, at risk from submarine attacks, which reached their peak in mid-1942. Only by spending enormous sums on providing sonar and other antisubmarine equip-

Loading lend-lease supplies at an eastcoast port.

U-boat detected while trying to attack an Atlantic convoy.

ment could the Allies overcome the u-boat threat. Even so, by the end of the war, Allied shipping losses amounted to over twenty million tons, mainly as a result of u-boat attacks. There were few important naval battles in the west; the only decisive contest was fought off Cape Matapan, in waters between Crete and Greece. This gave the Allies effective control of the Mediterranean.

War in the air

Although naval maneuvering continued to be important in the island-hopping war in the Pacific, air power was in general rather more decisive. Large, slow-moving ships proved vulnerable to attack by aircraft. The Battle of Britain had already shown that air superi-

President Roosevelt asking Congress for a declaration of war against Japan.

ority could have a decisive effect, and both the Allies and the Axis powers were pressing rapidly ahead with research into improved engines. Jet-powered aircraft were, however, only available in useful numbers from 1944 and had little effect on the course of the war. Other developments—in rocketry and in increasing the speeds and payloads of bombers—had far greater effect. Both sides attempted to use saturation bombing of cities in an attempt to cow the enemy, but this policy did not have the anticipated effect and only served to stiffen civilian resistance. World War II was above all a land war, and although the future importance of airplanes was fully

The City of London suffering air raid damage; seen from the dome of St. Paul's Cathedral.

recognized by both sides, their immediate importance tended to be much exaggerated.

The Russian front

Fighting during 1942 took place on three main fronts, and all three were dominated by land battles. In Russia, Marshal Zhukov's counteroffensive, launched in December, 1941, against Army Group Center, had a devastating effect as no defensive position had been prepared by the Germans. Hitler, refusing to admit the very possibility of serious defeat, dismissed the Commander in Chief, Heinrich von Brauchitsch (1881–1948), and took over command himself.

Nothing that Hitler could order, however, was able to prevent the

Russian counterattack from gathering momentum and in January, 1942, bowing finally to the inevitable, Hitler ordered a retreat in order to prevent the encirclement of his forces. But the retreat opened a gap between Army Groups North and Center, and it was only with difficulty that the Germans avoided a serious defeat before the Russian attack finally lost its impetus.

In the spring of 1942 Hitler saw that the capture of Leningrad and Moscow, while important in the long term, would be only of limited immediate value. He resolved to attack southeast into the Caucasus in order to capture the oil fields around Baku, which would give him a valuable new source of gasoline, which the German army needed urgently. Launching a new offensive, the Germans cut off a quarter of a million men around Kharkov. In order to hold the Caucasus the Germans needed to capture the strategically important city of Stalingrad on the lower Volga and Hitler ordered an offensive against the city in August. It was to prove a costly order, and Hitler's hope that Baku would be captured was quickly disappointed. The few oil fields that the Germans were able to occupy were of little value as the Russians sabotaged them.

Surrender in Singapore

On the day after Pearl Harbor, the Japanese invaded Malaya,

smashing the complacent British, who had placed their hopes on the inadequate defenses of Singapore. There had been no civil defense preparations in the event of an air strike, and Japanese bombers were able to attack a brightly lit harbor. Churchill sent two of the British navy's most powerful ships, the battleship *Prince of Wales* and the battle cruiser *Repulse*, to aid the colony. Both were sunk by Japanese aircraft in the Strait of Malacca on December 10. This incident sealed the fate of Malaya and shattered the prestige of the Royal Navy.

With the U.S. Navy also crippled, the Japanese were free to fall on the British, Dutch and American possessions in the area. Guam fell on December 13, 1941; and Wake Island a week later; Hong Kong fell on Christmas Day, 1941; Manila one week later; and on January 11, 1942, attacks were launched against the Dutch East Indies. The British attempted to hold Singapore as a foothold in the Far East, but the city, which was prepared only for a sea attack, quickly capitulated to the Japanese troops who had hacked their way through the jungle and attacked from the rear. A huge contingent of British reinforcements, newly arrived in the city, were forced to surrender; they provided invaluable assistance to the Japanese who used them to build railroads. The surrender of Singapore on February 15 was one of the

Allies. At sea things were little better for the Allies, although the American victory over the Japanese in the Battle of the Coral Sea did something to help morale.

Defeating the Desert Fox

Depressed by Far Eastern defeats, the British could only view with alarm the situation in North Africa. The great gains of the Allies were threatened from April, 1941, by the arrival of German troops under Erwin Rommel, who rapidly proved himself to be one of the great generals of World War II. In May of 1942, Rommel's desert offensive had carried the Germans perilously close to Cairo. The victory would prove a costly one for the "Desert Fox," because General Bernard Montgomery, the commander of the British Eighth Army, realized that Rommel's lines of communication were too long and that it would now be possible to defeat him. He waited until October, slowly building up his forces, and then attacked the German forces at el Alamein to win the first decisive British victory of the war.

Triumph in the Pacific

As Rommel was plotting his assault on Cairo and Suez, the Japanese High Command was planning a second Pearl Harbor in

General Percival, the British commander at Singapore, on his way to surrender the city to the Japanese on February 15, 1942.

biggest defeats ever suffered by the British Empire. In March the Dutch East Indies were taken. Within a few months the Japanese dominated the whole of Eastern Asia, including Burma, much of China and half of New Guinea. Even India and Australia seemed threatened, and only in China, when the Nationalists won a decisive victory in the Kiangsi province in July, 1942, did there seem any ray of hope for the

the Pacific. That air strike, against the U.S. fleet's only mid-Pacific base, was designed to eliminate the remnants of the U.S. Navy and remove the last obstacle to an invasion of Australia. To achieve its goal, the Imperial Japanese Navy assembled the largest armada the world had ever seen and sent it steaming toward Midway Island. The ensuing sea battle was the turning point in the Pacific war.

Midway to Victory

After America's defeat at Pearl Harbor, President Roosevelt called for a declaration of war against the Axis powers, but even as he did so the Imperial Japanese Navy began to prepare a second massive strike against the Pacific Fleet. Unbeknown to the High Command, an extraordinary code-breaking coup had enabled American intelligence units to "read" the Japanese navy's top-secret communiqués. As Admiral Yamamoto's Carrier Striking Force— the largest such armada the world had ever seen—steamed toward Midway Island, the Americans closed in. This time the element of surprise was on their side, and in the ensuing battle Yamamoto's fleet was decimated and Japan's supremacy in the Pacific was ended. As Chester W.Nimitz, commander of the Pacific Fleet, observed, the U.S.Navy was "midway" to victory in the Pacific.

The Japanese Imperial High Command was infected, during the first half of 1942, with what several of its members characterized in postwar interviews as "victory disease." None of history's major empires were acquired with such ease and speed. Between 1940 and 1942, the myriad peoples of most of the Far East and the western Pacific became subjects of what Tokyo termed the Greater East Asia Co-Prosperity Sphere. The chief symptom of victory disease, according to its victims, was an arrogant assumption that whatever next step might be selected, victory was assured.

Early in 1942, some members of the Imperial High Command proposed an offensive against India and Ceylon. Others backed the strategy of isolating Australia—cutting its lifeline to the United States by seizing Fiji, New Caledonia and Samoa. Admiral Isoroku Yamamoto, Commander in Chief of the Imperial Japanese Navy, was of a different mind.

Yamamoto, who had studied at Harvard and served as naval attaché in Washington, had an abiding respect for America's industrial might. He argued that Japan's chances of consolidating its newly won empire depended upon an immediate naval victory over the United States—a victory of Pearl Harbor proportions—followed by a negotiated peace with Washington.

Yamamoto's hand was strengthened by the surprise Doolittle-Halsey raid on April 18, 1942, which caused little damage to Tokyo and other Japanese cities but severely damaged Japanese pride. Three weeks later, the Battle of the Coral Sea—the first naval action fought entirely by carrier aircraft, with the combatant ships never once sighting each other —proved that the U.S. Pacific Fleet was a dangerous foe, and Yamamoto's plan for a decisive naval engagement proceeded without further debate.

His timetable called for the great battle to take place early in June, almost exactly six months after Pearl Harbor. Yamamoto's objective was to smoke out the American fleet by threatening its one remaining important Pacific base, the Hawaiian Islands.

Operation MI, as it was designated, involved a primary objective, a diversionary thrust and four major striking forces. Yamamoto assembled the mightiest armada the world had ever seen: 162 major craft, including 8 aircraft carriers, 11 battleships, 22 cruisers, 67 destroyers, and 21 submarines. The diversion was aimed at the Aleutian Islands, which extend southwest from Alaska. The primary objective, involving the bulk of the Japanese Combined Fleet, was Midway Island, the westernmost outpost of the Hawaiian chain.

The core of the Midway Operation was Vice-Admiral Chuichi Nagumo's Carrier Striking Force —fleet carriers *Akagi, Kaga, Hiryu* and *Soryu*. All were veterans of Nagumo's Pearl Harbor attack. Backing up Nagumo was Yamamoto's Main Body, a powerful surface force that included seven battleships. Finally, there was the Occupation Force, a heavily escorted transport group that intended to seize Midway.

Yamamoto assumed that the Americans would be as surprised by Operation MI as they had been by the Pearl Harbor attack; that they would react instinctively and steam into one of the traps he was baiting at Midway and off the Aleutians; that whatever course the Americans chose, their movements would be shadowed and reported by a picket line of Japanese submarines stationed off Pearl Harbor. Every contingency was covered—as long as the Americans reacted as they were expected to react.

Quite unknown to Yamamoto, Admiral Chester W. Nimitz, commander of the U.S. Pacific Fleet at Pearl Harbor, was the beneficiary of a remarkable code-breaking achievement by the navy's Combat Intelligence Unit. The "black chamber" cryptanalysis operations had established that Midway was the objective of the Japanese Combined Fleet, had

Above The Mitsubishi Type O fighter—known as the Zero— used by the Japanese navy in its attack on Midway.

Opposite An American gun crew closing the breach of a 16-inch gun, from a painting by Lieutenant Commander Dwight C. Shepler.

The Battle of Midway June 4-5, 1942

At 04:30 Japanese bombers and fighters launched from 1 Carrier Striking Force to attack Midway inflicting heavy damage. Return attack by Midway-based bombers on Japanese carriers proves costly and ineffective.

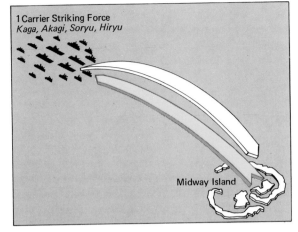

1 Carrier Striking Force
Kaga, Akagi, Soryu, Hiryu

Midway Island

At 10:25 thirty-five dive bombers from Task Forces 16 and 17 attack *Akagi, Soryu* and *Kaga*, and cripple them. A second strike, launched by Japanese dive bombers at 14:35 on *Yorktown*, destroys her.

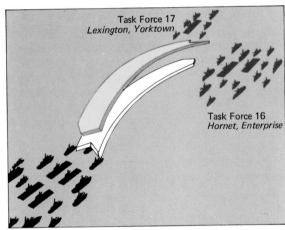

Task Force 17
Lexington, Yorktown

Task Force 16
Hornet, Enterprise

Shortly after 17:00, dive bombers from Task Force 16 attack *Hiryu* and cripple the carrier. The shattered *Yorktown* is protected by a screening force.

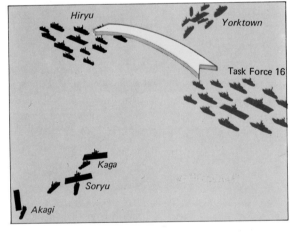

Hiryu

Yorktown

Task Force 16

Kaga

Soryu

Akagi

Apart from *Mikuma* of the Cruiser Division which was attacked by Midway-based bombers, 1 Carrier Striking Force was the only part of the Japanese fleet which took part in the action. Yamamoto's Main Body cruised hundreds of miles away from the carriers, thus depriving them of any aid.

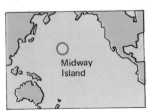

Midway Island

The course of the fleets
A 10:20 *Kaga, Akagi* crippled
B 10:25 *Soryu* crippled
C 14:35 *Yorktown* crippled
D 17:05 *Hiryu* crippled

Main Body (Yamamoto)

1 Carrier Striking Force (Nagumo)

11 Fleet (Kondo)

Cruiser Division (Kurita)

Task Force 17 (Fletcher)

Task Force 16 (Spruance)

Midway Island

400 300 200 100 miles

worked out in precise detail its composition, and had calculated its timetable with amazing accuracy.

Fleet carriers *Hornet* and *Enterprise* were recalled from the South Pacific, armed and fueled at Pearl Harbor, and dispatched toward Midway. The *Yorktown*, which had suffered severe internal damage from an aerial bomb in the Coral Sea action, was patched together by the prodigious efforts of Pearl Harbor's dockyard workers and sent off to join her two sister carriers.

By the afternoon of June 2, the U.S. battle fleet was on station well to the north of Midway. Task Force 17, composed of *Yorktown* and a cruiser-destroyer escort, was commanded by Rear Admiral Frank Jack Fletcher. Task Force 16, consisting of *Hornet* and *Enterprise* and their escorts, was under Rear Admiral Raymond A. Spruance. Fletcher, who had fought the Battle of the Coral Sea, was in tactical command. The combined strength of the two task forces was just 25 fighting vessels and 233 aircraft. Nimitz' strategy was to maintain the edge his intelligence officers had given him by secreting his forces until the last possible moment, relying on aircraft from Midway to locate the enemy. Nagumo's Carrier Striking Force was designated as the primary American target.

These rapid preliminary moves effectively canceled Yamamoto's contingency insurance. The picket line of Japanese submarines took position off the Hawaiian chain a full day too late to detect that Fletcher and Spruance had slipped out of Pearl Harbor. As the various elements of the Combined Fleet converged on Midway, the Japanese were blissfully unaware that the foe was reacting contrary to all their predictions.

Yamamoto's battle plan commenced precisely on schedule at dawn on June 3, 1942. The Aleutian strike force raided installations at Dutch Harbor and readied amphibious forces to seize the islands of Attu and Kiska at the tip of the Aleutian chain. Nimitz held Task Forces 16 and 17 on station, ignoring the gambit. The Occupation Force steamed along slowly, seven hundred miles west of Midway, marking time until the sea battle was decided. Angling in from the northwest was Nagumo's Carrier Striking Force, twenty-four hours' steaming time from the launching point for an air strike on the island. Some three hundred miles astern of Nagumo was Yamamoto's Main Body, waiting in the wings for the opportunity to draw the American fleet within range of its great naval rifles.

In midmorning on June 3, a Midway-based Catalina flying boat radioed that it had sighted Japanese ships due west of the island. Nimitz surmised that this was the Occupation Force: game far too small on which to waste his precious advantage of surprise.

The following morning, before dawn, eleven Catalinas lumbered off the Midway lagoon. *Yorktown* also launched a dawn search, but to the north, as a precaution. Everything pointed to the Carrier Striking Force's being to the northwest of Midway, and it was up to the Cats to locate it. At about the same time, Admiral Nagumo dispatched a 108-plane strike toward Midway. Almost as an afterthought, he ordered his cruisers to catapult seven float planes for a search to the north.

The early morning hours passed with agonizing slowness aboard the three American carriers. At 5:45 A.M. a message was intercepted from one of the Catalinas reporting "many enemy planes heading Midway." The tension increased. Then, eighteen minutes later, the key message came: the Carrier Striking Force had been sighted and tracked. The Cats had done their job. Spruance's Task Force 16 drove hard at twenty-five knots on a southwesterly course to bring its planes within range. After recovering *Yorktown*'s search planes, Fletcher followed.

At Midway, every plane that could fly was sent aloft, either to defend the island or to attack the enemy fleet. At 6:30 A.M. Midway came under heavy attack. Although the enemy bombers wrecked most of Midway's installations, they failed to crater the airfield enough to knock it out. The Japanese flight commander radioed Nagumo that a second strike would be required to neutralize Midway before any landing could be attempted.

At this point—it was now 7:15 A.M.—Nagumo made the first in a series of crucial decisions. He had prudently held back a one-hundred-plane reserve force in case any American ships were sighted. He now ordered those planes rearmed with fragmentation and incendiary bombs for a second strike.

Only a few minutes before, some 175 miles to the northeast, Raymond Spruance too had made a crucial decision. It was calculated that the Japanese carriers could be caught at an exceedingly vulnerable moment—rearming and refueling the returned Midway attack force—if Task Force 16 launched its planes immediately. Yet the range was still too great to assure the safe return of the relatively "short-legged" American fighters and bombers.

Spruance did not hesitate. He all but emptied *Enterprise* and *Hornet*, gambling everything on one single, massive surprise strike. Rear Admiral Fletcher launched a partial strike force from *Yorktown*, keeping back a half deck-load of dive

President Roosevelt (center), with General MacArthur (left), Admiral Chester Nimitz, and Admiral William Leahy (right) planning the final drive to liberate the Philippines.

bombers and fighters to deal with emergencies.

The Japanese Admiral, meanwhile, was undergoing increasing mental pressure. An uncoordinated but gallant series of attacks by Midway's airmen was forcing the Carrier Striking Force into radical defensive maneuvers, but only a handful survived the vicious Zeros and the antiaircraft fire.

In the midst of these attacks, one of the Japanese float planes launched earlier radioed a vague sighting: enemy ships to the northeast. Shortly after 8 A.M. the cruiser *Tone*'s search plane amplified the sighting by identifying one of the ships as a carrier. Nagumo hesitated. Contrary to all predictions, American ships had somehow slipped into the battle zone. Nagumo finally ordered the planes of his reserve force to be rearmed with torpedoes and armor-piercing bombs in anticipation of a naval action.

By this time, however, Nagumo's Midway strike force had returned, low on fuel and impatient to land. The Japanese Admiral was faced with yet another decision. He had thirty-odd dive bombers and torpedo planes on his decks, all properly armed for an immediate attack on the American ships. But his combat air patrol was too low on fuel to provide them with a fighter escort. With the harassing attacks from Midway driven off at last, Nagumo made his decision: he ordered the reserve force transferred below decks in order to take aboard the Midway strike force. Once all his aircraft were rearmed and refueled, he would launch a balanced, fully equipped

An artist's impression of the Battle of Midway shows the Japanese carrier *Kaga* being attacked by U.S. Dauntlesses.

U.S. aircraft carrier *Yorktown* receiving a direct hit from a Japanese plane. While being towed to Pearl Harbor after the battle, the *Yorktown* was torpedoed and sunk by Japanese submarines.

attack on the U.S. carrier that the *Tone*'s scout plane had sighted. As a precaution, he ordered a 90° course change, veering northeast—away from Midway and toward the American Task Force. Nagumo needed an hour's grace to prepare his new attack, and he anticipated that his course change would throw off any further enemy attacks.

Due to scattered clouds and haze—and the need to economize on fuel—the American squadrons had become badly scattered after taking off from their carriers. When they arrived over the expected intercept point one by one, they found nothing. The leader of *Hornet*'s dive bomber and fighter squadrons, assuming that the Japanese had held course but increased speed, turned toward Midway—and flew right out of the battle. The leaders of the other squadrons surmised that the Japanese had changed course and began to search to the northeast.

The first to sight the elusive Carrier Striking Force was the *Hornet*'s remaining squadron—Torpedo 8's fifteen Devastators. Even though he had no fighter escort, Lieutenant Commander John Waldron ordered an immediate attack. The lumbering, obsolete Devastators never had a chance. Patrolling Zeros shot down every one of Waldron's planes before they could get close enough for effective torpedo runs. One man survived.

Waldron's attack was made about 9:30 A.M. In the next forty-five minutes the torpedo squadrons from *Enterprise* and *Yorktown* tried their luck. None of their torpedoes found a target, and twenty more Devastators went cartwheeling into the sea. Free of attack once more, arming and refueling of their planes completed, *Akagi*, *Kaga*, *Hiryu* and *Soryu* turned into the wind to begin launching planes. By this time it was 10:20 A.M.

At that precise moment, Admiral Nagumo could not be blamed for feeling a surge of confidence. Despite more than three hours of intermittent attacks—eight of them in all—not one of his vessels had been even slightly damaged. Midway had been hit hard and nearly seventy U.S. planes had been shot down. He was about to hurl an overwhelming force against the American fleet—which was the objective of the whole massive operation.

But Nagumo's moment of confidence was brief. Some 14,000 feet above the Carrier Striking Force, the pilots and gunners of the dive-bomber squadrons from *Enterprise* and *Yorktown* were staring in frank amazement at the sight below. "This was the culmination of our hopes and dreams," recalled an *Enterprise* pilot.

As the Dauntless pilots carefully lined up their targets and rolled over into their dives, not a single Japanese fighter challenged them. Every Zero of the combat air patrol was far below, fresh from the slaughter of the U.S. torpedo bombers. Lacking radar, the first warning—the only warning—of impending doom for the men aboard the Japanese ships was the high-pitched shriek of diving planes.

The Douglas SBD Dauntless was a good scout plane and a superb dive bomber, with remarkable stability in even the steepest dive. Now, within the space of just six minutes on that fateful fourth of June, the forty-seven Dauntlesses exacted a frightful toll of the Carrier Striking Force.

The *Enterprise* pilots took *Akagi* and *Kaga* as their

A close-up of the Japanese cruiser *Mogame* showing its superstructure wrecked and burning after an attack by U.S. planes during the Battle of Midway.

targets and the *Yorktown* planes attacked *Soryu*; the fourth Japanese carrier *Hiryu*, was too far away to be reached with any chance of success.

Three bombs struck *Akagi*, two of them in the midst of the forty planes lined up for take-off. The fully armed and fueled planes exploded in a chain-reaction of destruction. In a matter of minutes Nagumo's flagship was aflame from stern to stern.

A similar grim fate overtook huge old *Kaga*. Rivers of blazing aviation gasoline spilled through the holed flight deck and ignited bomb and torpedo magazines. Nearly continuous explosions sent great gusts of flame and smoke in every direction. The *Yorktown* pilots were no less accurate. Three bombs tore *Soryu*'s flight deck apart, flinging planes overboard and spreading fires among the carelessly stowed bombs that the deck crews had failed to secure during the morning's frantic arming and re-arming. *Soryu*'s engines died and she wallowed to a stop.

As the Dauntlesses pulled out of their dives and raced for safety—pursued by the vengeful Zeros—they left behind a chaotic scene. Huge billows of black smoke from the three burning Japanese carriers stained the bright blue sky. Circled by anxious escorts, *Soryu* drifted aimlessly, her water mains ruptured and her fires beyond control. *Kaga* slowly lost headway and stopped, her hangar deck a white-hot inferno. *Akagi*, her rudder jammed, turned in slow circles like a wounded animal.

Despite the stunning turn of events, the battle was not yet over. Admiral Nagumo's surviving carrier, *Hiryu*, launched a strike force that tracked down Admiral Fletcher's *Yorktown*. Two waves of dive bombers and torpedo planes put three bombs and two torpedoes into the U.S. carrier. *Yorktown* lost power and took on a severe list; Fletcher, fearing she would capsize, ordered her abandoned.

Within two hours *Yorktown* was avenged. As soon as he had refueled and rearmed his planes, Spruance dispatched twenty-five Dauntlesses to attack *Hiryu* and once again the aim of the American pilots was deadly: four direct hits cut the carrier to pieces.

One by one, the once-proud carriers of Nagumo's command went to the bottom. Shortly after 7 P.M. *Soryu* slid stern-first under the calm sea; ten minutes later, *Kaga* followed. And at dawn on June 5 the still-burning hulks of *Akagi* and *Hiryu* were torpedoed by their own escorts.

A day later the battered *Yorktown* was discovered by a Japanese submarine as she was being towed toward Pearl Harbor. Two torpedoes sealed her fate; on June 7, sixteen hours later, she rolled over and sank.

Admiral Yamamoto had learned of the debacle shortly before 11 A.M. on June 4. Rallying quickly, he assembled a cruiser force to seek a night action with the American task forces—but to no avail. Finally, in the early hours of June 5, Yamamoto ordered a general retirement. The next day Spruance's airmen caught up with the lagging heavy cruiser *Mikuma* and sank her.

Nothing had prepared the Japanese for a defeat of such unimaginable proportions. Yamamoto was utterly disconsolate as the Combined Fleet steamed toward home waters. He had lost four fleet carriers, a heavy cruiser, over three hundred aircraft, and thirty-five hundred men.

On the American side, many shared credit for the decisive victory. The Combat Intelligence Unit's coup had made it possible for the United States to enter the battle as an underdog with a chance of victory. Knowing Japanese intentions and dispositions, the battle became a duel not between two mismatched battle fleets, but between Task Forces 16 and 17 and Nagumo's Carrier Striking Force—three carriers against four. Yamamoto's massive battleships might as well have stayed in Tokyo Bay for all they accomplished. Nimitz used his advantage brilliantly and decisively, and his commanders—Fletcher, and especially Spruance—directed the battle with equal brilliance.

Midway must be ranked with el Alamein and Stalingrad as one of World War II's turning points. On that glorious fourth of June the whole complexion of the war in the Pacific changed. Midway won America the time to mobilize its enormous war potential. Never again would the Imperial Navy sail the Pacific with safety or security. Two months later, at Guadalcanal in the Solomons, the United States took the offensive against Japan; six months later the initiative was firmly in American hands, never to be relinquished.   STEPHEN W. SEARS

Bottom American troops landing on the island of Okinawa, 350 miles from Japan, in 1945.

A memorial service for U.S. forces killed in the Battle of Midway. U.S. losses were light in comparison with the damage inflicted on the Japanese.

The End of the Beginning

Depressed by Far Eastern defeats, Britain viewed with alarm the situation in North Africa. In May, 1942, Rommel's desert offensive had carried the Germans perilously close to Cairo. This victory, however, would prove a costly one for the "Desert Fox."
With the arrival on August 13 of General Montgomery as commander of the Eighth Army, British morale rose. By October the Eighth Army was ready to attack the German forces at el Alamein and to win the first decisive British victory of the war—a victory that eliminated the threat to the Suez Canal and enabled the British to launch a counterattack. By November Rommel's Afrika Korps was in retreat.

Bernard Montgomery, commander of the Eighth Army in Egypt. His offensive at el Alamein constituted the first British land victory of the war.

Opposite A 25-pounder gun team in action on the el Alamein front, 1942, by John Berry. The offensive at el Alamein drove Rommel's forces out of Egypt, Libya and Tripolitania and eventually forced the Germans to abandon the Mareth Line in southern Tunisia.

On November 10, 1942, six days after Field Marshal Erwin Rommel, commanding the German and Italian troops in North Africa, had ordered a general retreat from the Alamein battlefield, Winston Churchill, the British Prime Minister, delivered a speech at the Mansion House in London. "This is not the end," he said. "It is not even the beginning of the end. But it is, perhaps, the end of the beginning." The Battle of el Alamein, fought in the sand of the Egyptian desert, devoid even of scrub, was one of the great "turning-point battles" of history. Indeed General Montgomery, who was in command of the British Eighth Army, had said as much—before the battle, when he stated categorically that it would be "one of the decisive battles of history. It will be the turning point of the war."

In the autumn of 1942 the British people and their allies, looking back to the beginning of the war that had broken out in September, 1939, could see little but a virtually unbroken chain of disasters. After Rommel's capture of Tobruk on June 21 he had been able to force the Eighth Army to withdraw to the defensive position of el Alamein, which took its name from the small railway station on the coastal line to Mersa Matruh, only some fifty-five miles from the Egyptian port of Alexandria on the delta of the Nile.

On July 1, after he had crossed the frontier between Libya and Egypt, Rommel was brought to a halt by the First South African Division and the Eighteenth Indian Infantry Brigade in the northern sector of the Alamein position, but by this time both sides were exhausted by the physical and administrative strains of prolonged desert fighting. The morale of the German and Italian troops under Rommel was high. Cairo and the valley of the Nile were almost in sight, and only a seemingly demoralized enemy barred their way. However, the morale of their enemy had risen since the arrival, on the morning of August 13, of General Montgomery, whose first objective had been to introduce an *esprit de corps* into the Eighth Army. Perhaps the greatest factor in raising morale was his declaration, on the very day he took over command, that there was to be no retreat from the Alamein position. Plans for a further withdrawal had been prepared and he gave orders for them to be burned. "If Alamein is lost," he said, "Egypt is lost. If we cannot stay at Alamein alive, we will stay there dead." He began to build up supplies of matériel in the forward areas and to reduce the enormous administrative "tail" of vehicles by sending them to the rear areas. Now the army could not withdraw—there was no transport.

On August 16 he moved his headquarters from the desert to a pleasant site by the sea at Burg el Arab alongside the headquarters of Air Marshal Coningham's Desert Air Force. Henceforth the liaison and cooperation between the ground and air forces were major factors in the success of Montgomery's desert war.

During the next ten days the Eighth Army was reinforced by the Forty-Fourth (Home Counties) Division and by artillery and tanks. At the same time a "deception" plan was put into effect, aimed at giving the enemy the impression that the southern sector of the defensive line was being greatly strengthened. Dummy tank regiments were moved into the Himeimat area, a dummy infantry brigade position was prepared just to the north of this and large dummy minefields were laid.

It was assumed Rommel would be aware of the reinforcing, refitting and reorganization of his enemy, and that if he were to break through to Cairo he must make the attempt soon, before the opposition increased to the point where an attack might invite defeat. It was estimated he would move at the time of the full moon, on August 26,

October 29, 1942: amid the dust and confusion of battle a German tank crew surrenders.

Opposite above Trucks carrying British infantry through a gap in enemy minefields come under heavy shellfire, October 27, 1942.

Opposite below A German Stuka destroyed by Allied antiaircraft fire.

when his spearhead, the famous *Afrika Korps* of two armored divisions and a motorized infantry division, could attack at night and see where it was going.

By the morning of August 26 the Eighth Army was in far better shape, materially and morally, to meet Rommel's anticipated assault. That afternoon, orders were issued to defend all positions to the last man and the last round of ammunition. Everyone was in a high state of readiness, and tension, but nothing happened. In some quarters it was believed that the deception plan had worked and there would be no attack. But Rommel's delay had nothing to do with deception.

His problems were almost entirely administrative. His army lay at the end of immensely long and constantly threatened lines of communication stretching along the north coast of Africa, across the Mediterranean to Sicily and Italy and back into Germany. His supply ships were menaced by British submarines and his transport aircraft by fighters from Malta and North Africa. Thousands of tons of fuel, ammunition, armor and "soft-skinned" vehicles never reached him. His target date for a major operation against the Alamein position had been forecast perfectly by the British, but everything depended on having adequate stocks of fuel and at least four days' supply of ammunition in addition to the first line holdings of his units. Reluctantly, assured of only one week's supply of fuel but with promises of more on the way, Rommel gave orders for the attack to go

in on the night of August 30, five days after the full moon.

Militarily, Rommel was a great gambler. He was also a great general. His attack has been described, accurately enough, as a gambler's last throw, a last desperate bid for Cairo, before it was too late. It was made against the southern sector of the defensive line, between Bare Ridge and Himeimat, and there is no evidence that he was in any way influenced by the careful British "deception." It progressed, slowly and painfully, past the southern flank of the Second New Zealand Division and finally broke against the Alam el Halfa ridge. In a hard-fought battle that went on for five days Rommel lost his last gamble, and he lost it on two main counts. He had thought the southern sector was not heavily mined and not held in strength, whereas the minefields were several kilometers deep and there were many obstacles. Second, the relentless day and night attacks by the Desert Air Force were far heavier than he had anticipated and not only caused great losses in men and matériel but seriously damaged the morale of his German and Italian troops. He began to withdraw on the evening of Saturday, September 2. A counterattack by the New Zealand Division on the night of September 3 failed to achieve any success, and by September 5, Rommel had gone back to his original starting lines and the battle was over.

From the point of view of the Allied soldiers holding the Alamein position, the Battle of Alam el

Halfa not only proved their ability to defeat Rommel but established in them a firm confidence in the high command. Montgomery had told them what was going to happen, and it had all happened virtually exactly as he had foreseen.

As soon as it became clear to Montgomery that Rommel had been beaten off, he and his three corps commanders, Lieutenant Generals Horrocks, Leese and Lumsden, and all the units under their command, continued their preparations for the far greater battle that lay ahead. The *Panzer Armee* could be crippled by supply problems, made almost insoluble by Allied attacks on its communications, but Rommel could only be driven out of Egypt by a massive counterattack. The Joint Intelligence Committee in Cairo, drawing up an appreciation of Rommel's situation, came to the conclusion that although for the moment he was in no position to attack, he could not withdraw, as he was unlikely to find a better defensive position than the one he now occupied, and could not attack before November.

It was Montgomery's intention to strike long before then. Because of the sea to the north and the Qattara Depression to the south, the operation he called "Lightfoot" would have to be a frontal attack against a strong defensive position, five miles deep, containing a network of infantry-defended localities, strongly supported by artillery and covering ground thickly sown with mines. Montgomery's aim was to destroy the enemy, trapping him where he was by attacks on both

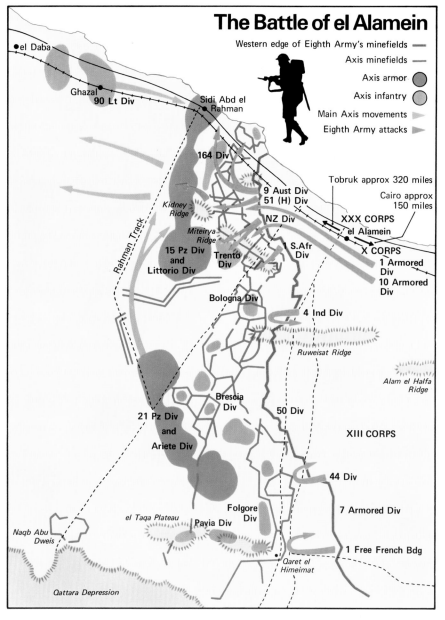

The Battle of el Alamein

Western edge of Eighth Army's minefields —
Axis minefields —
Axis armor ●
Axis infantry ●
Main Axis movements ▷
Eighth Army attacks ▷

el Daba

Ghazal
90 Lt Div

Sidi Abd el Rahman

164 Div

Tobruk approx 320 miles
Cairo approx 150 miles

9 Aust Div
51 (H) Div

Kidney Ridge

NZ Div

XXX CORPS
el Alamein

Miteirya Ridge

15 Pz Div and Littorio Div

Trento Div

1 S.Afr Div

X CORPS

1 Armored Div
10 Armored Div

Bologna Div

4 Ind Div

Rahman Track

Ruweisat Ridge

Alam el Halfa Ridge

Brescia Div

50 Div

21 Pz Div and Ariete Div

XIII CORPS

44 Div

Folgore Div

7 Armored Div

el Taqa Plateau

Pavia Div

Naqb Abu Dweis

1 Free French Bdg

Qaret el Himeimat

Qattara Depression

flanks, the main effort being in the northern sector.

The xxx Corps under General Leese would make two corridors in the north through which General Lumsden's x Corps could pass in order to confront Rommel's armor and destroy his tanks. At the same time, General Horrocks and his xiii Corps would attack in the south and, by drawing off enemy armor to support the Italian divisions in that sector, reduce the force Rommel would have available to use against Lumsden. Montgomery's primary target was Rommel's armor; once that had been dealt with there would be little difficulty in destroying the rest of his force.

This plan, in outline, was made known to formations on September 15, so that intensive training in the fighting of a full-scale, set-piece battle could begin. The date was secret, though it was clear that the initial stages of an attack must be made at night and therefore it was likely to coincide with the full moon. Montgomery decided to begin the battle on the eve of the full moon, October 23.

To fight the battle he had eleven divisions— about 210,000 men— 1,200 tanks, over 1,000 field and medium guns, adequate fuel and ammunition and a very short line of communication back to the base area. Rommel's army consisted of four German and eight Italian divisions and some independent units such as the Ramcke Parachute Brigade, which altogether amounted to about 180,000 men. He had between five and six hundred tanks, plenty of artillery and his defense in depth was strengthened with no less than five million mines.

Watching the training in the last few weeks before the battle, Montgomery began to feel his plan was perhaps too ambitious. Only two weeks before the battle he changed the whole concept of how it was to be fought, although he kept the general framework of the plan. The armored divisions were still to pass through the corridors but then they were to take up defensive positions at the western ends to hold off the inevitable counterattacks by the German armor while Rommel's infantry divisions were being methodically destroyed in what Montgomery himself described as "a crumbling process." When the German tanks attacked they would find the Allied armor in position and able to turn the German minefields to their own advantage. A particular feature of the "crumbling" tactics was the proposal, put forward by Major Williams, Montgomery's senior intelligence officer, to separate the intermingled German and Italian units along the enemy front. It would be easier to force a way through the Italians, who had been known to give way under pressure.

On September 19 General Stumme arrived at Rommel's headquarters to relieve the German Field Marshal who had been ill for some weeks and was badly in need of sick leave. Rommel left for Austria on September 24, but he said he would return at once if the British launched a major attack. Thus Stumme felt he was no more than a temporary caretaker; and he could never replace Rommel in the eyes of the men of the *Panzer Armee*.

Zero hour for Montgomery's attack on October 23 was fixed at 9:40 P.M. for the artillery bombardment and 10 P.M. for the infantry advance. The leading infantry had to spend the whole of October 23 in their assault positions, having moved there the previous night. It was an uncomfortable day of burning sun and infuriating flies. At 7 P.M., when it was dark, every man had a hot meal and an opportunity to work off the cramp of a long day spent in a narrow slit trench.

The Germans and Italians, after a succession of peaceful nights, were ill-prepared for what was to come. The night sky was cloudless and the moon brilliant, but shortly after 9:30 P.M. the silence of the desert was broken by the sound of distant aircraft engines. The bombers of the Desert Air Force were approaching their targets.

Exactly at the moment of zero hour every gun of the Eighth Army artillery opened fire.

The sound of the bombardment, unequaled since the massive barrages of World War I, struck the waiting Allied infantry with an almost tangible, earth-shaking force, and shells exploded at a combined rate of over one thousand rounds a minute on enemy gun positions and ammunition dumps. Amid the thunder of the guns came the heavy "crump" of bombs from the aircraft; the appalling noise and destruction went on for fifteen minutes. At 9:55 P.M. it ceased, as if switched off; there was complete silence while the gunners shortened the range to the line of the forward enemy positions. At 10 P.M. two searchlights pointed their beams into the sky and swung inward until they intersected to form an arch, dim in the moonlight. Simultaneously the guns began again, with even more furious intensity, concentrating this time on the enemy's infantry positions, and the long lines of steel-helmeted

Allied soldiers, their bayonets gleaming in the light of the moon, moved forward from their start lines into the dust and smoke of battle.

By first light next morning, Saturday, October 24, the assaulting infantry had not succeeded in opening the two corridors in the north, so the x Corps was not yet able to pass through and take

Erwin Rommel, the "Desert Fox." Commander of the German forces in Africa he captured Tobruk from the British and before el Alamein was poised to take Cairo.

Left Breaking through the last minefield at el Alamein, October 4, 1942; by A. Ingram.

Opposite Loading up bombs during the Battle of Egypt in 1942; by Arthur Gross.

October 26, 1942; the Alamein line illuminated by the shelling of the 25-pounders.

up defensive positions in the open country beyond. But the armored divisions began to fight their way forward and in the southwestern part of the northern sector the New Zealand Division started the "crumbling" operation. The first real crisis came that night. In the northernmost of the two corridors the First Armored Division had broken out into the open and was being heavily attacked by the German armor—as Montgomery wanted— but in the southern corridor the Tenth Armored Division was suffering heavy casualties on the Miteiriya Ridge and it seemed as if, in this area, Montgomery's plan might fail. The commanders of both the x and the xxx Corps went to Montgomery's tactical headquarters at 2:30 A.M. on Sunday, October 25, and were told categorically that there would be no change in the original plan.

This was perhaps the supreme test of Montgomery's generalship. Had he weakened at that vital moment and abandoned the attempt in the southern corridor, the whole battle might well have been lost.

As it was, later that morning both corridors were forced through and the leading elements of all the armor were out in the open beyond. That afternoon it became apparent that the "crumbling" operations in the southwest were resulting in unacceptably heavy casualties to the New Zealand Division, and Montgomery decided to switch the main effort to the area of the Ninth Australian Division that was fighting its way north, toward the coast, which took the Germans by surprise.

The *Panzer Armee* had in fact had a number of surprises. The tremendous initial bombardment was worse than anything they had imagined and it had destroyed their communications systems almost entirely along their front. Concerned about the shortage of ammunition, Stumme had hesitated to retaliate and so there had been no shelling of Allied assembly positions. The fire of the Eighth Army gunners was extremely accurate; it caused what Rommel himself described as "enormous casualties" and destroyed most of the infantry's heavy weapons. Without communications no one knew what was happening. Stumme died while attempting to find out what the situation was.

Rommel returned on October 25 to find that his army, now commanded by Lieutenant General von Thoma, was engaged in repeated attacks against Allied armor and infantry in an area known as Kidney Ridge. Losses were severe and no real progress was being made. On the Allied side, the brunt of this fighting was being borne by the First Armored Division, the Ninth Australian Division and the Rifle Brigade, whose valor set the course for victory. During the night of October 27–28 Montgomery carried out a major regrouping and pulled the First Armored Division and the New Zealand Division into reserve to rest and refit; they were to be the instrument for the final breakout through the enemy's defensive position.

He had deliberately given Rommel the impression that this breakout would be in the north, along the line of the coast, because he knew that Rommel, to whom this area was both vital and vulnerable, would make every effort to defend it. It was possible that in doing so he would concentrate his German units there, and Major Williams' hope that the German and Italian units would thus become separated would be realized.

Rommel reacted as Montgomery had anticipated. All the German troops who were stiffening— or in Major Williams' term, "corsetting"—the Italian formations in the south, were drawn to the north and on the morning of October 29 Montgomery made the decision to aim the final, knockout blow on the boundary line between the Germans and the Italians.

Italian prisoners of war captured in the Alamein area, entering a barbed-wire compound, July 20, 1942.

This operation was nicknamed "Supercharge," and it began at 1 A.M. on the morning of November 2. When the initial infantry objectives were reached, the Ninth Armored Brigade passed through, attacked and destroyed the enemy's "last ditch" defenses and the artillery positions on the line of the Rahman track and around Tel el Aqqaqir. In a fierce battle this brigade lost 113 out of its 132 tanks, but it opened the way for the First Armored Division to continue the fight.

The Germans made repeated counterattacks but were unable to stem the penetration south of Kidney Ridge. Rommel, realizing his position was now untenable, decided to withdraw, and notified Adolf Hitler accordingly. But the battle went on all the following day although it was now clear the *Panzer Armee* had been smashed. That evening Hitler countermanded the orders Rommel had given for the withdrawal.

At 2 A.M. on November 4 Montgomery launched further attacks in the main breakout area against enemy attempts to prevent the Allies from widening the gap they had blown through the entire position. A major battle developed between the First Armored Division and the *Afrika Korps* in the Tel el Aqqaqir area, but the Seventh Armored Division and the New Zealand Division broke out further south, outflanking Rommel who now, regardless of Hitler's instructions, was forced to order a general withdrawal if anything of his army was to be saved.

In the southern sector, where General Horrocks commanding the XIII Corps had attacked in the Himeimat area with steady success, the Italian divisions could not escape because the Germans had taken all their transport.

By the evening of November 4 Rommel's army was in full retreat. Montgomery left the XIII Corps to clear up the somewhat confused situation in the southern sector; the XXX Corps had orders to reorganize to the west of the main breakout area, ready to move forward at short notice; and the X Corps was to be in the van of the pursuit of Rommel's defeated army.

The battle had in fact been won on November 3—the twelfth day of the offensive. In his address on October 20 to all officers down to the rank of lieutenant-colonel, Montgomery, explaining the general conduct of the battle, had said, "The whole affair will last about twelve days." Yet, in writing of the battle many years afterward he confessed that up until November 2, when "Supercharge" began to succeed, there was no single moment when victory seemed certain. It had been a long and desperately hard struggle. The Eighth Army's casualties numbered 13,500, just under eight percent. German and Italian casualties totaled about 50,000, nearly fifty percent of the troops actually engaged in the battle, of whom some 30,000 were taken prisoner.

The problem at Alamein was remarkably similar to that of the Somme in July, 1916. Neither had been battles of maneuver, only of attrition, wearing the enemy down until at last he gave way and the breakthrough was possible. Montgomery succeeded in twelve days at the cost of 13,500 casualties. In 1916 Haig and Rawlinson failed after five months of endeavor and the loss of 600,000 men. Both battles were turning points of history; the Somme almost imperceptible at the time, Alamein a vivid and inspiring stroke, halting the tide of defeat. Montgomery himself said: "Final victory depends on the courage and will to conquer of regimental officers and men." The victory at Alamein also depended on the professional skill, determination, stamina and mental robustness of the Army Commander.

JOCK HASWELL

Ordeal at Stalingrad

"The Russians are done for," Adolf Hitler assured his Chief of Staff in June of 1942—and by all rights they should have been. Seventy percent of Hitler's military might was committed to the 1,250-mile-long Eastern front, and nothing seemed capable of stopping the German army as it swept eastward toward the vital oil fields of the Caucasus. Indeed, the campaign in the southeast was meeting with so little opposition that the Führer decided to launch a simultaneous campaign against Stalingrad, a major industrial city on the Volga River. And there, for the first time, Hitler's armies ran into stiff resistance. The siege of Stalingrad lasted from August until February, 1943, and when it ended 85 percent of the city lay in ruins, close to 150,000 German troops were dead, 60,000 Sixth Army vehicles had been captured or destroyed, and the Wehrmacht's eastward thrust had been halted.

Joseph Stalin, Russian dictator after whom Stalingrad was named.

Opposite Russian soldiers defending a ruined building in Stalingrad, November, 1942.

The Battle of Stalingrad was one of the most costly and catastrophic reverses ever suffered by German arms. It marked the limit of the Wehrmacht's advance into Russia and the eastward limit of the Red Army's long retreat. More significantly, the German army's defeat at Stalingrad proved to be the turning point not only in the struggle between Hitler's Third Reich and the Soviet Union but also in World War II in Europe, for Germany had committed 70 percent of its military strength to the disastrous campaign on the Eastern front. After Stalingrad, the strategic initiative remained with the Russian commanders who steadily advanced to Berlin despite two major German counterblows.

By June of 1942, one year after Hitler's invasion of the U.S.S.R., over 3 million of his troops—Italian, Rumanian, Hungarian and Finnish as well as German—were deployed along a 1,250-mile front from Finland to the Sea of Azov. Hitler was convinced that the Russians had spent their main reserves in attempts to regain lost territory, notably around Kharkov, where three armies had been encircled and mauled in May. "The Russians are done for," the German leader assured his Chief of Staff.

There seemed to be little to halt Germany's eastward drive. But which objective should have priority? German troops could take Stalingrad, then wheel north and cut the communications of the Soviet forces defending Moscow, the very heart of Russia. That was one alternative. Another was to push south to the oil fields of the Caucasus. Germany needed oil to prosecute the war and had already drawn heavily on its reserves. Capture of those supplies would not only solve Hitler's oil shortage but would also cripple the Red Army's mobility.

Thus the oil fields of Maikop, Grozny and Baku beckoned as tempting—and plausible—German targets, provided that the northern flank of a thrust between the Black Sea and the Caspian Sea could be protected. To some extent the Don and Volga rivers did afford such protection, but the gap between the rivers would have to be held, and to achieve that goal the Wehrmacht must seize Stalingrad. That was the other alternative.

The German High Command should have chosen one or the other—the Caucasus or Stalingrad. Instead, they resolved to tackle both simultaneously, and in so doing they eventually stretched their resources to the limit and beyond. The ease of their advance had induced overconfidence, and the unexpectedly quick fall of Rostov on July 23, 1942, merely reinforced this optimism. Hitler had already decided it was no longer essential to take Stalingrad and cover the northern flank *before* Field Marshal Siegmund List's Army Group A headed south for the Caucasus. While List forged south, Field Marshal Maximilian von Weichs' Army Group B was to form a defensive front on the middle Don, cut off the narrow isthmus between the Don and Volga rivers, and advance on Stalingrad.

The Sixth Army, which was commanded by a fifty-two-year-old Hessian named Friedrich Paulus, was to lead the way. Originally, General Hermann Hoth's Fourth Panzer Army was to have had that honor, but at the last minute it was directed to help Army Group A across the lower Don east of Rostov. Only then did Hoth's troops turn northeast to Kotelnikovo, seventy miles from Stalingrad. As a result, the Sixth Army's progress was slower than desired, and the Russians were given more time to organize the defenses of what was to become the most famous city of the war.

Joseph Stalin had been sent to the city in 1918 (when it was still named Tsaritsyn after a local river) to serve as commissioner for food supplies in southern Russia. He soon organized the irregular Red units there, transformed them into the first regular regiments of the Red Army, and beat off three attacks by a White Russian force. From 1925 to 1962, when it was renamed Volgograd, the town was called Stalingrad, and by 1939 it had grown into the third largest industrial center in the U.S.S.R., with nearly half a

Above A gun crew at work amid the smoke and dust of Stalingrad's factory area.

Nikita Khrushchev (right) listening to an artillery officer's report on the fighting.

million inhabitants. Standing as it did at one end of the canal that linked the Volga and Don rivers, the city became a major river port for timber, oil, iron and steel. A vital center, to be sure—yet one wonders whether the Germans, and Hitler in particular, would have become so obsessed with the place had its name still been Tsaritsyn.

The main German summer offensive of 1942 opened on June 28, with two separate army groups being launched against widely divergent targets. In North Africa, General Erwin Rommel had just achieved a disrupting victory and was heading for the Nile. In southern Russia, the many Germans who despised the African campaign as a sideshow looked forward to an even more spectacular success.

The Sixth Army, moving across the open, almost treeless steppe between the Don and the Volga, met little resistance until Stalingrad came into view. Late on August 23, leading units broke through the northern suburbs and reached the Volga. That night the Luftwaffe systematically bombed the city. Tens of thousands of Russian civilians were left homeless, and thousands more were killed or injured in that

terror raid. The Germans then seeded the Volga with mines. They hoped to close the vital river and strangle the flow of supplies and reinforcements, but the Russians destroyed the mines.

The Russians formed a new "Stalingrad front" under General Andrei Yeremenko, whose three-man military council included, as party representative, the energetic Nikita Khrushchev, afterward Prime Minister of the U.S.S.R. Yeremenko had three armies under his command. The most notable of them was the Sixty-Second, which was led by the future Marshal Vasily Chuikov, who was responsible for the defense of Stalingrad.

In the city itself a desperate struggle was fought for every street and house, for every square, cellar, factory and gutted building. The destruction was so great that when the battle was finally over, 85 percent of Stalingrad lay in ruins, and it was called "the city without an address."

The Germans, who had failed to take the city by storm, believed that they were winning the war of attrition—when all the time they were wearing down their own strength and committing more troops to the battle than the Russians were. During September and October, reinforcement of Stalingrad's defending forces was kept to the necessary minimum, and it barely covered Russian losses. This was partly deliberate policy, for the defenders of Stalingrad were fighting to give the Russian High Command time in which to assemble a force large enough to inflict a decisive counterstroke.

Indeed, a million troops, 900 tanks, 1,100 aircraft and over 1,300 guns were assembled north of the Don under command of Marshal Georgi Zhukov, and the secret of their presence was maintained. In addition General Paulus failed to wipe out several Russian bridgeheads on the right bank of the Don during his advance on Stalingrad in

August. Paulus' omission left his northern flank vulnerable to attack.

That attack came on November 19 when Konstantin Rokossovski's Sixty-Fifth Soviet Army stormed out of the Kletskaya bridgehead, eighty miles northwest of Stalingrad, and struck the weak Third Rumanian Army guarding Paulus' left flank. In four days the Rumanians lost 75,000 men, 34,000 horses and the heavy weapons of 5 divisions. At the same time the other prong of the mammoth Russian offensive, which aimed at encircling and then annihilating all the troops under Paulus' command, swept out of a bridgehead just south of Stalingrad and attacked the Fourth Rumanian Army. Here too the Russians broke through and captured the bridge on which the Sixth Army relied for all supplies.

As a result of the Soviet pincer movement, some 330,000 German and Rumanian troops were trapped between the Don and Volga rivers. When Hitler heard of the encirclement and of a proposal that Paulus be allowed to fight his way out to the west, he banged his fist on the table and twice shouted: *"Ich bleibe an der Wolga!"* ("I stay on the Volga!") On November 22 Hitler designated Stalingrad a fortress that must be held at all costs and canceled the orders from Army Group B for a breakout.

Hitler next summoned the brilliant General Erich von Manstein, whose army had captured Sevastopol in July, and ordered him to take command of the newly created Army Group Don, comprising the Sixth Army, the Fourth Panzer Army and what remained of the two Rumanian armies. Eleven divisions were hurried in from France, Poland, Germany and other parts of Russia. Manstein, who believed that Paulus could no longer break out unaided, planned to cut a south-north corridor through which the Sixth Army could be replenished (and thus enabled to hold out longer). To this he obtained the Führer's agreement, but Manstein also planned to order Paulus to push south to aid the rescue operation, and then, having restored the Sixth Army's mobility with stocks of fuel from his column of vehicles laden with supplies, he would fetch the troops out of the Stalingrad "cauldron."

After several postponements, Hoth's Fourth Panzer Army struck northeast from Kotelnikovo on December 12 and at once encountered fierce opposition. With seventy-five miles to go, Hoth forced his way across the Aksay River, and on December 19 his battered force reached the Myshkova River. The German spearhead was barely thirty miles from the cauldron's southern edge, and the encircled German soldiers at Stalingrad grew more hopeful when they heard the distant gunfire. Hoth's troops had suffered immense losses, however, and his offensive strength dwindled rapidly—so much so that Manstein felt he could not get through by himself.

Manstein had come to believe that Paulus and the Sixth Army must concentrate against one short length of the perimeter and blast a way through to meet the rescuers. Accordingly, he ordered Paulus to break out. When Paulus collected his sixty remaining tanks and several hundred trucks, he found

A group of German generals captured during the battle.

German Field Marshal Paulus arriving at Red Army Headquarters for interrogation after the German surrender.

that the vehicles had fuel for twenty miles at most. The gap between the two armies was thirty miles. What if Hoth failed to advance any further? What if his own columns became stuck halfway through? The risks were great, of course, especially while he was keeping back the Russians. But not to use this slender chance meant abandoning all hope of saving the trapped Sixth Army.

Paulus felt that unless Manstein could extract from Hitler permission for a total breakout—and by December 22 he had not done so—he would not risk

Defeated German troops in the snow near Stalingrad.

The red flag of victory being raised over a shattered Stalingrad.

The new Russian threat to Rostov also placed the whole operation of List's Army Group A in jeopardy. In August Group A had captured the oil fields at Maikop, but it had failed to reach the Black Sea at Tuapse or to secure Grozny, let alone to advance to Baku on the Caspian. Army Group A had been starved of equipment and reinforcements because of the Stalingrad battle, and the Wehrmacht's resources were simply not adequate to sustain the three-pronged advance against the Caucasian oil fields while the worsening situation on the Volga embroiled more and more troops. And so, two days after the Fourth Panzer Army had retreated over the Aksay to the Don, Hitler decided to order Army Group A to begin a withdrawal.

Inside the irrevocably isolated Fortress Stalingrad, which Hitler had taken under personal (albeit long-distance) command, most of the soldiers were without special winter clothing. Morale had deteriorated since the failure of Manstein's rescue attempt, and the men, cold outside, were also cold within for lack of food. During December, nearly 80,000 troops under Paulus' command were lost through death, disease, wounds or sheer hunger and cold, thereby reducing his force to 250,000. For the Germans the situation was already past redemption, but for Hitler, who had become obsessed by the struggle, Stalingrad's retention was a matter of political as well as military prestige. Although it could be argued that the Sixth Army tied down huge Russian forces, this was a diminishing return, and not nearly enough of the Red Army had been drawn in to prevent the whole of Germany's southern sector of the Eastern front from collapsing.

The Russians, lucidly aware that matters lay to their advantage, addressed terms of surrender to General Paulus on January 8, 1943. The German commander rejected the terms, whereupon the Soviets launched an all-out concentric offensive. Since Zhukov had nearly half a million men along the Stalingrad perimeter, Paulus was outnumbered

Right Drive the Nazi German villains from our land—an appeal to patriotism.

Forward to Victory, a Russian army poster.

the venture. The last opportunity for retreat passed, and in mid-December a new and admirably timed Soviet offensive smashed through the Italian Eighth Army below Voronezh on the middle Don and pushed south toward Millerovo and the Donets River. This advance promptly sealed the fate of Paulus' Sixth Army, because Manstein was compelled to detach part of his force to counter the new threat and also to build up a front to guard Rostov. As a result the depleted Fourth Panzer Army, which had failed to breach the Russians' Myshkova River-line defenses, was driven back over the Aksay to Kotelnikovo, its point of departure, on December 27. The rescue bid had failed, at a cost of 300 tanks and 16,000 troops.

78

German Mastery of Europe 1942

Greater Germany
Occupied by Germany
Occupied by Italy
(dates show when occupied)
Allied to Germany
Opposing Germany
Neutral

FINLAND
NORWAY 1940
SWEDEN
ESTONIA
GREAT BRITAIN
LATVIA 1941
DENMARK 1940
LITHUANIA 1941
EIRE
HOLLAND 1940
Leningrad
London
Moscow
U.S.S.R.
Berlin
GERMANY
POLAND 1939
UKRAINE 1941
Maximum advance of German armies
1940
Prague
Warsaw
CZECHOSLOVAKIA
Kiev
Stalingrad
BELGIUM
Paris
FRANCE 1940
Vienna
Rostov
Vichy
AUSTRIA
HUNGARY
SWITZERLAND
ITALY 1941
RUMANIA
SERBIA
YUGOSLAVIA
SPAIN
1941
BULGARIA
TURKEY
1941
ALBANIA 1939
GREECE

by two to one. Suffering grievously from malnutrition and frostbite, Paulus' exhausted men could not hold off the Russian tanks.

On January 24, Paulus signaled to Hitler that effective command was no longer possible, further defense was senseless, and collapse inevitable. As expected, the Führer refused to countenance surrender, insisting still that the Sixth Army hold its positions to the last.

Four days later the Red Army broke through to the Volga from the west, and entire German battalions were wiped out or silenced. Declaring that there was no record of a German marshal's having been taken prisoner, Hitler promoted Paulus to the rank of field marshal—but his action could not prevent Paulus from surrendering on the last day of January. On February 2 the final pocket of resistance —six mangled divisions—yielded in the face of a massive assault. Some 90,000 prisoners fell into Russian hands, and 85,000 of them never returned to their homes. Close to 150,000 German and Rumanian troops perished within the cauldron as it dwindled in size and split apart.

When the radio announced the Sixth Army's surrender, a hush fell over the German people, who only days before had read posters that declared: *Stalingrad—unsterbliches Vorbild deutschen Kämpfertums* (Stalingrad—immortal example of German fighting spirit). Four days of national mourning were ordered, and places of entertainment closed for that period. The catastrophe undermined Germany's influence with neutral countries, heartened resistance movements in occupied territory, and encouraged anti-Nazi groups within Germany and the Wehrmacht. Many intelligent senior officers by then realized that ultimate defeat was inevitable, and they were converted to the belief that "something must be done"—by which they meant that Hitler must be removed from power.

On January 24, the Allies announced their policy of unconditional surrender at Casablanca, a move that complicated the work of conspirators. This new development was largely offset by the disasters at Stalingrad and by the defeats in North Africa. In the latter theater, the Eighth Army reached Tripoli by January 23. Tunis fell on May 7, and 250,000 Axis troops were obliged to lay down their arms.

Defeat at Stalingrad irrevocably shattered the myth of German invincibility that had already been severely shaken at the Battle of el Alamein three months earlier. It was now the Russians' turn to be overconfident when they regained Kursk and Kharkov. Barely three weeks after Stalingrad, the brilliant Manstein launched a counterblow that was so effective that the Red Army was compelled to relinquish Kharkov and 6,000 square miles of recently regained territory.

The German army's resilience demonstrated what a close-run battle Stalingrad had been. Had the Germans taken the city and thwarted the great Russian counteroffensive, their attack on the oil fields could have been reinforced as well as protected. And Army Group A might well have captured not only Grozny and Baku but the Caucasus as well. Indeed, it might have fought its way into Persia and Iraq and headed for the rich oil fields around Mosul and Kirkuk. Had such a threat developed in November it is not impossible that General Bernard Montgomery's Eighth Army would have been obliged to call off its pursuit of Rommel's defeated troops and that the whole course of the war might have been altered.

ANTONY BRETT-JAMES

The memorial to the dead of Stalingrad.

The worm turns

By February 2, 1943, when Germany conceded that it had lost the Battle of Stalingrad, all significant Axis advances had been checked. Thereafter, the Allied problem was to recapture territory seized earlier by the Germans and Japanese. Throughout the rest of 1943, the Axis powers were rolled steadily back, and by 1944, they were being regularly defeated in every theater of the war. In the Far East the Japanese had tried to compensate for the defeat at Midway by an attack on the American force in the Solomon Islands at Guadalcanal. But they overextended their lines of communication; in November of 1942 the Japanese suffered a sizeable naval defeat off the Solomons, and in February, 1943, they evacuated their remaining troops from Guadalcanal.

General MacArthur (*left*) inspecting a southwest Pacific marine base.

portance of the Burma Road, on which the Nationalist Chinese depended for supplies. Until the route was reopened in 1944 Chiang Kai-shek's forces were at an enormous disadvantage against

U.S. marines crossing a jungle stream on Guadalcanal early on in the campaign against the Japanese.

On the Asian mainland, too, the Japanese offensive seemed at last to have exhausted itself, signaling the end of any serious Japanese threat to the Indian subcontinent. British commandos, operating under the leadership of Orde Wingate (1903-44) in the Burmese jungle, helped to hold down the Japanese, and in 1944 an Allied offensive—the British Fourteenth Army and a Chinese-American force under General Joseph Stilwell (1883-1946)—reoccupied most of Burma. The fierceness of the fighting in Burma was due to the strategic im-

the better equipped Japanese.

As the war in the Pacific entered its final phase, a huge offensive was launched by General Douglas MacArthur. U.S. strategy consisted of knocking out major Japanese island bases and leaving the troops isolated and ineffective in between. The U.S. scheme was a brilliant and effective exploitation of Japan's overextension, and as early as April, 1944, Australian and U.S. troops had taken much of New Guinea. Their amphibious forces soon gained control of the Solomon and the Marshall Islands.

German problems stemmed from Hitler's abandonment of his early policy of limited objectives achieved one at a time, in favor of an all-out attempt to execute the wild schemes outlined in *Mein Kampf*. The invasion of Russia was a military blunder, and by strictly adhering to the principles of Nazism, the Germans complicated the campaign still further. As they advanced eastward, the Germans were welcomed by peoples who, out of expediency and a desire to free themselves from the rigors of Stalin's social policies, let them pass unhindered. But the Germans soon alienated these peoples. Rigidly following Hitler's plan for German expansion into eastern living space, Heinrich Himmler's dreaded secret police, the Gestapo, and the s.s. inaugurated a brutal policy of racial liquidation. Millions of Poles, Czechs and Russians perished through starvation or forced labor. As a result, the conquered peoples resisted the Germans even more bitterly. In most of the occupied countries, resistance movements sprang up and were sometimes able to operate with success. In Czechoslovakia for example, the resistance was responsible for the assassination of Reinhard Heydrich, the Gestapo leader there, in 1942.

The "final solution"

The most horrific task embarked upon by Himmler was the "final solution of the Jewish problem." This incomprehensibly monstrous scheme involved the arrest, deportation, internment and ultimate elimination, in the gas chambers and by other means, of roughly six million European Jews. For the most part, Himmler's program met little or no effective opposition. But in February, 1943, in a final, heroic—and doomed—gesture, the Jews who had been herded into the ghetto of Warsaw to starve rose up in arms against their tormentors. The ghetto was ultimately razed, and the survivors deported. Such brutality was not just the work of the secret police; atrocities against prisoners, particularly in Russia, were also committed by regular soldiers of the German army. In occupied Europe, the Nazis themselves did more than anyone to keep alive the resistance groups harassing the German forces.

Africa and Italy

The victory of the British at el Alamein made possible the destruction of Rommel's army. British naval power in the Mediterranean—the possession of Gibraltar and the much-bombed island of Malta, which was to be awarded the George Cross medal by the British government, helped the Allies in Africa enormously, insured that the Germans were short of supplies and made possible the invasion of Vichy-French northwest Africa. Consequently, on November 8, a massive Anglo-American assault force under General Dwight D. Eisenhower, disembarked in French Morocco and Algeria. Meanwhile the British Eighth Army moved rapidly across the desert, capturing Tripoli on January 24—covering over 1,350 miles in the eighty-one days after el Alamein. German control was now confined to Tunisia; this did not prevent Rommel from attempting a bold but costly counteroffensive, which brought the Allied advance to a halt for a time. On May 13, 1943, however, the German command surrendered and all of North Africa was in Allied hands. Although the responsibility for the victory was largely British, it had been facilitated by an American advance from Morocco.

The end of Axis power in North Africa allowed the Allies to launch a second-front offensive in Europe to help relieve the Russians who were still hard-pressed by the Germans despite the end of the siege of Stalingrad. Sicily was invaded on July 9, 1943. The prospect of imminent invasion (linked to a widespread revulsion against Fascism in general and the German occupation in particular) led to the downfall of Mussolini. And despite his fears of brutal German reprisals, Italy's new leader, Marshal Pietro Badoglio, began making overtures of surrender. Under the impression that Italy would fall without a struggle, Churchill pressed for an invasion of the mainland. The Americans, who preferred a landing in France, wavered. By the time agreement had been reached for a landing in September, the Germans had brought fresh troops into Italy. The expeditionary force that

Italian and German prisoners captured during the advance on Tripoli.

reached the Italian mainland on September 2 met stiff resistance, and the Allies could make only slow progress. After nine months of fierce fighting, in June, 1944, they finally entered Rome, the first European capital to be freed from Nazi rule.

The whole question of an Italian theater of war posed serious political problems for the Allies. Although the battle for Italy involved German troops, it hardly accorded with Russia's urgent demands for the opening of a second front. Once the Germans realized there was not going to be an attack on northern France,

they were able to release several divisions—twenty-seven according to Stalin—for the Russian front. Moreover, the shipping required for the Italian operation cut down Allied supplies to Russia and embittered Soviet-Western relations.

The Allies' failure to open what Stalin considered a genuine second front in Europe (until late in the war when the Russians were driving into Eastern Europe) convinced the Russians that Germany had been defeated largely through their own efforts. Russia, Stalin concluded, would have to depend on its own unilateral action to insure its future security.

The abbey on Monastery Hill above Cassino after the assault on Cassino.

Carving up Europe

It was for this reason that the Russians thought increasingly in terms of zones of influence, a topic discussed at the Allied foreign ministers' meeting that was held in Moscow in October, 1943. If nothing else, that meeting demonstrated that the Western Allies, as much as the Russians, thought in terms of spheres of influence. Earlier in the war, American leaders, fearful of upsetting millions of U.S. voters of Eastern European origin, had been reluctant to involve themselves in the carving up of Central and Eastern Europe. But as early

Red Army cavalrymen reporting to their commander after an action against German forces on the Russian front.

as 1942, Secretary of War Henry L. Stimson had come to the conclusion that "there is no doubt that the Soviet government has tremendous ambitions with regard to Europe."

The Russians push west

The year 1944 brought the Russians huge military successes. In a series of sweeps they pushed the Germans back into Eastern and Central Europe. The Allies' actions in Italy had established that the liberating country could determine the liberated nation's political,

social and economic future, and the Russians were determined to capitalize on the precedent. In January, they reached Poland; in March, Rumania. By the late summer, the Russians had pushed west as far as Warsaw and were about to take Yugoslavia and Bulgaria. By this time they had 225 infantry divisions in Central Europe—a military reality that inevitably affected the question of the political control of the liberated areas. The British, who recognized the Russian threat, favored a division of spheres of influence, which they said might save some of Eastern Europe from Communism.

The Americans, on the other hand, were reluctant to enter into any agreements that might prevent their challenging Soviet control of such areas after the war. However, with Roosevelt's acquiescence Churchill made a deal with Stalin.

Operation Overlord

In June, 1944, the Allies landed in northern France and began the push that would bring them face to face with the Russians in the middle of Germany. Operation Overlord, as the landing was called, was executed with extreme precision.

D-Day

On June 6, 1944, the long-deferred Anglo-American seaborne assault on Fortress Europe was launched. "Operation Overlord," as the landing was called, was executed with precision. A great flotilla ferried the 156,000 Allied troops to the beaches of Normandy. Deceived by dummy attacks on another part of the coast, the Germans were slow to react and missed a vital opportunity while the Allied forces were disembarking. By the end of D-Day the Allies had secured the beachhead and opened up a second front. This triumph of Allied arms, together with Russia's victories in the East, spelled the end of Germany's domination of Europe.

D-Day—June 6, 1944—on which the Western Allies launched their assault on Fortress Europe, was the culmination of many months, even years, of planning. As early as April, 1942, the Joint Chiefs of Staff had agreed that the ultimate objective of Allied strategy was to deliver an Anglo-American seaborne assault across the English Channel against the German forces in the West. This decision was never reversed; but in the spring of 1942 Allied resources fell far short of what was required for so large and hazardous an enterprise. Moreover, at that moment the situation on the Russian front had become critical, and the most urgent need was to force the Germans to disperse their forces as a means of relieving pressure on the Russians. Hence the decision to launch an invasion of North Africa (Operation "Torch"), and this in turn involved the postponement of D-Day to the indefinite future. The decision had serious political as well as military consequences. It created suspicions of Allied intentions both in the Russians and among left-wing opinion at home, and for the next two years demands for the opening of a second front in Europe became increasingly strident.

By January, 1943, the strategic position of the Allies had greatly improved. The North African campaign had been brought to a triumphant conclusion, and the Russians were preparing to go over to the offensive. At the Casablanca Conference it was decided to undertake the immediate invasion of Italy and to begin the task of planning the invasion of France. The cross-Channel operation was given the code-name of "Overlord," and a headquarters designated as COSSAC (Chief of Staff to the Supreme Allied Commander) was established to undertake the outline planning. At the same time, it was decided to launch a large-scale air offensive against Germany with the object of reducing her strength before the invasion.

Four months later, in Washington, it was confirmed that "Overlord" should be launched in the spring of 1944, and by August COSSAC had produced an outline plan which was approved at the Quebec Conference in that month.

COSSAC's outline plan was necessarily a highly provisional one, because as yet no commander had been appointed for the operation; but it embodied an immense amount of work which was later to prove invaluable. In particular it made the important recommendation that the target area for the operation should be not the Pas de Calais, but the coast of Normandy between roughly Carentan and Caen, which, although it involved a longer sea crossing, still lay within the range of British-based fighter cover. The plan thus laid the basis on which it was possible, during 1943, to undertake the construction of the cross-Channel pipelines and the two prefabricated harbors that were essential to the success of the operation.

At the two conferences held in 1943 in Cairo and Teheran, General Eisenhower was nominated Supreme Allied Commander, to the bitter disappointment of the American Chief of Staff, General George Marshall, who regarded "Overlord" as the culmination of his entire war strategy and had hoped to command it himself. General Montgomery, fresh from his African victories, was appointed Commander in Chief of the Anglo-American ground forces in the assault phase of the operation. The naval forces were placed under the command of Admiral Ramsay and the air forces under Air Marshal Leigh-Mallory. Thus the naval, army and air forces in the assault phase of the operation were all under British command. From this point of view D-Day may be said to mark the end of an historical era; it was the last great operation of war in which, as regards both command and the forces involved, Britain played a predominant part. It was, however, a potential

British commando coming ashore on D-Day.

Opposite Detail of a painting by Barnet Freedman of Normandy beach after the D-Day landing.

weakness in the chain of command that the American practice was not adopted of appointing a single task force commander for the assault.

By January 21, 1944, General Montgomery had produced a revised outline plan, which differed in several important respects from that of COSSAC. He extended the frontage of attack and increased the strength of the assault forces, in particular the strength of the airborne forces. COSSAC, however, had been limited by the naval forces available which, in addition to "Overlord," had to provide for an invasion in the south of France (Operation "Anvil"). Moreover, there was a shortage of trained naval crews for any additional shipping that might be allocated to "Overlord." The adoption of Montgomery's revised plan involved both the postponement of "Anvil" until August, thus releasing the shipping required for "Overlord," and the postponement of "Overlord" until the end of May, which allowed for the training of additional naval crews.

The revised plan provided for an assault on a front of fifty miles, on the right by two divisions of the First American Army (General Omar Bradley), on the left by three divisions of the Second British Army (General Miles Dempsey), with airborne landings on the flanks of the assault by the Eighty-Second and the Hundred-and-First U.S. Airborne Divisions and the Sixth British Airborne Division. The frontage of assault was extended to include the eastern coast of the Cotentin Peninsula. This had the advantage of bringing the Americans within closer striking distance of Cherbourg. It had the disadvantage that the land in the rear of the Cotentin beaches had been extensively inundated, and that the American assault forces would be divided by the Carentan estuary. The objective of "Overlord" was defined as:

> . . . to mount and carry out an operation, with forces and equipment established in the United Kingdom and with target date 31 May, 1944, to secure a lodgement on the Continent from which further offensive operations could be developed. The lodgement area must contain sufficient port facilities to maintain a force of some twenty-five to thirty divisions and enable that force to be augmented by follow-up shipments from the United States or elsewhere of additional divisions and supporting units at the rate of three to five divisions a month.

Montgomery's revised plan was approved on January 21, 1944. This left a little over four months for the detailed planning of "Overlord" and the issue of the necessary operation orders. They were months of feverish preparation which, as General Montgomery himself has said, by the time D-Day arrived left many of the staff involved in a state of exhaustion instead of being fresh for the battles that lay ahead.

The assault phase of "Overlord" involved the concentration of 175,000 men with their equipment and supporting weapons in their embarkation areas, and of the vast fleet required to carry them across the Channel. The actual transportation of the force across the Channel was to be in the

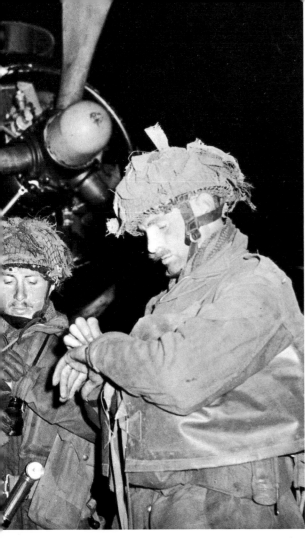

face of hostile action. It would have to disembark on open and heavily defended beaches in a condition fit to fight and to move immediately on selected objectives. This required the meticulous coordination of men and ships with the naval, air and air-landing operations designed to give cover and protection to the assault forces and to neutralize the coast defenses by preliminary bombardment of the target area. The fire plan for the assault included preliminary air attack on coast defenses by heavy and medium bombers, and naval bombardment that involved the use of weapons and techniques specially designed and developed for "Overlord"; as it happened, the Allied air forces flew 11,000 sorties on D-Day. The landing itself was supported by specially developed assault weapons, such as amphibious tanks, bridge-carrying tanks, mat-laying tanks, flail tanks for clearing mines and ramp tanks to enable other vehicles to climb sea walls. The assault phase of "Overlord" was in fact one of the most intricate and hazardous operations in the history of war. In the minds of those who planned it there lay the memory of the terrible lessons that had been learned from the catastrophic failure of the raid on Dieppe in 1942 and the determination that, if humanly possible, it should not be repeated.

It can be said that the organizational and technical problems involved in "Overlord" were triumphantly overcome; few operations of war have been so meticulously planned. Time, tide, weather, the phases of the moon are not subject to human control and these factors imposed on "Overlord" such strict limitations as to leave very little room for flexibility or maneuver; the operation orders constituted an immensely complicated timetable that had to be adhered to in the strictest detail if the operation was to be successful.

Moreover, while the planning of "Overlord" proceeded, the enemy had not been idle.

The German forces in France and the Low Countries, under the Commander in Chief of the West, Field Marshal von Rundstedt, comprised some sixty divisions; more than two-thirds of these were under the operational command of Army Group B, which consisted of the Seventh Army (Normandy and Brittany), the Fifteenth Army (Pas de Calais and Flanders) and the XXXVIII Corps (Holland). In February, 1944, Hitler appointed to the command of Army Group B Montgomery's old enemy, Field Marshal Rommel. He committed himself to a policy of defeating invasion on the beaches and immediately set about strengthening the beach defenses and reinforcing the coastal garrisons. In particular, Allied air reconnaissance showed in the months preceding D-Day that there was a rapid and continuous increase in the number of underwater obstacles. Lying below high-water mark these were armed with a variety of explosive charges that made them particularly dangerous to landing craft.

This proliferation of underwater obstacles added

Top British army officers synchronizing their watches before taking off for Normandy.

Bottom RAF gliders and tug aircraft crossing the Channel, part of the airborne armada of June 6, 1944.

85

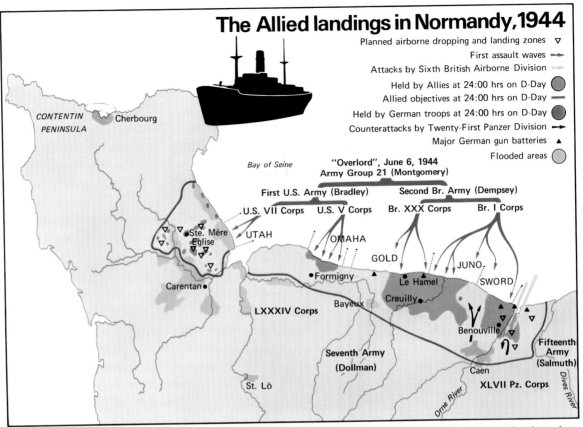

The Allied landings in Normandy, 1944

Planned airborne dropping and landing zones ▽
First assault waves ➞
Attacks by Sixth British Airborne Division ➞
Held by Allies at 24:00 hrs on D-Day ⬤
Allied objectives at 24:00 hrs on D-Day ▬
Held by German troops at 24:00 hrs on D-Day ⬤
Counterattacks by Twenty-First Panzer Division ➞
Major German gun batteries ▲
Flooded areas ⬤

CONTENTIN PENINSULA — Cherbourg

Bay of Seine

"Overlord", June 6, 1944
Army Group 21 (Montgomery)

First U.S. Army (Bradley) — Second Br. Army (Dempsey)

U.S. VII Corps — U.S. V Corps — Br. XXX Corps — Br. I Corps

Ste. Mère Eglise — UTAH — OMAHA — GOLD — JUNO — SWORD

Carentan — Formigny — Le Hamel — Creuilly — Benouville — Fifteenth Army (Salmuth)

LXXXIV Corps — Bayeux

Seventh Army (Dollman)

St. Lô — Caen — XLVII Pz. Corps

Orne River — Dives River

a further complication to an already complicated problem—the timing of H-Hour, the moment at which the first wave of assault craft would hit the beaches. The timing had to reconcile, as far as possible, the requirements of all the three services and it had been agreed that these would best be met by a landing in daylight at high tide after a moonlit night. Moonlight would enable the medium and heavy bombers to identify their targets with greater accuracy. The interval between nautical twilight (the time at which the first light of day is visible at sea) and daylight would give greater accuracy to the naval bombardment. A landing at high tide would expose the assault forces to enemy fire on the beaches for a minimum period. High water would, however, hinder the assault engineers in their task of destroying and disarming the underwater obstacles. H-Hour was therefore set at forty minutes after nautical twilight and three hours after high water.

This combination of requirements set a very narrow limit to the choice of D-Day, and the odds against them coinciding with a period of fine weather in the Channel were very high. In fact the first period that satisfied all the required conditions began on June 4. On June 4 nautical twilight was at 03:20 hours. D-Day was therefore provisionally fixed for June 4 and H-Hour for 04:00 hours.

Apart from the complication of time, tide and weather, there was the incalculable factor of the German reaction. Rommel's policy of defeating invasion on the beaches implied that, once the target had been identified, he would concentrate all available resources on throwing the invaders into the sea. Intelligence estimates of the German strength and reserves showed that under such conditions the build-up of Rommel's forces, including armored elements, in the target area would proceed at a higher rate than anything the Allies could hope to achieve in the first few days of the invasion; that in fact the position would change each day to the Germans' advantage. This was a risk that had to be accepted. The invasion plan, however, contained two provisions to reduce the rate of build-up of enemy forces behind the beaches. The first was a maximum effort, by air, and on the ground by the French resistance forces, to disrupt enemy communications and movement by road and rail into the target area. The second was an elaborate deception plan designed to make the Germans hesitate to commit their reserves to Normandy, by persuading them that "Overlord" was a diversion, and that the main thrust of the invasion would be directed at the Pas de Calais. Both these operations achieved remarkable success and effectively inhibited both the enemy's power of movement and power of decision. Indeed the deception plan coincided with and confirmed Hitler's fixed conviction that the main thrust of the invasion would be directed at the Pas de Calais.

In May, General Eisenhower, Admiral Ramsay and General Montgomery moved their headquarters to Portsmouth. Because of its dependence on its communications system, Air Marshal Leigh-Mallory's headquarters remained at Stanmore. By the end of the month, the final stages had been reached in the massive movement of men and ships that would, at length, permit "Overlord" to be launched; elaborate security precautions effectively sealed off the assault and follow-up forces from communication with the outside world. After months of preparation D-Day was at last at hand.

On D−1, however, June 4, the weather forecast for the following day was so bad that General Eisenhower ordered a twenty-four hour postponement. On June 5, the weather forecast, though still unfavorable, showed a slight improvement, and the brave and hazardous decision was made that the operation should take place the following day. "Overlord" was, in fact, launched under conditions that would not have been regarded as acceptable by any of the commanders involved during the long months of planning and preparation.

Weather indeed was the worst enemy that the invasion force encountered on its passage across the Channel. Neither at its embarkation ports, nor its assembly positions, nor during the sea crossing, did it meet with any opposition; the great invasion armada crossed the Channel with as little interference from the enemy as if it were a pleasure boat.

The seaborne assault at H-Hour was preceded by airborne landings. On the right (American) flank the Eighty-First and Hundred-and-First U.S. Airborne Divisions dropped at 01.30 and

A naval beach party flies the white ensign on the Normandy coast.

Top Planning "Operation Overlord" in London; left to right, Lieutenant General Omar Bradley (U.S.); Admiral Sir Bertram Ramsay (U.K.); Air Chief Marshal Sir Arthur Tedder (U.K.); General Dwight Eisenhower (U.S.); General Sir Bernard Montgomery (U.K.); Air Chief Marshal Sir Trafford Leigh-Mallory (U.K.); Lieutenant General Walter Smith (U.S.).

medium bombers. The air attack was accompanied by naval bombardment by the heavy ships of the fleet, and as the assault went in the troops were given cover by a variety of specially designed naval craft. The air and naval bombardment was less effective than had been hoped but it was successful in neutralizing the enemy's guns and in paralyzing his communication and radar system.

In the assault on the beaches, nature remained a worse enemy than the Germans and it was a notable feat of seamanship and determination that under such conditions the naval assault parties should have been able to keep their stations and, with few exceptions, put the troops ashore at the right time and in their correct positions. The high seas and surf and the strong onshore winds drove the tide far up on the beach and made it difficult for the clearance parties to deal with the underwater obstacles. Troops, many suffering from seasickness, were swept off their feet as they waded ashore and were in no condition to fight when they finally reached the beaches.

The plan for the assault divided the target area into five beach sectors, code named, from right to left, UTAH, OMAHA, GOLD, JUNO and SWORD, the initial letter of each code-name corresponding to the designation of the naval task forces responsible for the landing on each beach. UTAH and OMAHA, divided by the Carentan estuary, were the objectives of the United States First Army, GOLD, JUNO and SWORD of the British Second Army.

On UTAH beach the assault, delivered by a regimental combat team of the Fourth U.S. Infantry Division, benefited by being landed a thousand yards south of their planned position, where there were fewer underwater obstacles. A second regimental combat team quickly followed and the beachhead of four thousand yards was secured. During the day the troops penetrated ninety-six miles inland and successfully made contact with the Hundred-and-First Airborne Division. On OMAHA, however, the Americans were less fortunate. The air and naval bombardment had proved ineffective; the assault encountered high seas and a dense network of underwater obstacles, and on landing faced a German field division that was on a stand-to exercise as the assault went in. The assault force, and the two Ranger battalions on its right flank, suffered heavy casualties and for a time the position was critical, until a second regimental team succeeded in getting ashore and with great courage and determination the Americans regrouped and stormed the German positions. By nightfall they held a beachhead about a mile in depth and were pushing ahead to Formigny, two miles inland. OMAHA saw the fiercest fighting of D-Day and was the one beach on which for a time it appeared that the assault might fail.

In the British sector, the assault was delivered on GOLD beach by the famous Fiftieth (Tyne and

02:30 hours southeast of Ste. Mère Eglise and successfully achieved their primary objective of seizing the causeways across the flooded areas behind the coast. On the left flank, six gliders of the Sixth British Airborne Division landed at Benouville and seized the bridges over the Canal de Caen, followed at 02:30 hours by the Third and Fifth British Parachute Brigades, which reinforced the glider-borne detachments and blew up the bridges over the Dives River and its tributaries. While the airborne landings were in progress, over eleven hundred heavy bombers carried out the initial air bombardment provided for in the fire plan and by dawn nearly six thousand tons of bombs had been dropped on the coastal batteries.

The seaborne forces had a rough passage, with waves five to six feet high and winds approaching gale force; cloud conditions seriously handicapped the air bombardment by the heavy and

Tees) Division, one of the finest formations in the British army, of the XXX Corps; on JUNO by the Third Canadian Division and on SWORD by the Third British Division, both from the I Corps. On GOLD as on OMAHA the weather was extremely bad, with a stiff breeze that prevented the launching of amphibious tanks. Here also fighting was fierce, and strong opposition was encountered at Le Hamel; for a time the troops were unable to move off the beaches, until reinforced by the landing of a follow-up brigade. At the end of the day the Fiftieth Division had secured a narrow beachhead from Manvieu to Creuilly, with contact with the Third Canadian Division on their left but not, however, with the First U.S. Infantry Division on their right.

On JUNO, the fighting met with the same conditions as on GOLD and the landing was twenty minutes behind schedule. Ashore there was difficulty in clearing the exits to the beaches as enemy points had survived the preliminary bombardment, but having cleared the beaches the assault force pressed steadily forward throughout the day, at one point reaching the Caen-Bayeux road, its planned objective for D-Day.

On SWORD, on the extreme left of the British line, two squadrons of amphibious tanks were successfully launched in spite of the heavy seas and half of them were able to land abreast of the infantry. A follow-up brigade and a reserve brigade were landed during the course of the day. The assault met with severe opposition and was counterattacked by infantry and tanks, but successfully resisted; a firm beachhead was secured and contact was made with the Sixth Airborne Division at Benouville on the Orne River. East of the river, the Sixth Airborne Division was repeatedly counterattacked but was joined in the

course of the day by commandos of the First Brigade at 21:00.

The results achieved by the end of D-Day are perhaps best described by General Montgomery's succinct summary: "The Allies had obtained a foothold in Europe; and they were there to stay." It was not as large a foothold as they had hoped for, and the beachhead was neither as deep nor as continuous as had been planned. In particular, there was a gap in the American sector, across the Carentan estuary, and in the British sector it remained to capture Caen, which played a vital part in General Montgomery's plans for the development of the operation.

On the other hand, the expedition had survived the incalculable hazards involved and in particular the severe handicap imposed by the bad weather. By the end of D-Day, the Allies held a firm base from which they could pursue the three immediate objectives of the landing: to strike at, and capture, the great port of Cherbourg; to strike south to the open country south of St. Lô-Bayeux and secure the landing grounds essential to the Allied air forces; and to fight the Battle of Caen. This was as large a return from D-Day as anyone could have hoped for, and justified the immense efforts invested in organizing the operation and the lives lost in executing it; casualties were in fact much lower than had been expected and were regarded as acceptable.

D-Day was a genuine triumph for Allied arms. It confronted the enemy with the specter that had haunted the minds of the German General Staff since the foundation of the German Empire— the nightmare of a war on two fronts. Together with Russia's victories in the East, it spelled the end of Germany's domination of Europe.

GORONWY REES

View of an American bridgehead in Normandy.

German disillusionment

With the aid of the French resistance, a rapid push through France began in the weeks after Normandy. As the Western front collapsed, several high-ranking German officers attempted to pave the way for surrender by an abortive attempt on Hitler's life. By July, a few courageous officers, including Rommel, had formulated a plot to assassinate the Führer. Colonel Klaus Schenk, Count von Stauffenberg, planted a bomb in Hitler's headquarters, but through a freakish mischance the German leader escaped almost unhurt. Many others who were close to Hitler found their loyalty increasingly strained as a result of his irrational belief that victory could still be gained. Albert Speer, the minister in charge of war production, for example, considered poisoning the air in the Führer's bunker.

The Balkans

In the Balkans, too, German power was rapidly declining. In Yugoslavia the Allies had been hindered by the existence of two competing guerrilla groups—the partisans under Marshal Tito (Josip Broz) (1892–) and the Chetniks under General Draža Mihajlović (c. 1893–1946). Although they had at first been the main anti-Nazi group, the Chetniks lost ground steadily as a result of Communist successes in Dalmatia. The partisans accused the Chetniks of collaborating with the Germans, Italians and Bulgarians and refused to recognize the authority of King Peter II's Yugoslav government-in-exile, which was based in London and in which Mihajlović was the Minister of War. Partly because of the British government's unwillingness to back the declining power of Mihajlović against that of the Russian-influenced Tito, the Yugoslav government-in-exile left London and set up its headquarters in nominally neutral Cairo, which led to a further decline in its influence as it was so far from any major Allied center. Despite the increasing replacement of Italian troops by better trained and better equipped Germans, Tito was able

French housewives salvaging vegetable leaves at a Paris market, 1945. The food situation in Paris returned to normal as supplies and transport became organized.

to establish his control over the whole country by the end of 1944. By the beginning of 1945 he had already set about the task of restoring the shattered economy of his country.

In the other Balkan states, too, Axis power collapsed rapidly—in Bulgaria the government accepted an armistice, abandoning the Axis during 1944, but, as in Yugoslavia, there was often a split between pro-Western and pro-Communist guerrilla groups. Meanwhile, the German position in the west deteriorated and on August 23–24, Free French forces in the vanguard of General Patton's armored column liberated Paris.

V-E Day

The war in Europe was almost over. By January of 1945, a giant Russian offensive had thrust deeply into Germany, and Hitler had incarcerated himself in the Reich Chancellery in Berlin. While the confused Führer ordered nonexistent armies about, Marshal Georgi Zhukov's (1895–1974) forces pressed to within forty-five miles of Berlin itself. On the Western front the Allies advanced rapidly.

Yalta

Two issues remained to be decided in 1945: the war in the Far East had yet to be won, and the terms of a postwar settlement had yet to be reached. Both of these issues were central to the conference held by Roosevelt, Churchill and Stalin at the Crimean

coastal resort of Yalta in February. The Yalta settlement marked the high point of Soviet-American cooperation. Anxious to bring Russia into the war with Japan, the Americans made concessions to the Russians on several key issues. First was the division of Europe into spheres of influence. Second a government "friendly to the Soviet Union," would be set up in Poland. Third, Germany would be disarmed, demilitarized, partitioned and made subject to reparations, the details of which were to be worked out by a commission that would meet in Moscow. Roosevelt agreed to the partitioning of the Third Reich despite the opposition of many of his advisers, who were against granting spheres of influence to the Russians. The American Presi-

dent had little choice but to acquiesce, for the Russians were in all-but-total military control of Eastern Europe, and Roosevelt was really only recognizing a fait accompli. Many State Department officials who were secretly anxious to break this control hesitated to do so lest the Allies lose Russian support against the Japanese or provoke Stalin into signing a separate peace treaty with the Germans.

Japan's collapse

Meanwhile in the East, America's strength was gradually beginning to tell against the Japanese. By the beginning of 1945 the Allies had recaptured New Guinea and most of the small Pacific Islands; the Japanese were hard-pressed on every side by the Russians, Chinese and British—but it was the Americans who presented the main threat. As early as June, 1944, Japan itself had come under attack, but the Japanese had already shown signs of being willing to fight to the death. America felt that the use of a terrifying new weapon—the atom bomb—might frighten the Japanese into submission, thus preventing a long struggle and saving thousands of American lives. Oddly, it seems that such leaders as General Douglas MacArthur, the commander in chief of the U.S. Pacific Command, and others intimately connected with the struggle against Japan, were not consulted about using the bomb until

Churchill, Roosevelt and Stalin at Yalta in 1945.

The corpses of Mussolini and his mistress, Clara Petacci, hanging in Milan's Piazzale Loreto, in April, 1945.

American troops of the Eighty-Second Airborne Division and the Seven-Hundred-and-Fortieth Tank Battalion advancing near Herresbach, Belgium.

August 1: five days later an atomic bomb leveled Hiroshima.

Götterdämmerrung

In the west, on January 7, 1945, as the tide in the Battle of the Ardennes had begun to turn against the Germans, the British Field Marshal Montgomery, serving as commander in chief of an army group under the supreme command of General Eisenhower, gave a press conference summarizing the position. After quoting the message issued to the German armies before the battle by their commander General von Rundstedt, that the German counterattack was the "last great effort to win the war," Montgomery commented that even their resulting gains on the map would not save the situation for the enemy: "He is likely slowly but surely to lose it all; he must have scraped together every reserve he could lay hands on for this job, and he has not achieved a great deal."

The next few weeks were to prove Montgomery right. The Luftwaffe was by now losing its ability to defend the German ground forces against attack from the air, and the Allied armies pushed steadily forward. While the Americans, British and Canadians advanced toward the Rhine, the Red Army on the Eastern front took Warsaw in mid-January and crossed the German border into Silesia a few days later. German losses in the closing stages of the Ardennes battle were fifty thousand killed and wounded, and forty thousand taken prisoner; on the Eastern front, the losses were greater. There were also terrifyingly high figures for casualties among the civilian population, as the Allied air forces devastated one German city after another. Nuremberg, for instance, was bombed in January in a series of raids which destroyed most of the old city and caused immense loss of life; the following month Dresden was the target for incendiary raids which burned out the entire city and brought death to thousands of civilians, many of them refugees who had crowded into Dresden in their flight from the advancing Russians.

In their efforts to keep up the morale and fighting spirit of the German population, who had undergone the terrible experience of "total war," the leaders of the Third Reich resorted to desperate measures. The civilian population, including boys of twelve and thirteen, were drafted into the armed forces; savage punishment was inflicted on deserters, many of whom were hanged from trees and lamp posts; and special courts were set up to enforce discipline and obedience to the government.

By March, the military situation had worsened on all fronts. In the west, the Rhine had been crossed; in Italy and Greece, also, the Germans had been driven back; and on the Eastern front, from the Baltic down to the Balkans, the Red Army was pressing forward, while the nations that Hitler had occupied and enslaved in the early years of the war were now regaining their freedom. On April 30, Hitler, realizing at last that victory could not be salvaged from defeat, committed suicide.

Devastation caused by RAF bombers to a factory and railyards in the center of Hanover.

The Last Days of Hitler 1945

As Germany's defenses on all fronts crumbled before the Allied onslaught, Hitler withdrew from reality in his bunker beneath the Chancellery in Berlin. Deserted by all but his most loyal supporters, he was sustained for a while by desperate hopes and fantasies. When the pounding of Berlin's suburbs by Russian guns finally convinced him of Germany's defeat, he prepared a last testament to the German people, and together with his mistress staged an elaborate suicide. Thus ended the Reich that he had proudly boasted would last a thousand years.

In mid-January, 1945, the frontiers of Germany, and a good deal of territory beyond them, were still held by Hitler's armies; the Allies, though they had advanced on all fronts in the last months of 1944, had been forced to fight hard for every mile they gained, and they faced the prospect of even fiercer resistance by the Germans as the war was carried into their homeland. Five months later it was all over: Hitler had taken his own life; his main subordinates had either died, been captured, or disappeared; and the German people were under the rule of the victorious Allies.

Hitler received news of the snowballing military setbacks in his underground bunker at the Chancellery in Berlin. After the failure of the Ardennes offensive he had not returned to his wartime headquarters in the forests of East Prussia, but retired to his capital. Taking refuge in the underground rooms that came increasingly to resemble a tomb, he continued to issue impossible orders telling his generals to hold lines long since overrun by the enemy, and commanding nonexistent armies to counterattack. Oblivious of the Allied bomb attacks that were pulverizing the city above his head, and of the true state of affairs in a country where Germans were suffering and dying in their thousands, Hitler lived increasingly in a world of his own fantasies. One of the results of his withdrawal from effective action, as the "Thousand Years Reich" collapsed around him in ruins, was that the inherent conflicts and tensions within the regime became evident. Partly because Hitler had always been suspicious that one of his subordinates might become a rival, he had divided power among a number of rival "empires" each led by one of his chief lieutenants, and preserved his own power by playing them off against one another. Thus there were at least three rival "empires": the machinery of the central govern-

ment and civil service (controlled by Hermann Göring); the apparatus of the Nazi Party (ruled by Hitler's deputy Rudolf Hess until his flight to Scotland in 1941, and then by Martin Bormann); and the s.s., originally a Nazi Party security service, but now almost a state within a state (controlled by Heinrich Himmler). The conflicts between these rival authorities had seriously handicapped Germany's war effort (a striking disproof of the theory that dictatorships can always function more efficiently than democracies), despite the attempts of Albert Speer, originally Hitler's chief architect and now his armaments minister, to organize the planning and direction of the war on more rational lines. Now, with the guiding hand of Hitler weakened, the rival chieftains eyed each other with more jealousy than ever, and the conflict was made worse by the claims of other members of the Nazi hierarchy, among them the Foreign Minister Joachim von Ribbentrop. Of these leaders whose feuds marked the downfall of the Third Reich, Göring was to be disgraced and deprived of his office by Hitler for suggesting that he should take over power from the Führer. Himmler was to poison himself after Hitler's own death; Bormann, like the Führer's Propaganda Minister Josef Goebbels, was to perish with Hitler in the ruins of Berlin; and Ribbentrop was to be tried and executed as a war criminal. Göring later committed suicide in Allied captivity.

Hitler himself seems to have realized, at least with part of his mind, that the end was near. He summoned his mistress, Eva Braun, to come from Bavaria and join him in Berlin (they were to marry on April 29, the day before they took their lives), and he also turned his mind toward the last testament in which he was to abuse the German people who had proved unworthy of him. Right up to the end, however, Hitler continued to hope for some miracle that would save him and his

Hitler's ambition contrasted with the reality of Germany's destruction at the end of World War II.

A Soviet soldier on the steps of Berlin's Reichstag, with Russian graffiti on the wall.

regime. On April 12, as Vienna was falling to the Russians and the cities of the Ruhr and central Germany to the Western Allies, Hitler seized on the news of President Franklin D. Roosevelt's death as the salvation of Germany. Drugged by sedatives and influenced by sycophantic courtiers who encouraged his fantasies, he believed that the death of Roosevelt would bring a peace treaty between America and Germany in the same way as the death of Catherine of Russia in the Seven Years War two centuries before had brought to the throne a successor who had made a providential peace with Frederick the Great of Prussia. Hitler pinned his hopes on the fact that Roosevelt had played an important part as a conciliator between Churchill and Stalin—who had by now clashed on a number of issues, including the future of Poland and Greece—and chose to believe that with Roosevelt replaced by Truman, the Grand Alliance would fall apart. He even issued an Order of the Day on April 16 that treated Roosevelt's death as an act of providence: "From this moment when the greatest war criminal has been removed from this earth by fate, the war will take a decisive turn."

Hitler's hopes of a decisive turn of his fortunes for the better were, of course, illusory. On April 25, the advance units of the Russian and American armies met each other at Torgau on the Elbe, amid wild rejoicing. This meant that Germany's armed forces were split in half, and the end could only be a matter of days away.

Göring and other Nazi leaders were sent to the Bavarian mountains with the idea of setting up a center of resistance there; Hitler remained in Berlin with his loyal henchman Goebbels, who continued to broadcast appeals to the German people to resist to the utmost. It was at this stage that Hitler resolved not to let the Allies take any of Germany's remaining industrial installations intact. Orders were given that bridges and factories should be blown up as the enemy approached. This "scorched earth" policy was resisted by Albert Speer, who successfully foiled a number of demolitions that would have left the Berliners in a state of total chaos.

Hitler did, however, have his way in a number of final acts of destruction. One of these involved the Berlin subway system, through parts of which Russian forces were advancing. When Hitler heard of this, he ordered the flooding of the subway tunnels, even though this resulted in the drowning of many hundreds of Berliners who were sheltering in the tunnels from air raids.

Meanwhile, desperate hand-to-hand fighting was going on in the streets of Berlin, and the Russians were steadily approaching Hitler's Chancellery. The defense of Berlin was in the hands of elderly conscripts and teenage boys, who were ordered to halt the advance of Russian tanks by attaching grenades to them by hand. The fanatical bravery of these youngsters—stimulated by the threat of execution if they refused to fight, but also in part by genuine devotion to Hitler—was a remarkable feature of the last days of the Third Reich.

Inside the bunker, Hitler married Eva Braun—his mistress for many years—and they prepared to meet their deaths. Hitler's "Political Testament," which he dictated during his last hours, rejected any responsibility for the war that had cost the lives of 35 to 40 million people.

The testament went on to lay down Hitler's wishes for the future of the Reich. Grand Admiral Doenitz (the commander in chief of Germany's U-boat fleet) was to be Hitler's successor, aided by Bormann and Goebbels, and the new leadership was sworn by Hitler to "scrupulous observance of the racial laws and unmerciful resistance to the universal poisoner of all nations, international Jewry."

On April 30, with the Russians only a few streets away, Hitler called in the Chancellery staff to say farewell. His private pilot, Baur, protested passionately at Hitler's intention to "end it all," and offered to fly him to Argentina, to Japan, or to an Arab sheikdom, so that he could continue the struggle from there. Hitler, however, declared: "My generals have betrayed me, my soldiers don't want to go on, and I myself cannot carry on like that." He presented his pilot with a portrait of Frederick the Great, a portrait in whose magical powers he had trusted for years, and instructed Baur to cremate the bodies of himself and his wife before flying Bormann out of the doomed city of Berlin to continue the government of the Reich with Doenitz, who was at naval headquarters at Flensburg.

At 3:00 P.M., after saying goodbye to Goebbels and Bormann, Hitler shot himself through the mouth. Eva Braun, now Eva Hitler, took poison. Their two bodies were carried out into the courtyard of the Chancellery, soaked in gasoline, and burned, in accordance with the conclusion of Hitler's testament: "It is our wish that our bodies be burned immediately in the place where I have done the greater part of my daily work during the twelve years of service to my people."

Looking back over Hitler's last weeks in the bunker, the most amazing aspect of the whole drama is perhaps the degree to which the Führer was cut off from reality. The demonic inner drives that had enabled him to catch the mood of the German people from the 1920s onward were now, in the moment of total national collapse, turned inward into a private world of fantasy. Hitler's obsession with the changing fortunes of Frederick the Great—whose portrait, the one he presented to Baur before killing himself, was the only picture in his study—is a clear example of this. One of Hitler's favorite books was the *History of Frederick the Great* by the English historian Carlyle. Goebbels told his colleague Schwerin von Krosigk of an evening early in April, 1945, when he sat reading aloud to Hitler the section of the book dealing with the lowest point in Frederick's fortunes during the Seven Years War: how the great king, surrounded by his enemies, had told his ministers that if no improvement in his situation took place by February 15, he would give up hope and take poison. Then, Goebbels excitedly read to Hitler from Carlyle's account, on February 12 the Empress of Russia died, and Frederick's prospects improved dramatically.

Hitler's response to this encouraging historical parallel was to send for the records of two horoscopes, one his own—drawn up on the day he became Chancellor in January, 1933—and the other that of the German Republic, drawn up in 1918. Goebbels deduced from these documents—and convinced the unbalanced Hitler—that the fortunes of the Reich had been predestined to fall up to April, 1945, but that a dramatic rise in

Opposite top The Krupp works at Essen after an Allied bombing raid.

Opposite middle A British tank advancing through the ruins of the Dutch town of Uden during the advance toward Germany.

Opposite bottom The American and Russian troops meeting at Torgau in 1945.

The Russian Marshal Zhukov is decorated by Field Marshal Montgomery with the British Order of the Bath in Berlin, July 12, 1945.

Germany's power was equally inevitable from that moment on. On the strength of this historical "evidence," Goebbels urged Germany's retreating troops on to greater efforts, and it was this astrological "argument" that made Hitler so excited when Roosevelt died on April 12—an apparent repetition of the death of the Russian Empress two centuries earlier.

The same sort of delusions dominated Hitler's last attempts to direct military operations from his underground bunker. In the days following his birthday, on April 20, he repeatedly ordered counterattacks against the advancing Russians by the German forces still available on paper, but as these no longer existed as effective fighting units, his orders could not be carried out. Hitler's reaction to the nonexecution of his orders was not to accept the realities of the situation, but to blame his subordinates for disloyalty. Every one of his generals, so he screamed in a fit of rage on April 22, had deserted and betrayed him, and he was surrounded by treason, lies, corruption and cowardice.

None of Hitler's subordinates was spared his violent attacks in this last stage of his decline, even among those who continued to support him most loyally. It is true that some of his leading associates now deserted him, and tried to realize their own

ambitions at the expense of the doomed Führer. Göring, for instance, made a bid to take over power from Hitler, sending him a cable from the relative safety of Berchtesgaden (on the German-Austrian border) pressing his claim to succession along the lines laid down in a decree the Führer had issued in 1941. Hitler's response to this claim—and to the activities of Heinrich Himmler, now trying to negotiate a compromise peace with General Eisenhower through the office of neutral Sweden—was to denounce his former close associates as despicable traitors.

With those who were still within his power, his method was even more direct: he ordered the immediate execution of Hermann Fegelein, a high-ranking s.s. officer (and brother-in-law of Hitler's mistress Eva Braun), who had attempted to desert Hitler when he saw that the end was near.

Hitler's last testament of April 29 provides further evidence of how little the Führer understood the nature of the catastrophe he had brought upon Germany, or of its real causes. As we have seen, Hitler's testament placed the blame for the war on international "Jewish interests," and repudiated any German responsibility. The document also promised Germany, incredible as it may seem in the circumstances, a "glorious rebirth of the National Socialist movement of a truly united nation."

The successor named in Hitler's testament, Admiral Doenitz, was far from sharing the Führer's delusions about the possibility of a German military revival. As soon as Hitler and Goebbels had taken their lives, on April 30, Doenitz, from his headquarters in the north of Germany, began to make preparations for surrender to the Allies.

On May 7, at 2:41 in the morning, General Jodl and Admiral Friedeburg, on behalf of the Doenitz government, signed the document of unconditional surrender at the little schoolhouse in Reims where Eisenhower had his headquarters. The attempts of Doenitz to sign a separate peace with the Western powers alone, leaving Germany in effect on their side against what he called "the advancing Bolshevik enemy," had been doomed to failure by the unity with which the Allies insisted on a surrender with no conditions attached, and Doenitz bowed to the inevitable.

Thus the war in Europe ended on May 8, 1945. Millions of civilians had perished as well as men in the armed forces. With the death of Hitler, and the surrender of his successor, there ended the most appalling totalitarian regime of the twentieth century or any other. The shattered city of Berlin had once been among the leading capitals of European civilization. Under Hitler it had come to stand for oppression, suffering and destruction without parallel.   ROGER MORGAN

Opposite above One of Hitler's last conferences in his bunker at Berlin with Ribbentrop and Göring and generals Keitel and Jodl.

Opposite below The Soviet flag flying over the Reichstag.

Hitler's last moments.

Disagreement at Potsdam   1945

In the summer of 1945, the leaders of the United States, the United Kingdom and the Soviet Union met at Potsdam, Germany, to agree to the ending of World War II and the shape of the world to follow. Such questions as the future government and boundaries of Poland, the extent of the punishment and reparations to be meted out against Germany, the future of Austria and Greece and the administration of Berlin were to be discussed. These and other questions were hotly and endlessly debated. By the end of the conference it had become clear that agreement was neither possible nor even, perhaps, relevant. The harsh realities of the Cold War had become apparent.

The Potsdam Conference was held from July 17 to August 2, 1945, in the Soviet zone of Germany at Babelsberg in the suburbs of Berlin, where the palace of the German Crown Prince provided an excellent conference room for the three protagonists and their staffs. Churchill, feeling that the conference must mark the end of the long struggle on which Britain had embarked in 1939, chose the name Terminal. This was agreed to by Marshal Stalin and President Truman. This unimportant matter was the beginning and end of their agreement.

The conference marked the end of the European war, but not the beginning of peace in the hoped for sense of the word. Instead it marked the beginning of an uneasy and dangerous condition, afflicting almost the entire world, known as the Cold War: the confrontation of two bitterly opposed and irreconcilable systems of government.

The agenda facing the three heads of government and their foreign ministers was formidable, but it aroused no objections. The heart of Europe had suffered damage on an immense scale, and some sort of order quickly had to be fashioned out of chaos. Political and social disruption was almost total; starvation and human suffering demanded action. To the West it was soon clear that the problems, despite the rather loose agreements of Yalta, were insoluble in any terms appealing to the protagonists. The political and military pattern of Europe was rapidly taking shape in the face of Soviet, and of British and American, military power and occupation. The confrontation was absolute, but at the heart of the matter was the fate of Germany, for Germany was the hub of Europe. Ideas conceived in the heat and hate of war, such as cutting it up into powerless pieces, had to be abandoned. On the contrary, except for restoring its ability to wage war, Germany had to be restored. Her present and future had to be debated and hammered out at all costs.

The Soviet authorities were already plundering and pillaging in the regions over which they held sway—most gravely in the Soviet zone of Germany —regardless of the disastrous effect this would have on the industrial and economic recovery of the countries concerned. Plant and machinery were torn out and removed to the Soviet Union. Hungary, Rumania and Bulgaria were already under Soviet-installed puppet governments over which the Western Allies had not the power to mitigate, change, or even satisfactorily observe. In Poland, despite Soviet assurances, a Communist puppet government—the Lublin Poles—long nurtured and groomed by Moscow, was installed in Warsaw under its President, Boleslaw Bierut. With this the hopes of the Polish government-in-exile in Britain, together with the Polish nationals who had fought for the "liberation" of their country, were doomed. This was the nation for which Britain had gone to war.

On the question of Poland neither Britain nor the United States could accept the Soviet solution. A fight for a free or relatively free Poland and for the exiled Poles had to be made, and Soviet-Polish expansion westward had to be resisted with all the arguments possible. Polish occupation of large areas of Germany, including a vast acreage of arable land, vitally affected the survival of Germany, condemning tens of thousands to starvation. This situation added to the tasks facing the British in particular.

Thus bitter and often fruitless arguments involving the present and future of Germany, the Soviet demands for reparations, the Polish puppet government and Polish expansion westward, dominated the conference from beginning to end.

Churchill had feared some such pattern of development in Europe when he had pressed the

British Prime Minister Clement Attlee, who took over from Churchill during the conference : West European socialists, such as Attlee, found themselves out of sympathy with Stalin.

Opposite Churchill, Truman and Stalin at the opening of the Potsdam Conference.

Americans to advance to confront the Soviet armies as far to the east as possible, and for an early conference before positions had hardened irrevocably. The Americans had disagreed; first Roosevelt and then Truman, inheriting his policy, wooed the Soviet Union toward a declaration of war against Japan, and cajoled Stalin into permitting his uncompromising spokesman, Molotov, to take part in the San Francisco Conference to found the United Nations. Both Roosevelt and Truman were basically domestic politicians, and the affairs of Europe were not a part of their emotional and historical backgrounds. Moreover, Roosevelt had permitted himself dangerous illusions as regards the liberalization of Soviet Communism and the good nature of Stalin. These illusions had been induced by the euphoria of the "comrades-in-arms" relationship generated by the mutual struggle.

It is perhaps idle to speculate on what might have happened had Churchill persuaded the Americans in the last days of the war to occupy Prague, and as much of Austria as possible, and to permit the march on Berlin. Soviet aims—basically Russian strategic aims arising out of the experiences of one and a half centuries of history—were also Communist aims for profoundly military and political reasons. Soviet Communist ambitions ranged over vast areas from the Baltic to the Bosphorus, to the North African coast, and possibly to the Indian Ocean.

Apart from the central points of dispute, the Western Allies had to establish Allied Control Commissions to operate as effectively as possible in the occupied countries, to reach agreement on occupation zones in Germany and Austria, to establish the best possible access routes into Berlin through the Soviet zone, and to strive to establish Austria as a "special case," not to be confused with Germany. In these matters the Western Allies could not give ground.

It was, of course, impossible to modify Soviet power in the countries she occupied in Eastern Europe, or to "democratize" the systems of government already established. Nor, in fact, was it desirable. Free elections and forms of Western democratic government were alien to countries that had known nothing but tyranny.

Churchill arrived in a somber mood, and with a general election in progress in Britain marking the end of the wartime coalition. Truman, attending his first international conference, meeting Stalin and Churchill for the first time, was subdued and resolute, determined to tidy things up in the shortest possible time. He and the British Prime Minister had reached Potsdam on July 16, satisfied with the arrangements made and with good first impressions of each other; Stalin, excusing himself on the grounds of slight indisposition—believed to have been a mild heart attack—arrived a day late. He was in good humor, cool and bland, but, as Churchill knew, hard as steel.

Thus the conference opened. It was clear that Truman hoped to be a moderating influence. This was disturbing for the British even though Britain and the United States were bound to work closely together on many issues, notably the present and future of Germany and of Austria. The two Western heads of government had reached Berlin to be informed that the way was barred for the entry of their troops into Vienna. Moreover, Allied Control Councils could not be established effectively until British and American troops had withdrawn from what the Russians chose to call "their illegal occupation of Soviet territory." These matters were tiresome hindrances, mainly for the military commanders and their subordinates to resolve between them, but they were indicative of the difficulties in the four-

Postwar Europe, 1945-48

- - - - 1937 frontiers
- Allied control zones of Germany and Austria
- Ceded to Russia by Britain and America
- Annexed by Russia in 1945
- States which became Communist between 1945 and 1948
- Yugoslav gains from Italy, 1945
- Cities divided into 4 occupation zones
— The "Iron Curtain" from 1948
— German boundary since 1945

FINLAND
Viborg
Leningrad
ESTONIA
Pskov
SWEDEN
Riga
LATVIA
DENMARK
LITHUANIA
BALTIC SEA
Memel
Königsberg
Vilna
EAST
Minsk
PRUSSIA
Danzig
RUSSIA
American
Stettin
Bremen
Berlin
GERMANY
Poznan
Warsaw
Pinsk
British
Russian
POLAND
Erfurt
Breslau
French
Prague
Cracow
Lvov
Nuremberg
CZECHOSLOVAKIA
Uzhgorod
Czernowitz
FRANCE
Vienna
French
Russian
Kishinev
American
Budapest
French
AUSTRIA
HUNGARY
RUMANIA
SWITZERLAND
British
Trieste
(British and American
occupation 1945-55)
Bucharest
Pula
Belgrade
YUGOSLAVIA
BULGARIA
ITALY
ADRIATIC
SEA
Sofia
Communist activity 1946-49
ALBANIA
MEDITERRANEAN
SEA
AEGEAN
GREECE

power administration of Berlin. The French, although excluded from the conference, occupied a zone of Germany and would be given a hand in the final resolutions of the council of foreign ministers. Meanwhile the British and Americans had to do the best they could in spite of obstructions. In Vienna the British complained that they were hampered in their duties. They were nonetheless resolved that Austria should not fall into the Soviet net. Fortunately for them, the Austrians could not be persuaded to embrace Communism and thus provide the Soviets with a nucleus of support with which to establish a government.

Over the whole conference there lay the somber shadow of the atom bomb. On July 16, Truman was informed of the successful detonation of the bomb at Alamogordo. It had profoundly disturbed all those who had observed the explosion. The President was, in U.S. Secretary of War Stimson's words, "tremendously pepped up by it." It undoubtedly gave him confidence. Churchill's reaction was predictable: "This atomic bomb is the second coming in wrath!" According to Field Marshal Alan Brooke he felt it "no longer necessary to persuade the Russians to come into the Japanese war; the new explosive was sufficient to settle the matter."

That may have been true, but Churchill's optimism was premature and based on his conception of a kind of super "conventional" weapon. Field Marshal Alan Brooke, the British Chief of the Imperial General Staff, tried to moderate his elation. Meanwhile, with Churchill's agreement, Truman chose a period of relaxation at the end of a conference session to convey his news casually to Stalin. It seems probable that Stalin knew a great deal about it already, despite the immense secrecy with which the whole project had been surrounded. The Soviet leader merely remarked that he was glad to hear Truman's news, and hoped that the President would make good use of it against Japan. The political, social, moral and military effects of the bomb were unpredictable.

At the conference table an atmosphere of compromise was almost entirely lacking. Germany and Poland were at the heart of the matter, and from beginning to end occupied the center of the stage.

The condition of Germany cannot be expressed in terms of facts and statistics. The entire country was laid waste. The havoc caused, the misery and destruction she had wrought upon Europe and herself, were impossible to assess in terms of dollars in the immediate aftermath of war. Her ability to pay was impossible of assessment and if her remaining industrial assets in every department were to be removed physically, she might be rendered incapable of recovery for an indefinite period. Reparations is another name for loot. Thus the Soviet demand for $20 billion dollars had to be denied and the Soviet desire to destroy the means of ultimate German recovery, resisted.

Only the zones occupied by the Western Allies could be protected, and only by enabling Germany to produce and to trade could immediate and future disaster be avoided.

At the conference table the Soviets bargained, mainly through Foreign Minister Molotov, in anticipation of the riches to be gained from the industrial Ruhr in the British zone. The Russians regarded the total destruction of Germany and the misery and starvation of the German people with indifference; but the Western Allies, fearing that a divided Germany might prove an easy prey to Communism and become a threat to Western Europe, knew that the country had somehow to be rebuilt, and its ability to produce, to export and import, and to support itself, had to be restored as quickly as possible. Whether a surplus might be made available for reparations was a consideration for the future.

The task facing the Western Allies in Germany, and Britain in particular, in the first weeks seemed insurmountable. The physical state of the country was one of chaos and ruin. Hundreds of thousands of human beings, "displaced persons," searched for sustenance and shelter. Those Germans displaced from the huge areas the Soviets had annexed for Poland—four million, including children

Bottom The trial of Nazi leaders at Nuremberg, which was taking place during the conference.

The Cecilienhof at Potsdam, where the conference took place.

The problems of urban life in Berlin at the end of the war. The Potsdam Conference did not solve the German problem, but it helped to restore normal life in Germany.

and the aged and infirm—spilled into the British zone, and could not be denied.

Many towns had become heaps of masonry, steel, wood and earth, inhabited by "cave dwellers," burrowing into the rubble. Many small townships and villages had disappeared. The fertile earth remained, but the industrial situation would take many months to restore even to a minimum production of exportable goods to be exchanged mainly for grain.

The new boundaries of Poland, contrary to all that had been said at Yalta, ran from Swinoujscie on the Baltic, fixed firmly on the line of the Oder River, embracing Stettin and Breslau, and the Western Neisse River to the Czechoslovakian frontier. In no circumstances could or would the Western Allies agree, but they were, in the end, powerless. The area occupied by the Poles created in effect a fifth zone administered by Poland. Most of East Prussia, excluding Königsberg and a region in the north administered by Russia, was in Polish hands.

Thus the German and Polish problems were interlocked. Soviet demands that the coal mined from the Ruhr should be sent to Poland in exchange for nothing had to be rejected at all costs. Only the grain in the Polish-occupied east in the arable areas of Germany could keep the Germans fed. In the end the Russians were forced to accept from the ruined industrial Ruhr what they called a percentage of nothing. The loot which might or might not be available ultimately could not be given a money value in advance, nor, as Truman said, would the United States pay for Polish revenge.

The physical and moral ruin of Germany had revealed certain stark realities of the human condition; the fear, envy, greed, stupidity and cruelty of man had brought about this calamity. Qualities of compassion and even of heroism were manifest in individuals, but absent from collective man. Meanwhile the problems of Germany could only be solved by genuine realism purged of fear and hate. The Russians, appalled by the desolation and death wrought upon their own country, were motivated by fear and hate, and were without compassion. Moral considerations apart, however, the British sensed that Germany was, or must be, the citadel of Western Europe. If it should be permitted to fall to Communism, Europe would be lost.

The French had been excluded from the conference, even though their interests were great. However, together with the three great powers they occupied a zone in Germany, and would profit from their absence in the long run. Meanwhile the occupation and administration of Berlin painfully passed under Allied control, the British and Americans uneasily aware of their isolated position deep inside the Soviet zone of Germany. The Allied position might become precarious. Tact and patience in the highest degree, coupled with firmness, was the only hope for the future of the old capital.

Unaccustomed to international conferences, President Truman was immediately irritated and frustrated by the long discussions and by the failure to reach agreement. When Churchill tried to soothe him by suggesting that three or four main subjects should be prepared for debate each day, Truman replied that he was only interested in decisions. He had not wanted to come to the conference and the sooner he would be able to get away the happier he would be. Yet, even if the conference settled almost nothing, it did clarify the issues and confront the Allies with the bitter fruits of victory.

Churchill had properly invited the Deputy British Prime Minister, Clement Attlee, to accompany him to Potsdam. Attlee might become Prime Minister after the election. Thus for the first week Attlee watched as Churchill used all his gifts to deflect Stalin from his course, and to consolidate such gains as might be possible.

Soviet demands upon Turkey, pursued with serious military threats and annexations of territory, could not go unchallenged. Churchill, while conceding the basic "freedom of the seas" and access for Soviet shipping from the Black Sea by way of the Bosphorus to the Mediterranean, condemned the Soviet demand to dominate the narrow straits by "force."

It was at once apparent that a Soviet naval presence in the Mediterranean would pose grave problems for the future. At once Stalin wanted to know what would happen to the Italian colonies in Allied hands. He wanted Libya, he calmly demanded a hand in the administration of Tangier, and he rebuked the Western Allies for having anything to do with Spain. There were other sore spots in the West, notably the turbulence in Greece. Stalin scoffed when Churchill pointed out that at least observers could go and observe freely if they wished, a situation denied to Western observers in Communist-controlled territory.

Yugoslavia was also a serious British problem, with Tito pressing for control of his "beloved Istria" and Venezia Giulia. These delicate matters were finally resolved by the resolution and calm of General Alexander and the shrewd common sense of Tito. Yugoslavia was a country apart and it was difficult to foresee what its fate would be. Czechoslovakia seemed relatively safe from Communist rule for a time. President Beneš, head of the government-in-exile in Britain, returned to a great welcome, and something like democracy was established. Nevertheless it would have been a bold man who would have ventured an optimistic forecast of Czechoslovakia's ultimate fate.

The determination of the Western Allies to restore Italy and to bring her into the community of nations and a seat in the United Nations was treated with scorn by the Russians, whose demands for reparations were rejected.

Some of the matters discussed at Potsdam, such as the Soviet demands for a share of the German navy, were comparatively simple to deal with. But in the main, as deadlock succeeded deadlock, problems were passed to the council of foreign ministers of the five powers—the U.S.A., Great Britain, France, China and the Soviet Union—for final solution. The council was to prepare the way for a peace conference. Here again limitations were imposed by the Russians. From first to last the fate of Poland dominated the conference and could not be resolved. It was the most agonizing problem that Britain had to face, and this was especially true for Churchill. Before the conference Churchill had written to Stalin appealing for cooperation. The appeal was wasted. The Soviet Union had embraced and nurtured a Communist group led by Boleslaw Bierut and known as the Lublin government, and signed a mutual-aid pact with them. Without consulting the Western Allies the Soviet High Command had committed "President Bierut" and his government to the control of the whole of the new Poland to the Western Neisse. Soviet avowals that this would not affect the determination of Poland's future frontiers were a blatant lie. The hope that Britain might gain for the Polish government-in-exile in London any part in the affairs of their country was simply dissipated. The London Poles and the 180,000 still under arms in the Allied camp had few illusions. Stanislaw Mikolajczyk, head of the government-in-exile, was outraged that leaders of the Polish underground who had served under his orders were detained by the Russians. He distrusted Soviet assurances that they would be treated with leniency. Bierut, the Communist President, tried unsuccessfully to convince the British and Americans that he and his government had the support of the Polish people. Churchill confronted them at Potsdam in vain. Mikolajczyk, persuaded to visit Moscow and Potsdam to meet Bierut and the "Lublin Poles,"

Loading machinery for shipment from Germany to the Soviet Union. The U.S.S.R. demanded the payment of huge war reparations.

realized that he was faced with a hopeless situation. As Stalin insisted on Allied recognition of the Communist Polish government, General Anders, commanding the Polish forces in exile, knew that "it was the total surrender of even the semblance of political independence."

Nothing else illustrates more vividly the division of Europe than the impassioned debate on Poland. On July 24 Churchill said his last word, and returned to England to hear he had been replaced as the leader of the British people.

The new Prime Minister, Attlee, returned alone to Potsdam. Ably supported by his Foreign Minister, Ernest Bevin, Attlee put the British points of view as unequivocally as Churchill, if with less eloquence, and equally in vain. In the early hours of August 2 the conference ended, searching for a formula that would convey the idea to the world that it had been a success. But the end of "Terminal" was indeed bleak.

Churchill wrote in his memoirs: "During the course of the conference I allowed the differences that could not be adjusted either round the table or by the Foreign Ministers at their daily meetings to stand over. A formidable body of questions on which there was disagreement was in consequence piled upon the shelves." He emphasized that "the overrunning by the Russian armies of the territory up to and even beyond the Western Neisse was never and would never have been agreed to by any Government of which I was the head."

Agreement had become irrelevant. Perhaps the most important result of the Potsdam Conference was Truman's decision not to share knowledge of the atomic weapon with the Soviet Union and not to allow the Soviet government any part in the control of Japan. For the rest, the conference ended the hopes and illusions of the West, which now was faced with the harsh realities of the new Europe, and of the new world.   R. W. THOMPSON

Fireball over Hiroshima

At 2:45 a.m. on August 6, 1945, the American bomber Enola Gay *lifted off a runway in the Mariana Islands and swung north toward Japan. Some five and a half hours later, after a flight that was devoid of incident, the aircraft was over its target: Hiroshima, a major communications center for the Imperial Japanese Army. At seventeen seconds past 8:15, the* Enola Gay's *bomb doors opened and her cargo fell away. Forty-three seconds later Hiroshima was obliterated by the first major atomic explosion in world history. Some 78,500 persons were killed in the holocaust that followed, and the practice of war changed convulsively and irrevocably. As a four-mile-high mushroom cloud formed over the leveled city, the world entered the Atomic Age.*

Harry S Truman, who gave the order for atom bombs to be used against Japan.

Opposite An atomic explosion similar to the ones that devastated Hiroshima and Nagasaki.

For the first five thousand years of the history of war, the development of weapons followed a simple pattern of changes resulting from individual experience and made practicable only when technology made one of its limited advances. The first of the climactic inventions—gunpowder—required two hundred years to become effective in war and another four centuries to reach its zenith. Then, abruptly, in the mid-twentieth century, the pattern changed: at fifteen minutes past eight on the morning of August 6, 1945, an American aircraft released one bomb over the Japanese city of Hiroshima. Forty-three seconds later Hiroshima had been obliterated. The nature and practice of major war had changed convulsively, and the history of man had entered a new era.

The moment of origin of the atomic bomb can be argued. Indeed, it may lie in the very beginnings of nuclear physics; it seems more probable, however, that historians will eventually place it at Ernest Rutherford's brilliant determination of the internal structure of the atom at Cambridge University, England, in 1911. The precision of his experiments led, by an inevitable and almost automatic process, to the final bombardment and splitting of the uranium atom by Otto Hahn and Fritz Strassmann in Berlin in late 1938.

The importance of the Germans' achievement was not immediately apparent either to politicians or to military leaders, although it was to scientists. Rutherford warned Sir Maurice Hankey, Secretary to the British cabinet, that Hahn and Strassmann's experiment was a highly significant one. In America, members of the considerable group of scientists who had left Fascist Italy and Nazi Germany in previous years were shocked. In March, 1939, Enrico Fermi, the Italian Nobel Prize winner, was put in touch with the U.S. Navy Department to discuss experiments he had made that confirmed the Germans' work, but the discussions were without significant result. In midsummer, with Germany's attack on Poland imminent, the Hungarian physicists Leo

Szilard and Eugene Wigner approached Albert Einstein and asked him to urge President Franklin D. Roosevelt and the U.S. government to take steps to develop an atomic weapon. Einstein was reluctant at first, but in August, with the assistance of Szilard and another scientist, Edward Teller, he wrote to Roosevelt asking that the project be started.

Roosevelt ordered action, but initial efforts met with delays, difficulties and lack of funds. Not until two years later, on December 6, 1941, was Vannevar Bush, head of the U.S. Office of Scientific Research and Development, able to announce governmental consent to an all-out drive to develop an atomic weapon. On December 7, in grim coincidence, the Japanese navy launched its attack on Pearl Harbor.

By June, 1942, an almost inconceivably vast, top-secret program of atomic bomb development (called the Manhattan Project) had been initiated under the authoritarian command of Brigadier General Leslie Groves. By December Fermi had induced the first controlled nuclear chain reaction in an unused squash court at the University of Chicago, and J. Robert Oppenheimer had begun research on the explosive aspects of a bomb. In 1943 the giant experimental laboratories at Los Alamos were functioning, the Oak Ridge National Laboratory in Tennessee and other enormous components of production had been set up, and more than half a million were on the Manhattan Project's payroll.

A test device was in the final stages of completion on May 8, 1945—V-E Day—when Germany surrendered. On July 16, as Harry S Truman—who had become President after Roosevelt's death—was driving through the ruins of Berlin, an atomic bomb was triumphantly tested at Alamogordo in the desert of New Mexico. By that time, three billion dollars had been spent on the project. In the interim Italy had collapsed, Germany had gone down in absolute defeat, and Japan alone was left fighting.

Approximately a year previously, the Manhattan Project had organized its own separate "air force," with its own Boeing B-29 Superfortresses, its own

Enola Gay, the B-29 Superfortress that dropped the bomb on Hiroshima.

Right Little Boy, the bomb detonated over Hiroshima. The ten-foot-long bomb weighed 9000 pounds.

An aerial view of Hiroshima showing the extensive damage done by the bomb.

transport aircraft and armament section, its own training program and rules, and a strength of seventeen hundred officers and men. Only Colonel Paul Tibbets, Jr., its commanding officer, was fully briefed on its purpose: to drop the first atomic bomb. In February, 1945, Admiral Chester Nimitz, commander in chief of the U.S. Pacific Fleet, was told the plan. General Douglas MacArthur, commander of U.S. forces in the Pacific, had not been informed. Tinian Island in the Marianas, a site that was secure, strategically located, and had a major air base, was chosen for the use of the 509th Composite Group, the Manhattan Project's private air force.

American forces were already dangerously close to the Japanese homeland. Iwo Jima had long been in their hands; Okinawa collapsed by June 22; B-29 fire raids and naval carrier attacks were sweeping across Honshu. As early as April, the Japanese sent out peace feelers through Allen Dulles' Office of Strategic Services in Switzerland; the effort failed, however, for lack of support in Tokyo.

Two months later Koichi Kido, a member of Japan's government, approached Emperor Hirohito

himself and secured approval for a peace plan, to which the Japanese Supreme Council agreed on June 18. By coincidence, on that same day President Truman confirmed the plan for Olympic, the name for the opening assault on Japan due in November and the invasion of Honshu, the main island, in March, 1946.

As Okinawa fell, the Japanese made fresh approaches to the Russian ambassador to Tokyo; when the Japanese army objected, it was rebuked by the Emperor, in an exceptional intervention. The Russians were, in any event, uncooperative. On July 7, Hirohito ordered a fresh approach through Russia that dealt in part with the question of unconditional surrender, but this failed also.

Just two days before, the cruiser *Indianapolis* had left the San Francisco navy yard, carrying on board the charge for the first nuclear weapon. Ten days later the Allied powers meeting at Potsdam presented this ultimatum to Japan:

We call upon the government of Japan to proclaim now the unconditional surrender of all Japanese armed forces. . . . The alternative for Japan is prompt and utter destruction.

This was the atom warning, but no indication of the nature or the power of the weapon was given. Japan failed to respond. Procrastination in the Japanese government, furious opposition by army officers, and political refusals to acknowledge reality inhibited action.

The weapon had now acquired a dynamic of its own. Inexorably, the steps that led to its use were taken. The target had to be a substantial city, untouched by previous bombings but large enough to provide a convincing demonstration. Kyoto, the ancient capital of Japan, headed the first list of choices, which included Hiroshima and Kokura. Kyoto was spared, for although General Curtis LeMay believed the destruction of its temples and its palaces would be a compelling shock to Japan, Henry L. Stimson, the U.S. Secretary of War,

considered that its destruction would be impermissible vandalism. Hiroshima became the primary target, Kokura the second and Nagasaki was added.

The city was a major communications base. From it, Japanese armies had sailed for the China War. for the Russian War and for the invasion of Malaya. In 1945 it had been designated Japan's Southern Command Headquarters in preparation for the anticipated American invasion, and the Emperor was to move to it if Tokyo was threatened. Hiroshima's population was 340,000, but evacuation had reduced it to 245,000 at the time of the atomic attack.

While President Truman was at sea returning from the Potsdam Conference, the final moves were made. At 1:37 A.M. on August 6, three reconnaissance aircraft were dispatched—to Hiroshima, Nagasaki and Kokura—to ascertain cloud cover

A street scene in Hiroshima hours after the atomic blast, two miles from the center of the explosion. The photographer later died of injuries.

Emperor Hirohito inspects bomb damage in Tokyo.

over the targets. At 2:45, *Enola Gay*, the aircraft carrying the bomb, took off, with Colonel Tibbets using every desperate inch of Tinian's runway. At two-minute intervals the instrument and photographic planes followed. After them came a standby plane. Two hours later, two more photographic planes followed.

The flight was uneventful. At dawn Iwo Jima was distantly visible to the northeast, and at 4:55 the accompanying planes assumed a broad arrow formation. There was no sign of Japanese air activity. All three reconnaissance planes reached their target cities. Kokura was clear; Nagasaki and Hiroshima had some cloud cover. At 7:45 the pilot of the *Straight Flush*, the plane over Hiroshima, signaled: "Advice: bomb primary." Then he turned for home.

The *Enola Gay* was already at bombing altitude, six miles above the Pacific. At ten minutes to eight she crossed the coastline of Shikoku. As inexorably as the takeoff and the flight, the testing of the bomb's electrical circuits proceeded. There was no Japanese jamming on the frequency of the proximity fuse, no hang-up in the aircraft's electronics.

At nine minutes past eight, Tibbets said casually, "We are about to start the bomb run. Put on your goggles. When you hear the tone signal, pull the goggles over your eyes. ..." Two minutes later *Enola Gay* reached the starting point of the bomb run, only seventeen seconds late after traveling fifteen hundred miles. At exactly 8:15 and seventeen seconds the bomb doors opened, the bomb dropped, righted itself and fell away. As the nose of *Enola Gay* flung up, Tibbets jerked the plane around in a violent evasive maneuver and swung away. On his left the instrument plane dropped its three parachute loads of recording and transmitting gear and swung

urgently clear. There were just forty-three seconds in which to reach a safe distance.

The flash from the explosion all but blinded those who looked directly at it through special polarized glasses. The fireball was 1,800 feet across. The shock wave hit the *Enola Gay* a minute later. Afterward, as they turned to fly past the southern outskirts of Hiroshima, the co-pilot, staring at the boiling dust and flame that roared up into the four-mile cloud, said quietly: "My God, what have we done?"

There had been no second air alert in Hiroshima. The first had been canceled after the *Straight Flush* left the area and the *Enola Gay*'s run was assumed to be just another reconnaissance. It would have made small difference. A few people saw parachutes in the sky—the instrument parachutes. No one saw the bomb, only the blinding, inconceivable flash that seared consciousness.

It is not possible to say how many died in the first instant of the flame that engulfed the central area of Hiroshima. The fire that followed was fed by thousands of little charcoal cooking fires burning in the flimsy houses that collapsed in flames in a circle three miles across. Those trapped in the wreckage died as the fire storm grew. Those wandering—blinded, scorched, with the skin peeling off them and their faces in shreds from the first horror of that flame—died in the fire storm also. But most of those in the center were killed by the blast itself.

It is believed that 78,500 people perished on the first morning. How many died later is unclear; people are still dying from causes attributable to the blast. Medical attention was all but impossible. Half the city's doctors were dead and most of the rest were wounded: 1,650 of the city's nurses were dead or injured. Ten thousand people crawled or

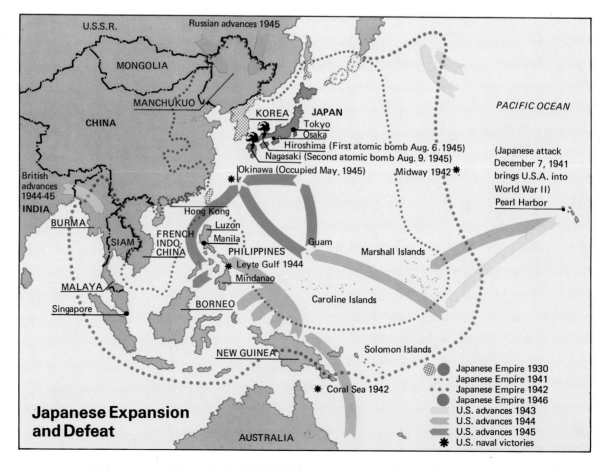

Japanese Expansion and Defeat

Russian advances 1945

U.S.S.R.

MONGOLIA

MANCHUKUO

CHINA

KOREA   JAPAN
Tokyo
Ōsaka
Hiroshima (First atomic bomb Aug. 6. 1945)
Nagasaki (Second atomic bomb Aug. 9. 1945)

PACIFIC OCEAN

British advances 1944-45
INDIA

Okinawa (Occupied May, 1945)   Midway 1942 ✳

(Japanese attack December 7, 1941 brings U.S.A. into World War II)

BURMA

Hong Kong

Pearl Harbor

SIAM   FRENCH INDO-CHINA
Luzon
Manila

Guam

Marshall Islands

PHILIPPINES
✳ Leyte Gulf 1944
Mindanao

MALAYA

Caroline Islands

Singapore

BORNEO

NEW GUINEA

Solomon Islands

✳ Coral Sea 1942

AUSTRALIA

Japanese Empire 1930
Japanese Empire 1941
Japanese Empire 1942
Japanese Empire 1946
U.S. advances 1943
U.S. advances 1944
U.S. advances 1945
✳ U.S. naval victories

were carried to the one surviving hospital. Medicine, drugs and bandages were destroyed, food was burned or inedible, water over large areas was undrinkable. Aid from outside was slow in coming, relief incompetent (Japan, it is necessary to remember, was a shattered country even before Hiroshima).

It is at this point that the moral questions begin. Was the bomb inhuman? In Tokyo on the night of March 9–10, 1945, at least 83,800 had died in uncontrollable fires. In February the RAF had killed 25,000 in Dresden (35,000 more were missing). The bomb dropped on Hiroshima was inhuman, but it was neither less nor more inhuman as an instrument of slaughter than the conventional systems it superseded.

Was the bomb necessary? The situation that existed in Japan for three days after the bomb had fallen was incomprehensible to Western minds. Despite the shattering proof of the weapon's potential, the absolute deadlock between the two sides in control of Tokyo continued. In the end the crisis required the personal intervention of the Emperor to resolve it, and even his decision was unacceptable to sections of the army, the navy and the air force. Indeed, elements of the army committed the sacrilege of seizing the Imperial Palace in an attempt to prevent the Emperor from invoking the ancient precedent of The Voice of the Crane—the act of speaking directly to the nation—through the modern device of broadcasting.

Had the army imposed its will on the Emperor or had the Emperor decided to fight on, the consequences would have been immeasurable. Japan was already defeated, but substantial forces still existed in the homeland, adequate quantities

The Industrial Promotion Center in Hiroshima has been left in its damaged state as a memorial to the victims of the first atomic bomb.

of ammunition and equipment were available and preparation for fanatical resistance had been made. No one who had watched the Japanese garrison on Iwo Jima accept annihilation or had seen the bitter desolation of Okinawa could believe that a Japan under the control of Korechika Anami, the War Minister, and the navy and army chiefs of staff, Admiral Toyoda and General Umezu—and backed (genuinely or under duress) by the Emperor—would not have fought the most terrible defensive battle of history. To break such resistance would have required fire storms in every remaining city and town in Japan and the annihilation of whole populations, as well as the destruction of the armed forces by conventional means.

The horror of the first atomic bomb lies not in the death and desolation of Hiroshima, nor even in the subsequent destruction of Nagasaki by the second bomb, but in the scientific and the technological potential that it unleashed. It made possible the unthinkable. Even before Hiroshima, men at the Los Alamos atomic center were talking of the "super" bomb. At Hiroshima the explosion yielded a power equivalent to 13,000 tons of TNT (the early figure of 20,000 was inaccurate).

But even that was not enough. Spurred by the genius of Edward Teller, scientific research was even then moving irresistibly toward a hydrogen bomb. To measure the explosive power of this superbomb it was necessary that scientists coin a new unit—megaton—to enable military men to calculate its effect in terms of a million tons of TNT. To carry such a bomb, new delivery systems were necessary, for aircraft delivery was becoming obsolete. To satisfy these new needs, the 1944 development of the German v-2 rocket—deemed to have failed then because of the inadequacy of its explosives—became a dominant element of future war.

The involvement of the twentieth-century world in the consequences of nuclear physics, the extravagances of missile technologies, the phenomena of lunar and planetary exploration, and the possibility of total destruction, are the moral issues arising from Hiroshima.   DAVID DIVINE

On September 2, 1945, Japanese delegates sign an unconditional surrender on board the U.S.S. *Missouri* in Tokyo Bay. General Douglas MacArthur is standing at the microphones.

Superpower hegemony

The Japanese surrender after Hiroshima did not altogether end the war in the Far East. In some of the Pacific islands fighting went on; groups of Japanese soldiers often refused to believe that their government would ever surrender and continued to fight. As late as 1974 a Japanese soldier in the Philippines finally surrendered when his brother—who had been flown from Japan—proved to him that the war had ended almost thirty years before.

Foreign Minister Mamoru Shigemitsu (front row, in formal dress with a cane) standing with the Japanese delegation before signing the capitulation documents.

In the wake of Japan's surrender, Russia and the United States moved rapidly to consolidate their power and the ideological clash resulting from that confrontation soon became the dominant feature of the postwar world. This tense international situation would soon be com-

plicated by the Chinese Communists' victory in the civil war against Chiang Kai-shek and by the emergence of what has since come to be known as the Third World—the vast underdeveloped areas of the globe that owe political allegiance to neither of the great power blocs. The Third World eventually became a battleground for the "superpowers" but in the immediate postwar period the conflict was confined largely to Europe.

The United States assumed leadership of the Western bloc during the first months of the postwar period, largely as a

result of the decline of the United Kingdom, which in 1945 was nominally victorious but economically shattered. The trading mechanisms by which Britain earned her livelihood had been destroyed, and the Empire on which she had depended for much of her wealth had become

Clement Attlee speaking at Labour's meeting in London after the 1945 election.

a burden (particularly because wartime propaganda had given colonial peoples a taste of freedom.) Many overseas investments had been sold to finance the war, gigantic debts had been contracted, and through wartime neglect capital assets—from industrial machinery to housing—had become run down. The British no longer had the power or the spirit to be an active imperialist power. The coalition government did not long survive the war. When the Labour Party under Clement Attlee was brought to power with an overall majority of nearly two hundred in the House of Commons in the general election of 1945, they made it clear that social improvements and economic recovery were more important than any continuance of dreams of empire. In the face of this abdication from world power, America, which had emerged from the war unscathed by Axis bombing and at the height of its industrial power, did not hesitate to take up the crown. Like Great Britain, other European states felt unwilling to reclaim their prewar role in the world. Only the French and the Dutch demanded the return of their colonies, thus creating a situation that was to throw Southeast Asia into turmoil for a good thirty years. What the war had done was to underline the fact that America, the war's main beneficiary, would be the world leader in the years to come. The only other country to gain substantially from the war was the Soviet Union, but, unlike America, Russia had first to repair the devastation that the war had caused.

Reconstruction in Russia

Some twenty million able-bodied Russian men had lost their lives during the war, and many millions more who survived were maimed or crippled. During 1945 the survivors began to return home from the Eastern front. The scene that greeted them was one of awful destruction: coal mines, steel mills and factories built during the Five Year Plan had been flooded, dismantled or razed, and countless homes destroyed. For years after the war twenty-five million people had to live in mud huts and dugouts, and to compound their misery, Russia was hit by a calamitous drought in 1946. Food rations were a quarter of what they had been in 1939, and industrial production was only fifty percent of the prewar figure. Between the end of the war and the declaration of the Truman Doctrine in 1947, the Russian leaders attempted to resolve the acute shortage of manpower by rapidly demobilizing their armies. That demobilization was undertaken with such alacrity that the number of men in uniform dropped from 11.5 million in 1945 to under 3 million in 1947. Allied fears notwithstanding, Russia was not in any position to launch a serious attack on Western Europe in the late 1940s.

By the terms of the agreement signed at the Yalta and Potsdam conferences, Stalin had committed himself to respect the predominance of capitalism in postwar Western Europe. And, at least initially, he seemed inclined to do just that. The Russian dictator prevailed upon the Communist parties in Italy and France to collaborate with centrist governments, and when the Greek revolt was crushed neither *Pravda* nor *Izvestia* made unfavorable comments. The Yugoslav Revolution was carried out by Tito against the instructions of Stalin (and while Stalin was advising Mao Tse-tung to yield to Chiang Kai-shek's Kuomintang). Even within the Russian sphere of influence in Eastern Europe the process of stalinization did not immediately follow the war. Fearful of antagonizing the West, Stalin allowed anti-Communist parties a brief representation in the coalition governments of Poland and of Hungary.

Concentration camps

Although the Germans had in general treated prisoners of war reasonably well, the Allies rapidly discovered that what many had suspected was true; there was a

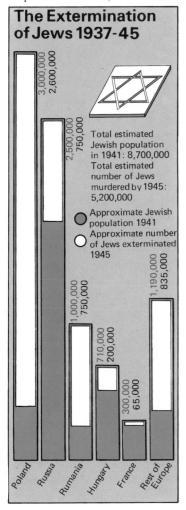

The Extermination of Jews 1937-45

Total estimated Jewish population in 1941: 8,700,000
Total estimated number of Jews murdered by 1945: 5,200,000

● Approximate Jewish population 1941
○ Approximate number of Jews exterminated 1945

	3,000,000 / 2,600,000	2,500,000 / 750,000	1,000,000 / 750,000	710,000 / 200,000	300,000 / 65,000	1,190,000 / 835,000
	Poland	Russia	Rumania	Hungary	France	Rest of Europe

whole arm of the German administration, the Gestapo, that had been able to operate without any regard for the law. As the Allies advanced they found concentration camps with thousands of starving anti-Nazis in many parts of Germany and the occupied territories. Worse still, they found extermination camps (such as that at Auschwitz) where the Nazis had sought from 1942 onward to impose their "final solution" to the "problem" of the Jews and other undesirable racial minorities, who were regarded as *untermenschen* (subhuman). Ironically, the desperate need of the Third Reich for slave labor had saved the lives of hundreds of thousands, but nonetheless millions had died in the gas chambers.

How far the German population was aware of what went on in the extermination and concentration camps is uncertain. The Nazi leadership had made considerable efforts to keep their activity secret, but many who were only indirectly concerned with the camps must have had an idea of what

Belsen after liberation. S.S. doctor Klein standing among his victims.

happened in them. In particular, German heavy industry had used the slave labor that the camps made available without question or criticism.

Even before the Allied advances into occupied territory had begun, it was clear that the Allies would have to institute procedures to insure that the Nazi leadership, who were primarily responsible, would be punished.

The Nuremberg trials

The Russians were already insisting that Germany be forced to pay enormous war reparations as compensation for the damage done

The accused at Nuremberg: in the front row (left to right) are Göring, Hess, Ribbentrop, Keitel, Kaltenbrunner, Rosenberg, Frank, Frick, Streicher, Funk and Schacht.

to Russia during the war. They also demanded that Nazi leaders be executed. As early as 1943 the Allied leaders had agreed in principle that those responsible for war crimes must be punished, but neither Churchill nor Roosevelt had much sympathy for Stalin's suggestion that at least fifty thousand Nazis be summarily executed without trial. In 1945 the Western Allies' view triumphed and an International Military Tribunal was set up.

From November, 1945, to October, 1946, the tribunal, which had one judge and one substitute from each of the four major Allied nations, sat at Nuremberg, the city that in the 1930s had been the scene of the great Nazi Party rallies. Twenty-one of the Nazi Party leaders were tried in person by the tribunal for conspiracy, crimes against peace and humanity and war crimes. Only two of those accused, Franz von Papen (1879–1969) and Hjalmar Schacht (1877–1970), were acquitted. Most of the others, including Göring, Ribbentrop and Streicher, were sentenced to death. Hess, who had spent most of the war in prison in Britain after an abortive peace mission in 1941, was sentenced to life imprisonment, and after the release of Speer in 1966 was the only prisoner in Berlin's huge Spandau prison. Martin Bormann was sentenced to death in absentia, and was sought in the South American jungles for years until his corpse was discovered in 1973, only yards from Hitler's bunker. As well as sentencing individuals, the tribunal found the Reich government, the Army

High Command and many Nazi Party organizations collectively guilty. The Nuremberg trials only dealt with the most important Nazi leaders, and other trials of lesser figures were held in the different occupation zones.

Despite the fairness with which the trials were actually conducted, many doubts were raised as to their justice in principle. Allied officers and politicians had, for example, ordered the massacre of innocent women and children in bombing raids against huge civilian targets rather than military centers, but they were not tried, and to some extent the trials assumed the collective guilt of the German people. Furthermore, since war crimes had not previously been incorporated into international statute, the trials also bore the taint of retrospective law. Nonetheless, the Nuremberg trials were an attempt to create a new standard of international justice, and to give practical expression to the ideals represented by a new international body, the United Nations, which was an offshoot of the Yalta Conference. The U.N. had functioned as a relief and rehabilitation bureau during the final years of the war and the immediate postwar period. On October 9, 1944, a group of delegates representing the Big Three powers and the Nationalist Chinese had met at Dumbarton Oaks to propose that the United Nations be established on a permanent basis; in the spring of 1945, the representatives of fifty nations convened in San Francisco to draw up a charter. In January, 1946, a general assembly of the new body met in London.

News Chronicle

No. 31,091 FRIDAY, JANUARY 11, 1946 ONE PENNY

LATE LONDON EDITION

Our ultimate aim is not just the negation of war but the creation of a world of security and freedom, of a world which is governed by justice and the moral law—*Mr. ATTLEE OPENING U.N. CONFERENCE*

BRITAIN'S PRIME MINISTER WELCOMES THE DELEGATES

With the great gold insignia of the United Nations dominating the scene, Mr. Clement Attlee makes his inaugural speech from the rostrum in Central Hall. Behind him at the presidential table sit Dr. Eduardo Zuleta Angel (Colombia), temporary Chairman, with Mr. H. M. Gladwyn Jebb, Executive Secretary, United Nations Preparatory Commission, on his right and Mr. A. Cordier (U.S.A.), chief of the General Assembly section, U.N. secretariat

U.N. Assembly elects Spaak, of Belgium, first President

By EDWARD MONTGOMERY, the Diplomatic Correspondent

IN TWO HOURS YESTERDAY AFTERNOON, IN CENTRAL HALL, WESTMINSTER, THE NEW WORLD ORGANISATION OF THE UNITED NATIONS WAS BORN.

During those two hours the representatives of the Governments of 51 nations, gathered for the first meeting of the United Nations General Assembly, were welcomed by their temporary chairman, Dr. Eduardo Zuleta Angel, of Colombia; listened to Mr. Clement Attlee, British Prime Minister and leader of the British delegation pleading with his calm sincerity for the creation of "a world of security and freedom, a world governed by justice and the moral law"; and elected as their President for the forthcoming session M. Paul-Henri Spaak, Belgian Foreign Minister and leader of the Belgian delegation.

It was precisely four o'clock when Dr. Zuleta rapped twice sharply with his gavel on the gold-draped President's desk and asked the 600-odd delegates, advisers and members of secretariat who crowded the floor of the hall to take their seats.

At three minutes past four

Gradually silence fell in the high, white-painted, brilliantly-lit hall, on the floor itself and in the galleries, crowded with the public, distinguished visitors and the Press.

Exactly three minutes' grace were to be given to the broadcasters, perched high up in their tiny glass-fronted booths over the public gallery, to tell the nations over a world-wide hook-up that the world organisation was ready to begin its work.

At exactly 4.03 Dr. Zuleta rose, rapped with his gavel and said: "La séance est ouverte." And duly the interpreter translated into English: "The meeting is called to order."

Rotund, be-spectacled, immensely dignified, Dr. Zuleta began his speech by quoting first phrase of the preamble of the United Nations Charter, written by Field-Marshal Smuts at San Francisco:

"Determined to save succeeding generations from the scourge of war, which twice in our lifetime has brought untold sorrow to mankind. . . ."

Mr. Attlee takes the floor

At 4.15 Dr. Zuleta had finished and his speech was translated into English. Then he rose again and said: 'La parole est au Premier Ministre du Royaume Uni, M. Attlee," and as the interpreter translated "The Prime Minister of the United Kingdom, Mr. Attlee, has the floor," Mr. Attlee walked to the speaker's tribune below the President's desk amid the applause of the hall.

While Mr. Attlee spoke he was brilliantly lit by the floodlights from the two big camera booths over the gallery entrances where the newsreel cameras were recording the scene for the world's cinema audiences.

Mr. Attlee was a little hard to hear—from the Press gallery, at least—for there is a bad echo in the hall, which even the elaborate public address system which had been installed, with two golden microphones on either side of the speaker's desk, had not been able to overcome.

Surprise Russian nomination

But his speech was listened to in attentive silence, and it was clear that what he had to say about the need for the United Nations to become "the overriding factor in foreign policy," and to deliver common people all over the world from the fear of economic insecurity, made a deep impression upon the delegates.

When M. Mathieu, chief interpreter of the United Nations Secretariat, had finished his translation of Mr. Attlee's speech into French, Dr. Zuleta Angel called upon the Assembly to elect its President for the forthcoming session.

It had been generally believed that there was wide agreement among most of the delegations on the choice of M. Spaak, Belgium's Foreign Minister, for the Presidency.

The election was to be by secret ballot, without nomination—that is, the head of each delegation would simply write the name of his delegation's candidate for the Presidency on a slip of paper and place it in the ballot-box.

As it turned out, the procedure came as something of a surprise.

Continued Back Page (B)

Premier on the choice now offered to mankind

MR. ATTLEE, the Prime Minister, in his speech at the opening of the General Assembly, said: "I have the honour today of welcoming to London this great Assembly of Delegates of the United Nations."

"It will be our endeavour to make you feel at home in this our capital city, so that you may speak as freely and frankly as if you were meeting in some special territory under international control. We shall do our best to make your stay here pleasant, within the limit of our means.

"We wish we could do more, but I am sure that all of you in the course of your stay will realise that anything that is lacking in your entertainment is not due to any absence of good will, but to the effect of the malice our enemies wreaked upon this ancient city.

ON PAGE TWO
This Day Shapes Our Destiny, by A. J. Cummings; M. Spaak, by Vernon Bartlett; What the public thought of the Conference.

ON PAGE THREE
More pictures of the first day of the United Nations Conference

Act of faith

"The evidences of this you will see around you.

"Last night we listened to an inspiring speech by his Majesty the King, in which he set before us in a few words the nature of the task which we have to accomplish, the vital importance of the issues at stake, and the keen desire of all the nations of the British Commonwealth, for whom he spoke, to make this first meeting of the United Nations Organisation a complete success.

"I had the privilege of taking part in the discussions at San Francisco from which was evolved the Charter of the United Nations.

"The initiation of these discussions, while our enemies were still in the field against us, was at once an act of faith in our victory and an acknowledgment of the cause for which we were fighting.

Mankind's choice

"The purposes and principles set down in the Preamble and in Article I of the Charter have the wholehearted support of his Majesty's Government and, I believe, of the whole of the people of this country, to whatever political party they belong.

"We realise that, as perhaps never before, a choice is offered to mankind.

"Twice in my lifetime a war has brought untold sorrow to mankind.

"Should there be a third world war, the long upward progress towards civilisation may be halted for generations, and the work of myriads of men and women through the centuries be brought to nought.

"The Preamble to the Charter of the United Nations admirably sets out the ideals for which men and women laid down their lives during the war.

"But the affirmation of principles is easy, the translation into action, the making of a working reality out of an ideal, is very difficult.

The single aim

"In the stress and strain of war it is possible to fuse the ideal aim with practical effort.

"When in the summer of 1940 this country was left open to the imminent danger of invasion, the whole of the people were animated by one single aim, and that aim was immediately translated into action.

"Every man and woman leaped forward to serve wherever needed, and the strength of that purpose endured through five years of war.

"During those five years, as nation after nation joined in the struggle, the efforts of the Fighting Forces, of the workers behind the line, of the resistance movements in so many countries, were all co-ordinated and directed to the single purpose of victory.

"Private interests and individual national aspirations were sunk in the common endeavour.

"Now today, when victory has crowned our arms, we have to bring to the task of creating permanent conditions of peace the same sense of urgency, the same self-sacrifice and the same willingness to subordinate sectional interests to the common good as brought us through the crisis of war.

Rule of law

"We all, therefore, must approach our work with a realisation of its outstanding and vital importance.

"The United Nations Organisation must become the overriding factor in foreign policy.

"After the first world war there was a tendency to regard the League of Nations as something outside the ordinary range of foreign policy.

"Governments continued on the old lines, pursuing individual aims, and following the path of power politics, not understanding that the world had passed into a new epoch.

"In just such a spirit in times past in these islands, great nobles and their retainers used to practise private war in disregard of the authority of the central Government.

"The time came when private armies were abolished, when the rule of law was established throughout the length and breadth of this island.

"What has been done in Britain and in other countries on a small stage has now to be effected throughout the whole world.

Breakdown

"We must all now today recognise the truth proclaimed by the Foreign Minister of the U.S.S.R. at Geneva—'Peace is indivisible.'

"Looking back on past years we can trace the origins of the late war to acts of aggression, the significance of which was not realised at the time.

"Failure to deal with the Japanese adventure in the Far East, and with the acts of aggression of the Fascist rulers of Germany and Italy, led inevitably to the breakdown of the rule of law and to the second world war.

"In the last five years the aggression of Hitler in Europe drew eventually into the contest men from all the continents and from the islands of the sea.

"It should make us all realise that the welfare of every one of us is bound up with the welfare of the world as a whole, and that we are all members one of another.

Social justice

"I am glad that the Charter of the United Nations does not deal only with Governments and States, or with politics and war, but with the simple, elemental needs of human beings, whatever be their race, their colour or their creed.

"In the Charter we reaffirm our faith in fundamental human rights.

"We see the freedom of the individual in the State as an essential complement to the freedom of the State in the world community of nations.

"We stress, too, that social justice, and the best possible standards of life for all, are essential factors in promoting and maintaining the peace of the world.

"I have said that the solution of the problem of establishing

Continued Back Page (A)

TODAY'S WEATHER

Dull, with occasional rain or drizzle, especially on coasts; mild

Page One News, briefly

Civil war in China ends

HOSTILITIES between forces of the Chinese Central Government and Chinese Communists are to cease immediately, ending the civil strife which broke out soon after the Japanese surrender last September.

This was stated in Chungking yesterday by Generalissimo Chiang Kai-shek, at the conference of the People's Consultative Council, called to bring about Chinese unity.

★

One Jew was killed and others injured in a clash between Arab and Jewish workers near Ramleh, between Jerusalem and Tel-Aviv. British airborne troops restored order after three hours.

U.S will be without phones

AMERICA'S telephone system is threatened with complete breakdown by strikes due to start today. There is little doubt that by the end of the week no calls will be put through in the U.S. The White House yesterday had to use military lines.

There is rising hope that negotiations will avert the strike of 700,000 steel workers.

★

Premier Sophoulis of Greece has made it clear that neither he nor the Liberal Party as a whole was involved in the Venizelos pact with the Populists (Royalists). The general strike has not materialised.

★

Abdul Hagir, Finance Minister, announced in Parliament yesterday that Persia would reject the Anglo-U.S. proposal that a Tri-Partite Commission investigate Persian internal affairs. Five persons were killed in political clashes in Northern Persia.

Demob riots by U.S. troops

A CALCUTTA demonstration by 5,000 G.I.s and riots at Marseilles in which gendarmes intervened, are the latest signs of U.S. troops' discontent. New York radio said that Gen. Eisenhower, reporting to President Truman on demobilisation, declared that troops who demonstrated at Manila were in no way guilty of indiscipline.

★

King Ibn Saud, of Saudi Arabia, arrived in Cairo yesterday on a 12-day State visit to Egypt.

★

A 73ft. dinosaurus has been unearthed at Mangabeira, Brazil.

★

Two new ranges of Utility furniture will be available in a few months. One will be comparable with good pre-war articles, the other similar to mass-produced pre-war pieces.

He spoke to the world

The delegates of 51 nations, sitting in a semi-circle, three delegations at each 40ft.-long table, listen as Mr. Attlee speaks. Above them in the galleries are distinguished visitors, representatives of the world's Press and members of the public. And through the microphones before him, Mr. Attlee's words were broadcast to the world

GERMAN INDUSTRY: ALLIED COUNCIL DECIDES

BERLIN, Thursday.

THE Allied Control Council in Berlin decided in 1hr. 20min. today one of the most difficult problems facing it—the future level of German industry.

But nearly six hours after the meeting Public Relations of the four military governors were still trying to draft a communique on the decision.

The session was described as "highly successful" by Col. James Williams, U.S. Public Relations officer, who promised a communique tomorrow night.

LATE NEWS

HUNGARIAN QUISLING DIES

Dr. Laszlo de Bardossy, Hungarian Prime Minister under the Germans, was hanged yesterday in Budapest.—Budapest Radio.

Lighting-up time, 4.43 p.m.

1s. hour more for U.S. motor workers

From Our Own Correspondent
[By Transatlantic telephone]

NEW YORK.

PRESIDENT TRUMAN'S fact-finding board investigating the 50-day-old General Motors strike today recommended a wage increase of 19½ cents (about 1s.) an hour. This represents an increase of approximately 17½ per cent., compared with the union's demand for a 30 per cent. increase, and the company's offer of a 10 per cent. increase.

President Truman said the report would "commend itself to the good judgment of the American public."

First Meeting of the U.N. General Assembly   1946

The failure of the League of Nations to prevent World War II sealed the fate of the institution, but everyone agreed that some international body was needed. The Anglo-American Atlantic Charter of 1941 was a modest start, followed by the declaration of twenty-six Allied nations that they would pursue the war together. With preliminary talks held at Dumbarton Oaks and a full convention in San Francisco, an organization to be known as the United Nations slowly took shape. As outlined it would comprise a Security Council of five permanent and six rotating elective members who would rule on threats to world peace and a General Assembly in which all members would be represented. In January, 1946, in a converted Methodist church in London, England, the General Assembly was convened for the first time.

Dr. Zuleta Angel of Colombia, acting as President, banged his gavel and at 4 P.M. on January 10, 1946, exactly twenty-six years to the day after the birth of the League of Nations, the first session of the General Assembly began its work. Two hundred and twenty-four delegates from the fifty-one member states were present in the domed Central Hall, Westminster, temporarily converted from its usual function as London's largest Methodist church. Among the delegates were the foreign ministers of sixteen countries including the United Kingdom, the U.S.A., the U.S.S.R., and France as well as the prime ministers of the United Kingdom and New Zealand and the world-famous Eleanor Roosevelt. For months war-torn London had been preparing for this great event. The Central Hall itself had been cleaned and redecorated and special temporary broadcasting studios built to take the news to the world. Over two thousand visitors, delegates and their staffs had descended on this part of London and somehow had been accommodated in hotels and private homes. Food rationing was still part of the daily lives of Londoners and bomb damage could be seen almost everywhere, but there was an atmosphere of optimism. This was none the less real for being limited. The war had been won and the peace could be too, but after the experience of the previous quarter century, it was going to be a very difficult task.

The mood in the conference chamber was not so very different when the British Prime Minister Clement Attlee welcomed the delegates. He spoke of the atomic bomb and the urgency it brought to the Assembly, describing it as "the last of a series of warnings to mankind." Mr. Attlee went on to warn of the dangers of leaving the United Nations outside the ordinary range of foreign policy as had been done with the League and said that "the United Nations must become the overriding factor

in foreign policy." Of at least equal importance was his statement that freedom from want was as important as freedom from fear and that the ultimate aim should not be the negation of war, but "the creation of a world of security and freedom governed by justice and the moral law."

The assembly was now ready to begin its first sessions. It had come a long way from its origins just five years earlier.

In August, 1941, President Roosevelt and Prime Minister Churchill had met in mid-Atlantic and expressed in the Atlantic Charter their hope "to see established a peace . . ." that would assure "that all men in all the lands may live out their lives in freedom from fear and want." On January 1, 1942, following the Japanese attack on Pearl Harbor, the U.S. joined the U.K., the U.S.S.R., China and twenty-two other countries engaged in war with the Axis powers, in making the Declaration of the United Nations, which bound them to continue the war together and not to make a separate peace. This was the first use of the title "United Nations" and it serves as a reminder that the word "united" in this instance related to unity in war, rather than in peace.

In October, 1943, the foreign ministers of the U.K., U.S. and U.S.S.R. meeting in Moscow issued a joint declaration together with the representative of China. They agreed that after the war, a new international organization should be established to replace the League of Nations. There were good reasons relating both to the Soviet Union and the United States for this step. The first great blow to the League, and a continuing weakness, was the absence of the United States, following the Senate's rejection of the Versailles Treaty of which the League of Nations Covenant was part. American involvement in a postwar international security organization was seen as vital to its success and it was thought to be easier to secure

John Foster Dulles as U.S. delegate addressing the U.N. General Assembly in Paris, 1948. American participation in the new world body insured it an effectiveness the old League of Nations lacked.

Opposite Front-page reportage of the opening meeting in London of the United Nations General Assembly in 1946.

113

Meeting of the preparatory commission of the United Nations consisting of all the signatories of the Charter under the chairmanship of Dr. Zuleta Angel of Colombia. Its task was to bring into being the main organs of the United Nations.

the support of the U.S. Senate for American membership of a new organization than for the old. In December, 1939, the Soviet Union had been expelled from the League following her invasion of Finland. As a direct consequence the U.S.S.R. was unwilling to face the humiliation of a reapplication for League membership and later was even opposed to a return to Geneva. In 1944, at Dumbarton Oaks, a secluded mansion in the suburbs of Washington, the broad outline of what was to become the United Nations Charter was agreed to by the U.K., the U.S. and the U.S.S.R. After the meetings of the representatives of these three countries had reached agreement, China replaced the Soviet Union at the conference table and endorsed what were by then the Dumbarton Oaks Proposals. This unusual course was necessary because the U.S.S.R. was unwilling to sit at the same table as China.

These proposals were very comprehensive and since they were subsequently adopted with few changes, it would be better at this stage to note that there remained but two major issues to be decided. The first was the voting procedure of the Security Council, which was to be responsible for international peace. The main organs of the League had

had a unanimity rule: a resolution required agreement by all, and every member of the Assembly or Council had the right of veto. The Security Council, it was agreed, should consist of five permanent members—China, France, the U.K., U.S. and U.S.S.R.—plus six elected members. It had been agreed at Moscow that the new organization should be based on the unanimity of the U.K., U.S. and U.S.S.R. This was extended to include France, and it was agreed that the Security Council should vote by a majority of seven out of eleven, including the votes of the permanent members. Two points regarding the voting procedure, however, remained unresolved: Should a permanent member who was a party to a dispute be permitted to vote and exercise its veto? Further, should the veto apply to procedural votes and enable a permanent member to prevent a dispute being placed on the agenda? Even on these issues there were discussions that led to agreements at a later date. In these preliminary discussions it became clear that what Russia feared was not the discussion of any issue, but collective action against a permanent member. The British delegation suggested a possible compromise whereby there would be no veto on procedural votes or on those under the chapter dealing with the specific settlement of disputes (later to be Chapter 6 of the Charter). Shortly after Dumbarton Oaks this suggestion was adopted by President Roosevelt, who made it an official U.S. proposal. By the end of January it had been accepted by the U.K., and at Yalta the Soviet Union finally gave its approval.

The second unresolved problem was the extent to which Russian claims for the representation of their constituent republics were to be met. These two outstanding issues were not unconnected. Russia's attitude to the veto might well depend on the acceptance, at least in part, of its demands for the socialist soviet republics. These constituent members of the Russian federal state (the Union of Soviet Socialist Republics), it was claimed, should have separate membership in the United Nations as well as that of the federal government itself. This, too, had to await the Yalta meeting before it was finally resolved.

The Dumbarton Oaks Conference began on August 21, 1944, and ended on October 7. On September 29 China had replaced the Soviet Union at the conference table. In this period of seven weeks, a remarkable degree of agreement was reached. The Dumbarton Oaks Proposals, which were to be the basis of the United Nations Charter, represented the joint views of the four powers on the purposes, principles, structure and operation of the new organization.

The conference attended by Churchill, Roosevelt and Stalin at Yalta from February 3–11, 1945, had been primarily concerned with the postwar European settlement. It was agreed, however, that procedural votes of the Security Council should be taken by a majority of seven and on other matters by the same majority, but with the proviso that it must include the votes of the permanent members. It was further agreed that in relation to the pacific settlement of disputes, as opposed to international action, a party to a dispute should abstain from voting. On the subject of membership it was agreed that in addition to the U.S.S.R. itself the Byelorussian and the Ukrainian Soviet Socialist Republics should be admitted.

Thus in 1945 invitations were sent by the sponsoring powers (China, the U.K., U.S., U.S.S.R.) to those nations that had declared war on Germany or Japan by March 1, 1945, and had signed the Declaration of the United Nations, to meet at San Francisco. At the beginning of the conference invitations were sent to Argentina, the Byelorussian Soviet Socialist Republic, the Ukrainian Soviet Socialist Republic and Denmark. This brought the number of participating states to fifty. No invitation was sent to Poland even though it had signed the Declaration, as the sponsoring powers had been unable to agree on which of the two governments should be recognized. Yalta had produced a merger plan by which the Russian-sponsored Lublin government would be enlarged to include representatives of the London-based Polish government-in-exile. Conflict over Poland, whose invasion by Nazi Germany had begun World War II, became a major source of disagreement among the Allies and it was not until June 23, 1945, that five members of the London Polish government joined the Lublin government.

Now, for the first time, fifty countries looked at the proposals made by four of their number for an international organization on which rested mankind's hopes for freedom from war and want. The proposed security system was based on the "realistic" approach. The "realism" was a recognition of the existing power structures in the world and the consequent limitation of the role of an international organization. Power resided in a small number of countries and if agreement could be reached among these, then the United Nations could be a means of channeling their collective will and making it effective. If, however, the great powers were divided or, even worse, were determined to go to war with one another, then no international organization could hope to prevent it. This was the thinking underlying the principle of the unanimity of the sponsoring powers and the voting procedures in the Security Council.

The U.K., U.S., U.S.S.R. and China had jointly declared at Moscow in October, 1943, "that their united action, pledged for the prosecution of the war against their respective enemies, will be continued for the organization and maintenance of peace and security." While the idea of unity in peace as well as war was an attractive one, it will be seen that the principle of great power unanimity had foundations in political realities as well as having a potential oratorical appeal.

Sir Charles Webster, professor of international history, and a member of U.K. delegations to the

General view of part of the conference hall as delegates take their seats prior to the opening of the U.N. Assembly by Prime Minister Attlee.

Left Mr. Trygve Lie, the first Secretary-General of the United Nations, addressing a press conference in London, 1948.

Dumbarton Oaks and San Francisco conferences, maintained years later that if the minutes of the San Francisco meetings were divided into two piles, one dealing with all aspects of the veto and the other with all other matters, they would be approximately the same size. Though the measurement of this dramatic illustration might be questioned, there can be no doubt of the importance of the issue. The small powers were at first resolutely opposed to the privileged position the sponsoring powers had given themselves and made their views known in no uncertain terms. Gradually it became apparent that the great powers were unwilling to become members unless they had the power of veto in the Security Council: the right to prevent unilaterally the passage of resolutions, including those to initiate or end collective action. This was of great importance since the Charter system of security was to depend on decisions to a greater extent than that of the Covenant, which was based on the keeping of promises. The differences were in the field of sanctions. If under the Covenant a member of the League resorted to war in disregard of the articles dealing with the pacific settlement of disputes, it was deemed to be an act of war against all the other members. They were

Ernest Bevin, British Secretary of State for Foreign Affairs, addressing the General Assembly in January, 1946.

TO
THE·GLORY·OF·GOD
AND·IN
PRAYER·FOR·PEACE·ON·EARTH
THIS·TABLET·COMMEMORATES
THE·FIRST·MEETING
OF·THE
GENERAL·ASSEMBLY
OF·THE
UNITED·NATIONS
IN·THE
METHODIST·CENTRAL·HALL
WESTMINSTER
JAN.10-FEB.14,1946

The plaque on Central Hall, Westminster, commemorating the first meeting of the General Assembly.

ment answering a total of twenty-three questions on the Yalta formula for voting in the Security Council, which they had "presented to this Conference as essential if an international organization is to be created . . . for the maintenance of international peace and security." France associated itself with the statement and though the debate continued through five more meetings of a main committee, the sponsoring powers finally won the day.

One of the most significant differences between the Charter and the Covenant was its emphasis on economic and social questions and the machinery it established for this purpose. The International Labor Organization had been established under the League system with its own constitution and membership. The League's main activities in the social field, however, such as securing and supervising the execution of agreements on white slave traffic in women, child healthcare, and dangerous drugs, were part of the League system itself. This work was to be extended. An Economic and Social Council consisting of eighteen members was to be elected for three-year terms. The International Labor Organization had survived the war and the new Food and Agriculture Organization and the International Bank for Reconstruction and Development were expected to be in operation by the time the Charter was in force. It was decided to "initiate negotiations . . . for the creation of any new specialized agencies required for the accomplishment of the purposes" of the organization and to bring them into relationship with the United Nations and coordinate their activities through the Economic and Social Council.

The Charter was signed on June 26, 1945, and on the same day a preparatory commission consisting of all the Charter signatories was set up under the chairmanship of Dr. Zuleta Angel of Colombia. Its task was to make provisional arrangements to bring into operation the main organs of the United Nations, including, of course, the General Assembly. Gladwyn Jebb of the U.K. became its Executive Secretary, offices were established at Church House, Westminster, an initial Secretariat formed, committees, including an all important Executive of fourteen, began to operate and by December 23 the great task had been completed and the final report adopted.

The first business on the agenda after Clement Attlee's welcome was the election of the President. There were no formal nominations, but it was expected that Paul Henri Spaak, the Belgian Foreign Minister, would be elected. Andrei Gromyko, acting head of the Soviet delegation, caused some surprise by nominating Trygve Lie, the Norwegian Foreign Minister, despite his declared unwillingness to serve. The surprise turned to concern when Dr. Manuilsky, head of the Ukrainian delegation, suggested that a ballot was unnecessary and Trygve Lie could be elected by acclamation. The Assembly, however, decided

bound under Article 16 to "immediately" sever "all trade or financial relations" and prohibit "all intercourse between their nationals and the nationals of the covenant breaking State." The experience of the League, where these obligations were often ignored, led to a different system. This gave power to the Security Council to determine the existence of a "threat to the peace," a breach of the peace or an act of aggression, and to decide on the measures to be taken. These were to include the "complete or partial interruption of economic relations," communications and "diplomatic relations" as well as, where necessary, military action.

On June 8, toward the end of the San Francisco Conference, the sponsoring powers issued a state-on a secret ballot and a useful precedent was created. Spaak was elected by a vote of twenty-eight to twenty-three.

Elections of the nonpermanent members of the Security Council, the eighteen members of the Economic and Social Council and the judges of the International Court of Justice followed as did that of Trygve Lie as the first Secretary-General. It proved impossible to reach agreement regarding membership of the Trusteeship Council. Three days had been spent in the preparatory commission on the question of the seat of the new organization and proposals as far ranging as Scotland, Danzig and a luxury ship on the high seas were considered. The vote eventually went to the United States: thirty for, fourteen against, with six abstentions. This decision was confirmed by the assembly where it was decided that the headquarters of the U.N. should be in New York.

Though by no means occupying a major part of Assembly time, the terrible threat of the atomic bomb, first used the previous August on Hiroshima and Nagasaki, hung over the whole conference. It was mentioned by Attlee in his welcoming speech and was often referred to in the debates. An Atomic Energy Commission, consisting of the members of the Security Council and Canada, was set up by a unanimous vote, to inquire into all phases of the problem of the international regulation of atomic energy and to make specific recommendations to the Security Council.

The existence of nuclear weapons threatened the very future of the United Nations as a security organization. The Charter, prepared by men who were unaware of the new weapon, had been based on a system of collective security centered around five great powers. Under the League, members had not been prepared to risk the immediate possibility of war for the long-term advantage of a secure world. Now they would be asked not merely to risk the horror of war, but to accept the possibility that it might bring the end of civilization. Either there had to be comprehensive disarmament, including atomic weapons, to unprecedentedly low levels, or a new security role had to be found for the United Nations.

In March, shortly after the end of the London session of the first Assembly on February 15, Winston Churchill made his famous "Iron Curtain" speech at Fulton, Missouri. The will to cooperate, on which the success of Dumbarton Oaks depended, had declined since that time. Efforts to maintain the wartime alliance continued, but by the end of the following year, the world was divided into rival camps and the Cold War had become a reality. The security system of the Charter, based on permanent member unanimity, was now in ruins, but by the end of the decade the first signs of a new role for the United Nations were beginning to emerge. In Kashmir in 1948 and in the Middle East in 1949, the U.N. established a small corps of observers. In the following decade they were to be followed by peacekeeping forces,

The Methodist Central Hall, Westminster, where the first meeting of the U.N. General Assembly took place.

as the idea of preventive diplomacy gradually developed. The new role, unlike the old, was not to be a guarantee against war, but rather a contribution to peace. The sights had to be lowered, but the process of adaptation to changing events was beginning.

The first speaker called by the President at that first Assembly had been James Byrnes, U.S. Secretary of State. It was a dramatic moment when the United States began to participate in the world body, whose precursor had suffered so greatly from American absence. Byrnes thought the United Nations should "adapt itself to the changing needs of a changing world." "I believe it will live," he said "because it springs from the impelling necessities of the age."   FRANK FIELD

Postwar America

Faced with the problem of converting from a wartime to a peacetime economy, America desperately needed to reopen its old trade outlets and find new ones. The war had brought an industrial boom that had virtually eliminated unemployment, and if wartime increases in industrial capacity were not to produce another crisis of overproduction, overseas markets would have to be maintained and extended. This necessity brought conflict with Russia, as W. C. Bullitt, U.S. Ambassador in Russia, observed in 1946: "Every time the Soviet Union extends its power over another area or state, the United States and Great Britain lose another normal market." The Allies' search for outlets for the goods produced by their overheated postwar economies was both intense and risky. It led, almost immediately, to a confrontation with Russia in Eastern Europe, and the desire to roll back Soviet domination in that region had some basis in Allied economic interests.

"Stalinization"

In response to this approach the Russians sought security in "Stalinization," the total subjection of Eastern Europe to Russia's political and economic needs. The Kremlin realized that a Communized Eastern Europe was necessary if the Russians were to block the penetration of U.S. capital and trade, let alone political ideas. In addition, it was a useful physical barrier against the danger of a revived Germany.

Throughout Eastern Europe, which was largely acknowledged by the Western Allies as Russia's sphere of influence, Stalin sought to insure that Communism would triumph. The greater Germany, the Reich that was to last a millennium, had fallen; Germany was partitioned among the Allies, and Stalin—supported by the French—was determined not to allow its reunification. The country was controlled by an Allied commission, but political parties began to press for some form of self-government. In the eastern zone the Social Democrats were

A Russian militiawoman controlling traffic at Brandenberger Tor in Berlin.

persuaded to join the Communists —who rapidly proved the stronger —in a United Workers' Party. In order to compensate the Poles for Russia's seizure of eastern Poland, East Germany was given a new border along the Oder River. From the beginning there were difficulties between the Russians and the Western powers.

Like Germany, the Austrian provinces and the city of Vienna were partitioned by the Allies. The Russians installed a provisional government under a Social Democrat Chancellor, and the pre-*Anschluss* constitution was reintroduced. At the end of 1945 elections were held, which gave the Roman Catholic Peoples' Party a majority. As in Germany, the Russians and the Western Allies found many points on which they could not agree, although no formal partitioning of the country took place, and it was not until 1955 that the Allied occupation of Austria ended.

Further north, the Baltic states of Lithuania, Latvia and Estonia,

which had enjoyed a slightly precarious independence until they had fallen under Russian sway at the beginning of World War II, were absorbed into the U.S.S.R. Finland's large Communist Party joined in a coalition with other parties, but in 1948 the coalition collapsed and the Communists left the government. The ruling Social Democrat Party took a generally pro-Soviet line, however, and trade links with Russia remained very close.

In Poland, the government-in-exile in London was simply ignored by the Russians, who recognized instead the Communist-dominated Polish Workers' Party. Moreover, tension between the two governments was further exacerbated by the suspicion of the London government that a massacre of Nationalist Polish officers, whose bodies had been discovered in the forest of Katyn, might have been organized by the Russians (although the Russians blamed the Germans). The arrest and imprisonment by the Russians of the representatives of the London government who had come to Poland for talks, increased the tension. The general election of 1947 returned the Communist-dominated government, despite complaints—both by the United States and Great Britain—that there had been widespread intimidation and arrests of opponents of the government. It was one of the ironies of World War II that the Western Allies, who had declared war on Germany in order to protect

Poland, had to stand by at the end of the war while the Russians took over the country.

The story of Russia's growing domination was similar in most East European states. In Hungary a coalition government, in which the non-Communist Smallholders' Party was the dominant member, had been elected in 1945. This government faced serious economic difficulties—not helped by the continued presence of a large Russian army of occupation, nor by the United States' refusal to return Hungary's gold reserves. In 1947, members of the Smallholders' Party found themselves under increasing Communist attack. The Prime Minister, Ferenc Nagy, was persuaded to resign. In elections held in 1947 the ruling coalition was reelected, but the Communists were now by far the largest party and Hungary rapidly came under Soviet sway.

Stalin's brusque and sometimes brutal program of "consolidation" in Eastern Europe met its first significant resistance in Czechoslovakia, where President Eduard Beneš' Social Democrat Party categorically refused to merge with the Communists. In July, 1947, the Beneš government momentarily accepted and then, under intense pressure from Moscow, rejected an offer of Western aid. The Czech move so disconcerted the Russians that they engineered a coup d'état the following February. A Communist-dominated government replaced the Beneš government and a sweeping purge eliminated all

King Michael of Rumania at the wheel of a jeep, gift of Uncle Sam, in 1944.

Hungarian Communist Party poster advocating nationalization of the mines.

liberal opposition to the new regime. Among those who died was the Foreign Minister, Jan Masaryk, who accidentally fell out of a window in his ministry— according to the Russians. In the Balkans, Stalin's aims met with less success than in Eastern Europe generally. Bulgaria, which was at first governed by a Communist-dominated coalition, soon came under Russian control after a series of political trials of opposition leaders. At first it seemed likely that Rumania would avoid being drawn into the Russian web, owing to King Michael's timely capitulation to the victorious Allies toward the end of the war. The postwar settlement was favorable to Rumania, although the Russians insisted—as they did throughout Eastern Europe—on the payment of substantial reparation. The King failed, however, to veto the appointment of a Communist-dominated cabinet, which in 1946 forced him to

abdicate, and in 1948 the Communist Party absorbed the larger Socialist Party and took over the government.

In other Balkan countries the Russians found it much harder to impose their will. In Greece, civil war dragged on until 1949 before the Communists admitted defeat.

In Yugoslavia, where local Communists—rather than Soviet troops—had been instrumental in expelling the Nazis, "consolidation" proved impossible. The leader of the Yugoslav partisans, Marshal Tito, indicated a willingness to cooperate closely with Stalin but he refused to permit his country to become a Soviet pawn.

In the immediate postwar period, Albania was much influenced by Tito and therefore avoided Russian influence. In 1948, however, angered by Yugoslav attempts to control Albania's policy, Enver Hoxha, the Communist Party leader, turned to

Stalin for assistance and this contributed to the quarrel between Russia and Yugoslavia that burst out that year.

Stalin's attempts to increase Russia's sphere of influence were not confined to Europe. Ever conscious of being the successor to the imperialist tsars, he sought to emulate them by taking an interest in the government of Persia (Iran), where Allied troops, including Russians, were stationed. The Russian-influenced Tudeh Party demanded autonomy for the province of Azerbaijan and organized a revolt there. Russian troops eventually prevented the government from suppressing the Azerbaijan rebellion. It was only after the government agreed to the establishment of a joint Soviet and Persian oil company that the Russians withdrew their troops, thus bringing the Azerbaijan rebellion to an end. The Russians did not, however, benefit from their support of the rebels as the *Majlis* (Parliament) refused to ratify the oil company agreement.

Although Russia's gains in Eastern Europe were largely caused by military success in World War II and by economic and political blackmail, there was a real regard for the Soviet Union in many of the satellite states. There was also a general leftward political swing throughout Europe in the immediate postwar years, as there had been after World War I; all of which helped Stalin achieve his ambitions.

The Truman Doctrine

Seeing the situation, not wholly correctly, in purely military terms, the U.S. State Department inaugurated a policy of "containment" on a worldwide scale in order to counter Stalin's westward thrust. That program, first articulated by the noted Kremlinologist George F. Kennan in the winter of 1946, became official U.S. policy on March 12, 1947. On that date, President Truman called upon Congress to appropriate several hundred million dollars to be used to combat Communist incursions in Greece and Turkey.

The American President's request, which was triggered by news of civil warfare between antimonarchist forces and government troops in Greece, served as a basis for a statement of American global aims. The policy, which became known as the Truman Doctrine, asserted that the United States was committed to helping free peoples "maintain their institutions and their national integrity against aggressive movements that seek to impose on them totalitarian regimes."

In practice, the Truman Doctrine took the form of massive economic aid and joint military alliances. The first aspect of the Doctrine, which was officially known as the European Recovery Program and popularly as the Marshall Plan, was born some two months after Truman's 1947 speech.

Greek troops keeping a watch on a mountain pass during the civil war.

The Marshall Plan   1947

At the end of World War II, Europe's economy was shattered. Cities could no longer produce enough goods to pay for food and fuel and farmers were reducing their crops to near-subsistence levels. Governments were forced to use available capital to provide these essentials instead of investing in reconstruction. The Western powers were also troubled by Soviet attempts to set up Communist puppet governments in Greece and northern Iran, and by the threats being made against Turkey. When England revealed that she could no longer afford to help Greece and Iran, Washington was forced to act. In the face of neo-isolationist sentiment, the Truman administration proposed the Marshall Plan—a concerted broad-based effort to help European nations financially, with the nations themselves participating at all levels. The unprecedented plan not only helped rebuild Europe, it also paved the way for later cooperation, such as the European Common Market.

On June 5, 1947, Harvard University held its 296th commencement ceremony. In many ways the occasion was like those that had preceded it and those that were to follow: the Governor of Massachusetts, after being escorted as far as the Harvard Yard by a company of mounted lancers, joined the procession of graduates led by the university marshal, the president, professors and deans; the Harvard band played the traditional march as the procession entered; and the Tercentenary Theater—the outdoor auditorium in the quadrangle in front of the Widener Library—was filled with the relatives and guests of the 1947 graduating class. In one respect, however, the commencement exercises of 1947 were to be particularly memorable: the special guests who were to receive honorary degrees included—as well as General Omar Bradley, T. S. Eliot and J. Robert Oppenheimer—the Secretary of State, General George C. Marshall.

Marshall was introduced by Harvard's President James B. Conant as "an American to whom freedom owes an enduring debt of gratitude, a soldier and statesman whose ability and character brook only one comparison in the history of this nation." Freedom's debt to Marshall was to be increased before the day was out, since the speech he made, in the name of Harvard's honorary graduates of 1947, contained a pledge to international action unprecedented in the history of American foreign policy. The Secretary of State made a decidedly civilian proposal in his speech, directed to the desperate economic condition of Western Europe.

"The truth of the matter," said the Secretary of State in his brisk, soldier-like way, "is that Europe's requirements for the next three or four years of foreign food and other essential products—principally from America—are so much greater than her present ability to pay that she must have substantial additional help or face economic, social, and political deterioration of a very grave character." He went on to offer aid for a European reconstruction program on a scale quite without precedent in the peacetime history of the United States.

Marshall began his speech with a simple declaration: "I need not tell you gentlemen that the world situation is serious. That must be apparent to all intelligent people." He went on to sketch a bleak picture of the state of Western Europe, physically devastated by the war, with its economy dislocated and its will power debilitated, and with any prospect of immediate recovery removed by a particularly bad winter. The breakdown of Europe's business structure was complete, he explained, and the division of labor between cities and farms, the basis of modern society, was in danger of collapse. The industries of the cities were not producing enough goods to exchange for food with the farmer. The farmer, faced with this situation, was producing less food for sale, taking fields out of cultivation, feeding more grain to his livestock and consuming more of his food himself. This meant that cities were short of food and fuel, and that governments were being forced to use their foreign currency and credits to procure these necessities abroad, exhausting reserves that were urgently needed for reconstruction.

The remedy for this desperate situation, Marshall declared, must be for the United States to give substantial economic aid for the purpose of "breaking the vicious circle and restoring the confidence of the European people in the economic future of their own countries and of Europe as a whole." The Secretary of State asserted that "our policy is directed not against any country or doctrine but against hunger, poverty, desperation, and chaos." His offer of aid was made to Europe as a whole, including the Soviet Union. However,

General George C. Marshall, who lent his name to the Marshall Plan.

Opposite Design for Marshall Plan poster. The political aspects of American aid were little less important than the economic, and the stress on one Europe was meant as a blow to the Communist states.

the motive behind the proposal was in fact the fear of American policy-makers that a weak and demoralized Western Europe would fall under Communist influence and tilt the balance of world power against the United States.

His practical appeal was in effect directed toward the governments of Western Europe:

It is already evident that, before the United States can proceed much further in its efforts to alleviate the situation ... there must be some agreement among the countries of Europe as to the requirements of the situation and the part those countries themselves will take in order to give proper effect to whatever action might be undertaken by this government. ... The initiative, I think, must come from Europe. The role of this country should consist of friendly aid in the drafting of a European program and of later support of such a program so far as it may be practical for us to do so.

Thus the ball had clearly been passed to the Europeans, and one of their leaders, the British Foreign Secretary Ernest Bevin, was quick to seize it. Before considering the European reaction, however, the problems that Marshall's offer was designed to overcome should be examined more closely.

The year 1947 marked the final breakdown of the wartime cooperation between the United States and the Soviet Union; it saw the replacement of this cooperation by the situation that came to be called the Cold War.

Even before Nazi Germany was defeated in 1945, American and Soviet interests clearly conflicted in the Mediterranean. The civil war in Greece, which began in 1944, saw Communist and anti-Communist forces pitted against each other—a foretaste of what was to come. Even though the Greek situation appeared calmer by 1946, there was renewed tension between Stalin's Russia and the West over the control of the northern part of Iran. The Russians, who had occupied this part of the country during the war, now delayed in leaving it, and attempted to install a Communist satellite government in the province of Azerbaijan before they did so. It was only through strong diplomatic pressure from the Western powers, backed by a United Nations resolution and by the determination of the Iranian government, that the Russians were finally induced to leave. By this time, however, they had exerted their influence in a renewed outbreak of civil war in Greece, renewed their wartime demands on Turkey for greater rights in the Black Sea, and shown that they were not prepared to cooperate with the Western powers in rebuilding occupied Germany. It was against this tense background that General Marshall, President Truman's Secretary of State, went to the Moscow Conference of Foreign Ministers in March, 1947.

While Marshall, together with his British and French colleagues Bevin and Bidault, was engaged in fruitless debates with the Russians on the political and economic future of Germany—debates which ended in a deadlock as the Russians refused to give up their claims for large reparation payments from the Germans—things were on the move in Washington.

President Harry Truman, the tough-minded man from Missouri who had been elevated to the presidency by Roosevelt's death in 1945, had by now come to the conclusion that the Soviet government had to be handled more firmly. As he tartly expressed it at the end of 1946, "I'm tired of babying the Soviets," and when Russian pressure on Greece and Turkey continued in the early weeks of 1947, he and his administration prepared to respond in kind.

Washington was in fact alerted to the urgency of the problem in a peculiarly dramatic way— by a virtual ultimatum from the British government. On February 21, 1947, a member of the British embassy staff in Washington conveyed to the State Department the stark news that Britain's financial reserves were running out, and that she would be unable to continue her support for Greece and Turkey beyond March 31. As this British aid—in money and in weapons—had played a major role in helping the two countries resist Soviet pressure, the situation was critical. Washington had less than six weeks to take action.

The officials in the State Department, led by Secretary of State Marshall and Under-Secretary Dean Acheson, realized that the United States faced the choice of allowing Soviet influence to spread into the power vacuum created by the drastic decline in Britain's capacity to hold the balance, or moving American power forward to fill that vacuum.

Such a commitment of American power to Europe, less than two years after the greatest war in history, would not be easy. The Congress elected in November, 1946, while not in the strict sense isolationist, had strong views on the subject of devoting American military and financial resources to foreign countries. The Congress was controlled by the Republicans, who not only opposed Truman on party-political grounds but also, throughout January and February of 1947, had a particular objection to large government spending and high taxes. While the press and radio of the world were filled with stories of economic breakdown, of growing East-West conflict and of West European weakness, symbolized by Britain's decision to cut off aid to Greece and Turkey, the Republicans in Congress were demanding reductions in the budgets proposed by the Truman administration for the American armed forces.

Any attempt by the President to persuade Congress to increase its spending abroad would therefore require very considerable efforts of persuasion, even with the powerful arguments put forward by his talented officials and advisers— men such as Averell Harriman, the Secretary of Commerce, Will Clayton, Under-Secretary of State for Economic Affairs, and George Kennan, the first head of the State Department's newly

established Policy Planning Staff.

All the arguments advanced by Harriman, Clayton and Kennan, concerning the need for the United States to spend large sums of money in order to prevent Russian domination of the Eastern Mediterranean, would be wasted if Congress refused to vote the necessary funds. It was therefore crucial that Truman seek and find a trusted Republican ally in Senator Arthur H. Vandenberg,

Dutch houses rebuilt with American finance.

Top Europe-bound tractors on Wisconsin production line.

Opposite above Landing the first cargo of Caribbean sugar in Britain under Marshall Aid.

Opposite below House construction in Berlin.

123

PAR LE PLAN MARSHALL
COOPÉRATION INTEREUROPÉENNE
POUR UN NIVEAU DE VIE PLUS ÉLEVÉ

Marshall Aid poster
emphasizing the rebirth
of Europe.

Doctrine and his language was deliberately sharp. Speaking only nineteen days after the news that Britain would have to hand over responsibility for supporting Greece and Turkey, Truman defended the case for America's picking up the burden in forthright terms:

I am fully aware of the broad implications involved if the United States extends assistance to Greece and Turkey. . . . The United Nations is designed to make possible lasting freedom and independence for all its members. We shall not realize our objectives, however, unless we are willing to help free peoples to maintain their free institutions and their national integrity against aggressive movements that seek to impose upon them totalitarian regimes. . . . I believe that it must be the policy of the United States to support free peoples who are resisting attempted subjugation by armed minorities or by outside pressures.

After these fighting words—as Truman put it later, "I had to scare the pants off Congress"— it was possible for the necessary American commitment to Greece and Turkey to be made. Truman had indicated very clearly that military support was an essential contribution to holding the balance against further Soviet pressure, and the lines of the Cold War were beginning to be clearly drawn across Europe.

Not only Greece and Turkey needed America's help. On May 8, 1947, Under-Secretary of State Dean Acheson made a speech to the citizens of Cleveland, Mississippi, in which he spelled out the need for a vast program of American economic aid for Western Europe as a whole. By now American public opinion, including congressional opinion, was increasingly aware of the perils that such a program was designed to counteract, and the way was prepared for the full-scale presentation of the new foreign policy by Secretary of State Marshall at Harvard.

The personal background of Marshall's speech at Harvard was curious. He had not originally planned to accept an honorary degree from Harvard at all. He had been offered one when he was the Army Chief of Staff during the war, but felt that it was bad for the morale of combat troops to read of their generals receiving honorary degrees in the safety of the home front. However, since his colleagues on the Joint Chiefs of Staff had accepted Harvard degrees during his absence abroad, he had merely postponed taking the degree, rather than refusing it outright. Now, at the end of May, 1947, when he needed a platform for his restatement of American foreign policy, he sent a telegram to Harvard to say that he would like to come and accept his wartime degree at the commencement ceremony scheduled for June 5, and to make a short speech.

Thus it was that Marshall came to launch the plan that will always be associated with his name; but launching it alone was not enough. As we have seen, Marshall made it clear that the detailed proposals for the economic rebuilding of Europe would have to come from the Europeans them-

the senior senator from Michigan. Vandenberg, who had been an arch-isolationist in the 1930s, had been converted by the Japanese attack on Pearl Harbor in December, 1941. As he later wrote, Pearl Harbor "ended isolationism for any realist," and the internationalist policies of Roosevelt and Truman won his active support. Without Vandenberg's valiant encouragement and hard work in the Senate, the Truman administration would not have been able to carry through the revolution in American foreign policy of the year 1947.

Even with Vandenberg's support, Truman's words to Congress had to be tough. His speech on March 12, 1947, to a joint session of Congress contained what came to be called the Truman

First shipment of American dried eggs to England under the Marshall Plan. Agriculture as well as industry suffered as a result of World War II.

The Way Back, an American newspaper cartoon draws attention to the Russian threat lurking in the background as Europe struggles to better itself with assistance under the Marshall Plan.

selves. Fortunately, Dean Acheson, Marshall's deputy at the State Department, had insured that the text of the speech would be transmitted immediately to Ernest Bevin, the British Foreign Secretary, who, as he later said, "grabbed the lifeline with both hands."

Thanks to Bevin and his French colleague Georges Bidault, the Marshall Plan quickly became reality. A series of European conferences set up the structure of the European Recovery Program and the Organization for European Economic Cooperation, through which Marshall Aid was distributed.

The aid program laid the foundations of Europe's economic growth in the 1950s and 1960s, and gave Europeans the habits of working together that were to culminate in the institutions of the European Common Market. The critical weeks and months during early 1947, from the Truman Doctrine to the Marshall Plan, profoundly influenced the shape of the postwar international system, in which Western Europe and the United States have tried to work together for their common good. Looking back more than twenty years later on the events in which he had played an important part, Dean Acheson justly said that, thinking of the postwar world as a whole, he could claim to have been "present at the Creation." ROGER MORGAN

The Cold War is fought over Germany—

The decline of sterling

The Marshall Plan was merely one of a number of important economic measures that were necessary to prevent economic disaster in Europe. The foundation of the World Bank and the International Monetary Fund in 1945 were other aspects of the attempt that was made to create a new international monetary order. These measures assumed a fundamental change in the relationship between the United States and the United Kingdom; no longer was sterling the world's major reserve currency; it had been replaced by the U.S. dollar. Despite the goodwill that went into such measures, however, they met with only partial success. The British economy, which had been Europe's strongest, was very weak throughout the late 1940s, despite huge American loans. In order to improve their terms of trade the British government was forced to devalue the pound sterling in 1949, which led to further distrust of sterling internationally.

The beginnings of the Cold War

In practice, the Marshall Plan did very much more than merely provide money for Europe. It helped to break down European tariff barriers and to create a market for American exports. Soon it also came to play an important part in the growing division of Europe into pro-American and pro-Russian regions. The meeting of Russian and American troops on the banks of the Elbe River in 1945 represented a real change in Europe. The change was disguised in the immediate postwar period by more pressing problems, but some farsighted statesmen and thinkers had been disturbed by it from the first. In 1946, for example, Winston Churchill had spoken at Fulton, Missouri, of an "Iron Curtain" in Europe and by 1948 that curtain could no longer be ignored.

To the Russians inevitably it seemed that Marshall Aid was part of a nonmilitary war in Europe and that the Americans were seeking to use the power of the dollar for their own benefit. The first real sign of Communist

Winston Churchill and President Truman leaving Washington for Fulton, Missouri, where Churchill will make his "Iron Curtain" speech.

domination in Czechoslovakia was the government's refusal to accept American aid under the Marshall Plan. The Russians felt that any West European initiative that would allow the Americans to organize European economic recovery was a challenge to European sovereignty.

The Cold War, as it soon came to be called, was largely fought over Germany, because Germany's status had never been formalized after the end of World War II. In 1947 Allied disagreements over German reparations made it increasingly difficult for the Allied Control Commission to operate effectively, and in March, 1948, the Russians walked out of the Commission and cooperation effectively ended. Four months later, the Russian blockade at Berlin forced the Western Allies to begin a massive airlift. The blockade made it clear both to the Western Allies and to the Russians that the postwar era of cooperation had come to an end and in 1949 Germany's division was institutionalized with the formation of two separate states, the German Democratic Republic in the Eastern (Russian) zone

and the German Federal Republic in the Western zone.

NATO

As Cold War attitudes intensified, both West and East founded alliances and institutions to propagate their views and to buttress their positions. In Western Europe, for example, the offer of

aid under the Marshall Plan led to the setting up of an Organization for European Economic Cooperation in 1948, to be followed by many other international organizations.

In March, 1948, Britain, France, Holland, Belgium and Luxembourg signed the Brussels Treaty, which provided for joint military and economic cooperation in the event of an armed attack on Western Europe during the next half century. It went further, in proposing economic and social cooperation, but the emphasis was military. A provision of this treaty created a permanent military committee, which was staffed by representatives of the signatory powers. A year later, the North Atlantic Treaty emerged from this provision. It was signed in Washington, D.C. on April 4, 1949, and led to the now familiar Western defense organization, NATO. In ratifying the treaty, the United States committed itself to its first peacetime alliance and, rather more fundamentally, to defending the territorial integrity of the non-Communist world.

The Soviet Union was eventually to respond to the formation of American-dominated NATO by setting up its own military treaty, the Warsaw Pact, but during the 1940s its efforts were largely concerned with propaganda and economic links with its European satellites. The COMINFORM (Communist Information Bureau), established in 1947, provided a useful mechanism for the spread of information. But Stalin was increasingly angered by the atti-

First meeting of the North Atlantic Military Production and Supply Board in 1949.

Marshal Tito, the Communist President of Yugoslavia. He pursued an independent policy and refused to allow his country to become a Russian pawn.

...tude of President Tito of Yugoslavia. Relations between the two Communist leaders had become increasingly tense during 1947, and in the summer of 1948 Yugoslavia was thrown out of the COMINFORM. Ironically this was to prove economically beneficial to Yugoslavia as the West immediately stepped in with offers of aid.

Still more important than COMINFORM was COMECON (Council for Mutual Economic Assistance), which was designed to make possible the pooling of natural resources and manufactured goods between Russia and her satellites. Yet there was a certain irony in the fact that while both East and West were setting up mutually opposed trade organizations, trade between the Eastern and Western blocs continued to increase rapidly.

Political change

The increasing hostility between East and West led to a change in West European political attitudes. In the immediate postwar period, Socialist parties had enjoyed widespread electoral successes in many European states, and in both France and Italy the Communists had emerged as leading parties. Toward the end of the 1940s, however, electoral trends began to favor more conservative parties and in the 1950s most European countries—notably Britain, West Germany, France and Italy—were governed by conservative or centrist administrations while Socialists languished in opposition. This move away from socialism was, perhaps, inevitable in a period of confrontation—and was paralleled in the United States—but there is no reason to suppose that it was not encouraged by Stalin, who saw in the policies of Western Socialist parties a challenge far more dangerous to his style of government than that posed by a military build-up. Russia was not alone in purging dissidents. Both in Europe and the U.S.A. those who opposed their governments found that life was made very difficult, and the 1950s were to see the emergence of witch hunts for Communists in the United States.

Asia

World War II had concentrated the eyes of the world on Europe, despite the importance of the fighting that took place in Asia. The changes that the war brought were to be felt as much in Asia and Africa as they were in Europe. The collapse of Japanese power, the weakening hold of the Western democracies, the resurgence of Russian interests, and the extension of the role of the United States all made the situation in Asia very fluid. In addition, there was a new force, nationalism, at work.

In the Middle East—formerly part of the Ottoman Empire, which had collapsed at the end of World War I—the British and the French had been given League of Nations mandates to govern. Among the Arabs of Syria, Lebanon, Palestine and Transjordan there was widespread anger at the continued existence of the mandate powers. In the Lebanon and Syria foreign troops were withdrawn in 1946. The following year saw the last British troops leave Iraq, but in Palestine and Transjordan political conditions necessitated the continued presence of the British. This was mainly because of a problem that only arose in an acute form after World War II. Although nearly half a million Jews had migrated to Palestine before 1945, it was only after the holocaust of World War II had ended that immigration dramatically increased and the world, shocked by revelations of what had been done to the Jews by Nazi Germany, supported

Assembly building, New Delhi, where newly independent India's delegates met to deliberate upon her future.

the tide of immigration. Because of Arab protests the British attempted to hold back the tide of immigration—unsuccessfully. Conflict between the Jewish and Arab communities was intensified, particularly after the British made clear that they were no longer willing to continue upholding their responsibilities.

But it was, almost inevitably, in India—with an imperial tradition of its own long before the British Queen Victoria had added "Empress of India" to her many other titles in the nineteenth century—that the force of nationalism made itself felt most quickly. During the interwar period, largely as a result of the leadership of Mohandas K. Gandhi, the Indian National Congress had become the leading Hindu nationalist organization, and the British had begun to recognize that there was a case for independence.

After the war, friction between the British, the Congress and the Moslem League, which sought the establishment of a separate Islamic state, increased. The British saw that it would be impossible to prevent India from being given independence except at enormous cost and with enormous bloodshed. With United Nations assistance a partition plan was agreed, although neither the Moslem leader, Mohammed Ali Jinnah, nor the Hindu leader, Jawaharlal Nehru, had much confidence in it, and British India became the independent states of India and Pakistan in 1947. Without Gandhi's emphasis on nonviolence it is difficult to believe that the British would have left so easily, yet six months after India and Pakistan became independent, the apostle of nonviolence died at the hands of an assassin.

Murder of the Mahatma 1948

On January 30, 1948, a fanatic Hindu nationalist fired three shots at pointblank range into the frail body of Mohandas Karamchand Gandhi, the father of Indian independence. A day later some 2 million Indians gathered outside New Delhi to witness the ritual cremation of the man who had won the sovereignty of the subcontinent of India through nonviolent means. The terrible irony of Gandhi's violent death was not lost on his disciples and admirers around the world. The British Attorney General called the Mahatma "the most remarkable man of the century," and George Marshall, the U.S. Secretary of State, eulogized: "Gandhi was the spokesman for the conscience of all mankind." In thirty-four years of public life, Mahatma Gandhi had never held public office—and yet by the sheer force of his personal example he had liberated colonial India, quelled civil strife, and given the world a hopeful alternative to violence.

Jawaharlal Nehru, who had become India's Prime Minister on August 15, 1947, when India won its independence, did not see eye to eye on many issues with Vallabhbhai Patel, Deputy Prime Minister. Their dispute, like many others, had been dropped into the lap of Mohandas Karamchand Gandhi, the "super prime minister." On the afternoon of January 30, 1948, Patel conferred intensely with Gandhi at Birla House in New Delhi. Finally Gandhi tore himself away. He was scrupulously punctual, and the interview had made him late for his daily five o'clock prayer meeting. He walked with big strides toward the grounds of Birla House, where some five hundred persons had been waiting. As he approached, most of the worshipers rose. Some edged forward. Those nearest bent to kiss his feet. Gandhi pressed his palms together in the traditional Hindu greeting.

At that moment a young man stepped into Gandhi's path and fired three shots from a small automatic pistol. After the second bullet hit him, blood began to stain the Mahatma's white shoulder-wrap and shawl. He murmured, "*Hey, Rama*" ("Oh, God"). As the third shot struck, Gandhi collapsed on the ground dead.

The body was brought back into the house and washed and anointed according to Hindu rites. Suggestions were heard that the Mahatma be embalmed. His son Devadas and his closest disciples objected. They wanted no worship. It was decided to cremate Gandhi the next day.

A million people lined the route from Birla House to the banks of the sacred Jumna River, where a funeral pyre had been prepared. Another million assembled around the pyre. The Pope, the Dalai Lama, the Archbishop of Canterbury, the Chief Rabbi of England, the King of England, President Harry S Truman, the President of France and the governments of all major and minor countries telegraphed condolences. The United Nations lowered its flag to half-mast.

Gandhi's life was remarkable in that he had been an indifferent pupil, a mediocre law student in London, and a failure as an attorney in Bombay. He was made great by struggle. Made aware of the indignities suffered by Indians in South Africa, he launched a twenty-one-year campaign against inequality and prejudice. His weapons were truth, reason and peaceful determination. Together these merged into an arsenal of combat that he called "civil disobedience."

Gandhi was not, at the inception of his public career, a complete pacifist or an anti-imperialist. He enlisted in the British forces in South Africa to succor the wounded on Boer War battlefields, and he recruited Indians for the British army in World War I. But after his return to India in 1915 he gradually became the foremost fomenter of Indian nationalism.

As India neared independence, Gandhi's life became a tragedy. The Government of India Act of 1935 gave the eleven provinces of British India a degree of self-government subject to the veto of the British governors, extended the franchise to approximately 30 million persons and introduced separate electorates for religious communities. The act thus created a large battlefield where Hindus and Moslems could compete for political power. This opportunity tempted Mohammed Ali Jinnah, who had established a lucrative law practice in England and who had earlier cooperated with the Indian Congress Party of Gandhi, Nehru, Patel and Maulana Abul Kalam Azad, to return to India. In the 1937 elections, the first held under the act, the Indian Congress Party won overwhelmingly—even in the totally Moslem Northwest Frontier Province. The Congress Party used these victories to enhance its power at the expense of Jinnah's Moslem League. Relations between the two large religious communities were further exacerbated by social developments. In 1940 Pakistan—a separate Moslem state in the Indian subcontinent—became accepted

Jawaharlal Nehru, first Prime Minister of independent India.

Opposite Mohandas Gandhi, the Mahatma, "Spokesman for the conscience of all mankind."

Moslem League doctrine. Henceforth, riots between Hindus and Moslems grew in number and ferocity.

Mahatma Gandhi was a doer. His keen political sense told him that World War II was the appropriate time for Britain to liberate India. He therefore planned a "Quit India" civil disobedience movement. Challenged by those who felt that Britain could not leave the country just when the Japanese were knocking at India's eastern door and Field Marshal Rommel was moving on Suez, Gandhi, to the astonishment of some of his closest disciples, said the British armed services could stay and also run the railways and manage the ports. Either by clear thinking or by intuition, he felt that, given the rising tide of violence and Hindu-Moslem tension, it would be best to grant India self-government while British forces remained in the land to guarantee order. And indeed it would seem, in the light of what happened during the three years after the war, that independence during wartime could have prevented the partition of India and saved the lives of hundreds of thousands of persons. In June, 1942, Gandhi launched his "Quit India" movement; it quickly turned to violence and also turned into a fiasco. Gandhi and hundreds of Congress Party leaders were imprisoned.

After his release in 1944, Gandhi knew that only the constitutional, legal way to independence lay open to him; for with violence filling the Indian air, he could no longer resort to the method by which he had achieved most of his victories and acquired most of his influence.

Gandhi accordingly welcomed the announcement by Labour Prime Minister Clement R. Attlee in the House of Commons on February 20, 1947, that Britain would quit India "by a date not later than June, 1948." The fear that England, in her enfeebled postwar state, might face a rebellious India that had wrenched itself loose from Gandhi's control gave wings to the Labour government's desire to implement its ideological commitment to Indian independence. In pursuance of Attlee's statement, an impressive British cabinet mission arrived in New Delhi on March 24, 1946, to negotiate with all parties and outstanding personalities in India. On May 16 the mission published its plan for the independence of India.

The mission stated that it had examined "closely and impartially the possibility of a partition of India" and found that in the proposed West Pakistan 37.93 percent of the population would be non-Moslem (Hindus and Sikhs), and in the proposed East Pakistan the percentage of non-Moslems would be as high as 48.31, while 20 million Moslems would remain outside Pakistan in the Indian Union. "These figures show," the mission declared, "that the setting up of a separate state of Pakistan on the lines claimed by the Moslem League would not solve the communal minority problem." Therefore the mission was "unable to advise the British government that the power which at present resides in British hands should be handed over to two entirely separate sovereign states."

Instead, the mission plan provided for a federal system of government well suited to India's provincial fissures. The central authorities in New Delhi would deal with defense, foreign relations and communications, and presumably with currency and finance. India would be divided into three subfederations, one in the west, largely Moslem, a second in the east with a bare Moslem majority, and the core in the center, overwhelmingly Hindu.

Firmly denied Pakistan by the mission plan, the Moslem League, under Jinnah's presidency, unanimously accepted the three-subfederation scheme as the next best. The Congress Party hesitated. The socialists, then still members of the Congress Party, disliked the religious basis of the plan. Others were apprehensive that Hindu and Sikh regions might become encased in the western and eastern Moslem federations. Nehru suspected that the British again proposed to divide in order to rule. But Gandhi trusted the British government. The All-India Congress Committee approved the mission plan on July 7 by a vote of 200 to 51.

"Now happened one of those unfortunate events which changed the course of history," wrote Maulana Abul Kalam Azad, himself a Moslem, in *India Wins Freedom*:

CHINA

KASHMIR
Disputed between
India and
Pakistan

AFGHANISTAN

TIBET Occupied by China 1950

PUNJAB

WEST PAKISTAN

New Delhi

NEPAL

INDIA

EAST PAKISTAN

Karachi

Calcutta

BURMA
Independent
1948

Refused union with India:
occupied by India 1947
and annexed 1948

Bombay

HYDERABAD

GOA Portuguese:
occupied by India
1961

○ Predominantly Moslem
before partition

● Predominantly Hindu
before partition

○ Predominantly Buddhist
before partition

✳ Areas of intense
Hindu-Moslem fighting

⌒ Frontier of
British India

CEYLON
Independent
1948

**The Partition of India
1947**

On July 10, Jawaharlal [Nehru] held a press conference in Bombay in which he made a statement that Congress would enter the Constituent Assembly "completely unfettered by agreements and free to meet all situations as they arise. . . . Congress had agreed only to participate in the Constituent Assembly and regarded itself free to … modify the Cabinet Mission Plan as it thought best."

The consequences of Nehru's intervention are history. Because Nehru, the Congress Party President, had rejected the mission plan, Jinnah jumped to the fresh opportunity, rescinded the Moslem League's approval of the cabinet scheme and again proposed Pakistan on July 27. He then proclaimed August 16 Direct Action Day. Calcutta, India's most populous city, became the first victim. Moslems killed Hindus, Hindus retaliated, rioting continued for four days and nights and at least 5,000 persons were killed and 15,000 wounded.

Gandhi went to Calcutta to bid the waves of hate to recede. "I am not going to leave Bengal," he pledged, "until the last embers of trouble are stamped out. I may stay on here for a whole year or more. If necessary I will die here." From Calcutta he traveled to Noakhali in the water-logged delta of the Ganges and Brahmaputra rivers. Jinnah's Direct Action Day had rent the district with civil strife. Many villages were in ashes.

He remained in Noakhali from November 7, 1946, to March 2, 1947. During that period he lived in forty-nine villages. By the time the seventy-seven-year-old leader left Noakhali, he was satisfied with the signs of intercommunity peace.

The Mahatma would have remained in Bengal but for reports reaching him from Bihar, the province that borders Bengal, of Hindu retaliatory violence against Moslems. He moved on to Bihar, where he again proved to have a magic touch.

Admiral Lord Louis Mountbatten arrived in New Delhi on March 22, 1947, to become the twentieth and last British Viceroy of India. The next day Jinnah stated that unless Moslems received Pakistan, India faced "terrific disasters." He had it in his power to unloose them. Mountbatten summoned Gandhi from Bihar. The Mahatma and the Viceroy conferred for two and a quarter hours on March 31. Five additional talks followed in the next twelve days. Jinnah was received in audience an equal number of times.

His talks with Mountbatten concluded, Gandhi returned to Bihar. Unless he could prove that the two religious communities were living in amity, Jinnah was right and Pakistan inevitable. Gandhi foresaw that partition would not solve the problems of the Indian subcontinent or reduce the level of violence. Segregation, he knew from experience, intensified hostility. Hence his total commitment to building a Hindu-Moslem bridge rather than widening the chasm.

General Lord Wavell, the preceding Viceroy, had chosen a provisional, all-Indian government with Nehru as Prime Minister and with Moslem League participation. In view of the widespread disorders, the Congress Party blundered into giving

Above Gandhi's memorial at Cape Comorin in southern India; and (*below*) the centerpiece of the Gandhi memorial, which contains the Mahatma's ashes.

Gandhi as a young barrister in Johannesburg. The plight of South Africa's colored community sparked Gandhi's interest in social reform.

Right Mohammed Ali Jinnah with Lord Mountbatten. Jinnah led the campaign for a separate Moslem state of Pakistan, and he became Pakistan's first Governor-General.
Gandhi with the last Viceroy of India, Earl Mountbatten of Burma, and Lady Mountbatten, two months before independence.

Patel the Home Ministry to cope with and letting the finance portfolio go to Liaqat Ali Khan, Jinnah's first lieutenant. By every stratagem possible the Moslem Leaguers in the provisional cabinet made it their business to prove that the Congress Party and the Moslem League, in harness together, pulled in opposite directions and could not run India.

The person most responsible for the partition of India was Jinnah. Lord Mountbatten, addressing the Royal Empire Society in London on October 6, 1948 (after his withdrawal from office in New Delhi), told how it happened. "Mr. Jinnah made it abundantly clear from the first moment that so long as he lived he would never accept a United India. He demanded partition; he insisted on Pakistan." The Congress leaders, on the contrary, favored an undivided India, but they agreed they would accept partition to prevent civil war. Mountbatten was "convinced that the Moslem League would have fought." The question before them, Mountbatten declared, was how to partition. The Congress Party refused to let non-Moslem areas go to Pakistan. "That automatically meant a partition of the great provinces of the Punjab and Bengal," Mountbatten said. The Punjab was almost half Hindu and Sikh; Bengal almost half Hindu. Mountbatten continued:

When I told Mr. Jinnah that I had their provisional agreement [the agreement of Congress] to partition he was overjoyed. When I said that it logically followed that this would involve partition of the Punjab and Bengal he was horrified. He produced the strongest arguments why national characteristics and that partition would be disastrous. I agreed, but I said how much more must I now feel that the same considerations applied to the partitioning of the whole of India. He did not like that, and started explaining why India had to be partitioned, and so we went round and round the mulberry bush until finally he realized that either he could have a United India with an unpartitioned Punjab and Bengal or a divided India with a partitioned Punjab and Bengal, and he finally accepted the latter situation.

Jinnah was unable to crack Mountbatten's logic, but Gandhi had an answer. He, the champion of Indian independence, favored delayed independence. The British, he knew, could not surrender power to the Moslem minority. Therefore if they wanted to leave—and they so obviously did—they would have to hand over power to the Congress Party to rule an undivided India. Nehru and Krishna Menon did not share this faith. On the principle that half an India is better than none, they felt they must seize what the British offered.

So it happened that on August 15, 1947, India became free and divided: Pakistan, two lobes a thousand miles apart, hung like elephant's ears from the body of India. The day that should have marked his crowning achievement was to Gandhi a day of mourning.

The trisection of India had provoked an immediate catastrophe: a great migration commenced. Fifteen million people, crazed by fear and horrified by mass atrocities, rushed from their ancestral homes —Moslems out of India into Pakistan, Hindus and Sikhs out of Pakistan into India. The fertile Punjab, rent in two by partition, poured forth a column of half-starved humanity fifty-seven miles long, crawling in the direction of Delhi to escape death. Vultures hovered overhead, waiting for the many who would collapse by the wayside. The Nehru government set up camps to catch the Punjabis before they reached the capital, but endless thousands eluded the thin cordons. In Delhi they slept on pavements, in doorways, in deserted homes. Anything belonging to a departed or lingering Moslem was fair loot.

Gandhi plunged into the eye of this tornado of madness determined to still the storm with counsels of love and peace. Slowly, in part through exhaustion, in part as a result of Gandhi's untiring talking, Delhi seemed to become an oasis of peace. Yet Gandhi was not satisfied; Moslems still were afraid to walk through the capital city of free India.

On January 13, 1948, he decided to fast. On the third day of the fast Gandhi dictated a statement asking the government of India to pay Pakistan 550 million rupees (approximately $180 million), a huge sum for the nearly empty treasury of New Delhi, as Pakistan's share of the assets of prepartitioned India. The Nehru cabinet had previously refused to pay. On Gandhi's demand, it did.

The day after his fast the Mahatma was carried in a chair to the prayer meeting in the grounds of Birla House, where he had been staying. The next day he was again carried to prayers. During prayers a handmade bomb was hurled at him, but Gandhi was not injured. The young man who had thrown the bomb, Madan Lal, was a Hindu refugee from the Punjab who had found shelter in a Delhi mosque only to be evicted when, in deference to Gandhi's wishes, the police began returning mosques to Moslem worshipers. He had seen Hindus shot down in Punjab towns.

After Madan Lal's failure, Nathuram Godse came up from Bombay. He was a thirty-five-year-old editor and publisher of a Hindu Mahasabha weekly and a high-degree Brahman. He began loitering about Birla House. In the pocket of his khaki jacket he carried a small automatic pistol. Godse said at his trial that he was exasperated by India's payment of half a billion rupees to Pakistan. "I sat brooding intensely," he told the court, "on the atrocities perpetuated on Hinduism and on its dark and deadly future if left to face Islam outside and Gandhi inside." On the afternoon of January 30, he killed Mohandas K. Gandhi.

Godse and eight others found guilty of conspiracy were hanged. Gandhi, who opposed every manner of killing, would not have approved. Nonviolence had been his banner and civil disobedience his ultimate weapon. The latter helped him achieve the liberation of India, and for him the freedom of India was the prelude to the rise of free Indians, countrymen free of corruption in politics and devoted to Gandhian ideals. In this goal he failed. India remains a democracy thanks to the legacy of the British, the heritage of Gandhi and the turbulent personality of Nehru, the Westernized infidel. But although all official Indians and many unofficial Indians pay lip service to Gandhi, he is dead in India except in the hearts of the very few. "Generations to come will scarce believe," Albert Einstein once said of Gandhi, "that such a one as this ever in flesh and blood walked upon this earth."

LOUIS FISCHER

Gandhi's cremation on the bank of the Jumna River on January 31, 1948.

Gandhi's personal possessions: sandals, watch, glasses, bowls, spoons and a book of songs.

133

Israeli Independence 1948

Six months before the State of Israel officially came into being, it was already fighting for its life against attacks by Arab commandos. At the time, Palestine was still under British mandate and the Palestine Jews had no legal army. The task of defending the substantial Jewish population of the region was therefore entrusted to an irregular army known as the Haganah. Then, on November 29, 1947, the United Nations General Assembly voted 33 to 12 to partition Palestine in such a way as to create a separate Jewish state. The Arabs' reaction was immediate and violent, and during the first phase of the war that followed, the Arabs gained several substantial victories. The united Arab offensive was finally brought to a halt in the spring of 1949, and later that year Israel concluded armistice terms with her neighbors. Israel joined the family of nations—and intermittent guerrilla warfare became a fact of life in the Middle East.

At dawn on May 14, 1948, dozens of workmen were swarming over the modest building that housed the Tel Aviv Museum on the Boulevard Rothschild. They hurriedly converted the main hall of the museum, set up a platform with tables and chairs in the middle, hung two enormous flags on the wall, and placed between them a large portrait of Theodore Herzl. Rows of seats were hastily installed on the balcony to accommodate the Philharmonic Orchestra.

At four o'clock in the afternoon, the car carrying David Ben-Gurion, the President of the National Directory, stopped in front of the museum. The stocky figure with the legendary mane of white hair saluted the guard of honor and ran up the steps of the building. He entered the main hall, where the other members of the Directory, those of the National Council, more than a hundred guests, notables, journalists and photographers were waiting. Ben-Gurion rose and read out Israel's declaration of independence to a visibly moved audience:

... On November 29, 1947, the General Assembly of the United Nations adopted a resolution providing for an independent Jewish state in Palestine, and invited the inhabitants of the country to take the necessary steps to put this plan into effect.

As a result, we, the members of the National Council, representing the Jewish people in Palestine and the world Zionist movement, are united today at a solemn assembly. In the light of natural law and the history of the Jewish people, as well as in accordance with the resolution of the United Nations, we proclaim the foundation of the Jewish state in the Holy Land which will bear henceforth the name of the State of Israel.

... The State of Israel will be open for the immigration of Jews from every country in which they have been dispersed. It will develop the country for the benefit of all its inhabitants. It will be founded on the principles of liberty, justice and peace, just as they were conceived by the prophets of Israel. It will respect the complete social and political equality of all its citizens, without distinction of religion, race or sex. It will guarantee freedom of religion,

conscience, education and culture. It will protect the holy places of all religious faiths, and it will sincerely apply the principles of the Charter of the United Nations.

... We wish for peace and good neighborliness, and we offer our hand to all those states which surround us. We invite them to cooperate with the independent Jewish nation for the common benefit of all.

At the end of the reading, the document was signed by the thirty-seven members of the National Council, and Ben-Gurion became Prime Minister of the State of Israel. Notably absent from the ceremony was the aged and ailing Dr. Chaim Weizmann, the future President of the State of Israel. At the time of the signing, Weizmann was visiting the United States, where he was directing all his efforts toward persuading President Truman to give the new state official recognition.

The efforts of this celebrated scholar and Zionist leader were not in vain. At two o'clock in the morning of May 15, Ben-Gurion was suddenly awakened by his aide-de-camp, who brought him a telegram. The United States had just recognized Israel. Some hours later a second telegram brought the news that Israel had also been recognized by the Soviet Union.

The Jewish state might well have been created ten years earlier, even before World War II. At that time there were some 450,000 Jews in Palestine, and they had the support of Great Britain, the mandatory power in Palestine. Successive British governments had been generally faithful to the Balfour Declaration of November 2, 1917, which advocated the establishment of a Jewish "national home" in the Holy Land.

The honeymoon between Zionism and His Majesty's government came to an end in February, 1939, during a conference at St. James's Palace in London. That conference, which brought together both Jewish and Arab delegates, was presided over by Neville Chamberlain. Great Britain, which was

The Israeli Declaration of Independence, signed by the thirty-seven members of the National Council in the Tel Aviv Museum on May 14, 1948.

Opposite Jewish immigrants arriving illegally at Haifa in 1947. After World War II, Jewish immigration to Palestine increased rapidly despite British attempts to limit the influx.

Jaffa during the 1948 war. The battle for the port town was complicated by the presence of the British. When the last British troops left on May 13, the Arab forces finally surrendered to the Jews.

Planting the Israeli flag at Eilat during the 1948 war. Eilat is Israel's only port on the Gulf of Aqaba and is the terminus of an oil pipeline.

preoccupied with the deteriorating international situation, decided to initiate a rapprochement with the Arab peoples of the Middle East at the expense of the Jews in Palestine. A white paper was published that announced a series of severe new measures, all disadvantageous to the Jews. They included the lowering of the immigration figures, a ban on the Jews' acquiring further territory, and the confirmation of the minority status of Jews in Palestine. From this time on, the Jewish leaders in Palestine were to engage more and more in a policy of resistance to England, whom they accused of duplicity.

More than 30,000 Palestinian Jewish men and women enlisted in the British army in the war against Hitler, but they were also actively engaged in fighting the white paper. An extraordinary congress, organized by the American Committee for Zionist Affairs, took place in the Biltmore Hotel in New York on May 12, 1942. With one abstention, the six hundred delegates voted for the proposal that Ben-Gurion had brought from Palestine, a proposal that after the war Palestine be transformed into a "Jewish Commonwealth integrated into the new structure of world affairs." Zionism had made a further step forward. Until now it had been content with a national home in Palestine. It was now demanding an independent state.

The real fight for the creation of that state began at the end of World War II. In the new state of world affairs, the Palestinian Jews had the advantage of some firm alliances: the new President of the United States, Harry S Truman, was a confirmed friend of the Zionist cause; the Soviet Union was coming to the conclusion that by assisting in the creation of a Jewish state in Palestine it would be able to supplant British influence in this area of the world; and world opinion had turned a favorable eye upon the national aspirations of the Jews after the terrible slaughter that had cost 6 million of them their lives.

The Arabs vigorously resisted the establishment of a Jewish state in Palestine. Here Arab rioters are burning goods in Jaffa harbor.

On the other hand, the attitude of the new Labour government in Great Britain hardened, and it refused to budge. Had England shown a little flexibility, history might well have been different, but in the face of British intransigence the Jews were forced toward more and more extreme behavior.

On February 14, 1947, Great Britain referred the matter to the United Nations. The international organization sent a commission of inquiry to Palestine that was composed of representatives from Canada, Uruguay, Guatemala, Peru, India, Iran, Holland, Sweden, Yugoslavia, Czechoslovakia and Australia. And in September the commission published its recommendations. By eight votes to three, it proposed the partition of Palestine into a Jewish state and an Arab state. On November 29, by thirty-three votes to twelve, the General Assembly of the United Nations adopted the plan of partition.

The territory allotted to the Jews by the United Nations comprised three narrow strips of land: part of Galilee, a narrow strip extending along the coast, and the Negev Desert (which stretched south to the Gulf of Aqaba). These three separate territories were linked together by tiny points of contact called "kissing points." Similar points united the remaining parts of Palestine, which had been allocated to the Arabs. Jerusalem was to become an international city.

The Arabs refused to accept the plan, and on the day following the voting they went into action. Apparently unconcerned about the presence of 100,000 British soldiers in Palestine, Arab commandos killed seven Jewish travelers on the roads. And thus the war of independence in Israel broke out, six months before the Jewish state came into being.

In 1949 the war came to an end, and the State of Israel had to be accepted as a fact. Through the mediation of Dr. Ralph Bunche, Israel concluded armistice terms with her neighbors. There were those in Israel who were sufficiently naïve to believe that the armistice was the prelude to a final peace between the Jewish state and her Arab neighbors, but they were soon disillusioned. The Arabs, smarting under their defeat, refused to conclude peace with Israel.

There were two principal stumbling blocks to improvement in the atmosphere between Israel and her neighbors: the question of the frontiers and the tragic question of the refugees. Hundreds of thousands of Arab refugees who had left their homes during the fighting were anxious to return. Israel refused to consider their return unless in the context of a negotiated peace settlement. However a family reunion scheme was implemented and $11 million in refugees' blocked accounts were transferred by Israel to the banks of countries technically at war with her. But the fate of the mass of the Palestinian refugees was by now firmly linked to the political conflict.

The Arab states also refused to integrate the refugees into their populations and their economies. They preferred to keep them clustered in wretched camps along the frontiers of the Jewish state and to use them as a political weapon. Out of these wretched conditions there developed a Palestinian national consciousness that would find expression in desperate acts of terror.

As time passed, the situation along the demarcation lines of the armistice agreement became more and more precarious, and military incidents between Israelis and Arabs established themselves as a normal occurrence in Middle East affairs. In spite of the insecurity that prevailed along the frontiers, and in spite of her difficult economic situation, Israel embarked upon a historic enterprise—the ingathering of the exiles. The young state opened its doors wide to immigration. In accordance with the Law of Return voted by the Israeli parliament, every Jew in the world had the right to be an immigrant.

Haj Amin el-Husseini, former Mufti of Jerusalem and Palestinian Arab leader. Focal point of Arab discontent during the Mandate, he played a leading part in the campaign of violence following the U.N. partition decision of 1947.

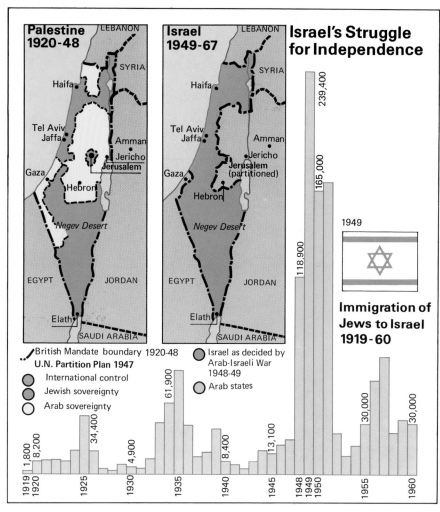

Israel's Struggle for Independence

Palestine 1920-48

LEBANON
SYRIA
Haifa
Tel Aviv
Jaffa
Amman
Jericho
Jerusalem
Gaza
Hebron
Negev Desert
EGYPT
JORDAN
Elath
SAUDI ARABIA

Israel 1949-67

LEBANON
SYRIA
Haifa
Tel Aviv
Jaffa
Amman
Jericho
Jerusalem (partitioned)
Gaza
Hebron
Negev Desert
EGYPT
JORDAN
Elath
SAUDI ARABIA

British Mandate boundary 1920-48
U.N. Partition Plan 1947
○ International control
○ Jewish sovereignty
○ Arab sovereignty

● Israel as decided by Arab-Israeli War 1948-49
○ Arab states

Immigration of Jews to Israel 1919-60

1949

1919 1,800
1920 8,200
1925 34,400
1930 4,900
1935 61,900
1940 8,400
1945 13,100
118,900
1948 239,400
1949 165,000
1950
1955 30,000
1960 30,000

Top right David Ben Gurion, Israel's first Prime Minister.

Bottom right The walled city of Jerusalem viewed from the Rockefeller Museum. During the 1948 war the Arab Legion captured the Old City and cut off western Jerusalem from the rest of the Jewish population. The siege was broken by the secret construction of a "Burma Road" —an alternative route from the coast south of Latrun.

Opposite above Ben Gurion presiding over the first Israeli cabinet meeting after the general election of 1949.

Opposite below Jews of different nationalities. Unrestricted Jewish immigration was encouraged despite the strain on the country's resources. The integration of diverse ethnic elements into a new Israeli identity was actually helped by the continuing Arab hostility.

intention was to set an example for the nation's youth and attract those youths to the pioneer work of reclaiming the desert, but his example was not followed. Ben-Gurion was replaced as President of the Council by Moshe Sharett, who also held the office of Foreign Secretary. Sharett, who was a far more moderate man than Ben-Gurion, was to be bitterly disappointed in his efforts to find a basis for agreement with the Arabs. In February, 1955,

Experts predicted that Israel's wide-open immigration policy would result in an economic catastrophe. They maintained that the State of Israel was incapable of absorbing so many people, to whom it could offer neither homes nor jobs. Their fears were in part borne out, for during the first years of the "return" the new arrivals did live in appalling conditions. Camps of tents and huts covered the countryside, an austere economic regime was put into operation, and the budget was balanced only by donations and loans from abroad. In spite of all those difficulties, Israel succeeded in integrating the returnees. Between 1948 and 1969, some 1,280,000 immigrants arrived in Israel, whose Jewish population now totals almost 2.5 million.

Israel's basic problem was that of defense. From 1948 on, military experts thought little of the chances of 1 or 2 million Jews holding their own against tens of millions of Arabs. But as the years passed, Israel not only succeeded in defending itself against its enemies but even asserted an undeniable military ascendancy. The Israeli army, which had been forged in the course of the war of independence, was organized and consolidated under the aegis of David Ben-Gurion, President of the Council and Minister of Defense from 1948 to 1953.

In 1953 Ben-Gurion resigned from office and settled in the kibbutz of Sde Boker in the Negev. His

Sharett's Minister of Defense resigned, and Ben-Gurion was asked to fill the vacant post. Following the general election of August, 1955, he once more became President of the Council.

At that time, an explosive situation was building up on the country's frontiers. Infiltrators, commandos who called themselves Volunteers for Death, and even regular units of the Egyptian army were broadcasting terror in Israel, and the situation was the same on the Jordanian and Syrian frontiers. The Arab states were acting in concert against Israel. Ben-Gurion strongly advocated a firm line, and the Israeli army, led by its commander in chief, General Moshe Dayan, reacted to every case of provocation with harsh reprisals against the neighboring states. Those provocations and reprisals soon became a vicious circle, one in which cause and effect were indistinguishable.

By creating a completely new nation, the beleaguered and, when necessary, bellicose State of Israel has brought about a profound change in the lives of millions of Jews scattered around the world. At the same time, its emergence has profoundly upset the established order and social structure of the surrounding states and has created a hotbed of unresolved tension in the Middle East.

MICHAEL BAR-ZOHAR

The Berlin Airlift 1948

Postwar Berlin was a city divided into Eastern and Western zones in the midst of Communist East Germany. All supplies to West Berlin had to go through East Germany, and in the spring of 1948—following bitter disputes over reparations and the future of Germany—the railways and roads leading to the city were subject to delays and harassments. The future—even the survival—of West Berlin was jeopardized. In June all traffic into the city was suspended, and soon after British transports flew the first vital supplies into the beleaguered city. From then until September, 1949, after the Communists had realized defeat and negotiated a reopening of the ground routes, the Allies airlifted more than two and a quarter million tons of supplies, eventually even exceeding the city's normal needs. A victory for the West, the airlift was a victory for peace—it was a major Cold War dispute that was ultimately settled by diplomatic means.

In April, 1948, when the Soviet authorities began petty restrictions against passenger traffic moving between Berlin and the West, they made the first overt move to coincide with the political offensive already under way. They were initiating, in fact, a carefully calculated program designed to create a crisis out of which Communism would emerge as the dominant force in Europe. Throughout the winter months the propaganda of vilification was intensified, its underlying theme being the need for a unified Germany and the cessation of four-power government by the major powers. Convinced, for their part, that the Soviets were determined to obstruct a settlement of the German problem, the three Western powers moved toward the notion of a purely Western German government. The two sides parted ways. On March 20, a meeting of the Allied Control Council was broken off by a walkout of the Soviet representatives.

The vast majority of traffic moved into Berlin through the Soviet sector by barge, rail and road along routes that had been carefully defined by treaty in the postwar years. There was only minor employment of air transport along three corridors that had been settled by an agreement signed by the four powers on November 30, 1945, and implemented in 1946. A sophisticated air-control system had been installed by the Western powers, however, and no major troubles experienced. Relatively little important cargo went that way. Thus when the Soviets on April 1 suddenly introduced obstructive control measures that severely curtailed the movement of land traffic into Berlin, it was apparent that the life and economy of the city might be dangerously threatened. At issue was not simply the feeding of people in Berlin but maintenance of the rise in living standards that had already taken place and making it clear to the majority of German people, who abhorred Communism, that a Western presence would remain. If

the industry of West Berlin was allowed to break down, unemployment would follow and with it the wholesale collapse of Western morale that the Soviets sought as a prerequisite to European domination.

From the outset the British garrison commander contemplated using transport aircraft to supply the members and families of his garrison, but nothing of this sort was attempted while the political game was being played and a modicum of supplies was being allowed through. On June 2 it was decided by the West to unify economically the three Western zones; on June 4 the Soviets introduced new restrictions on freight moving to Berlin and in the following week closed road bridges, ostensibly for "repairs," and began an almost total holdup of rail traffic. On June 18 the West announced unilateral currency reform for the Western zones; three days later all barge traffic was stopped, and on the following day a similar ban on rail traffic was imposed. Berlin was virtually isolated by land. The following day British aircraft delivered six and a half tons of supplies to the beleaguered city.

It was only the Americans who had the capacity to mount a really significant air-supply operation. British transport aircraft had been given low priority during the war, whereas the Americans had built a colossal fleet and had largely supported their allies' air transport effort. Most of the British air fleet consisted of twin-engined Dakota aircraft (U.S. c-47s) with a three-ton payload, supplemented by a slowly increasing number of four-engined transports, some derived from military types, others of original design. The U.S. had many c-47s available and could quickly reinforce them with four-engined c-54s, which had a ten-ton capacity. The French could offer no assistance. General Lucius Clay, the U.S. military governor, was convinced that Berlin must be sustained—a

Emblem worn by workers of the Berlin airlift: the inscription reads *Luftbrücke* (airbridge) *Berlin*. Other decorations have the British and U.S. flags suspended underneath.

Opposite Approach to Tempelhof, by Bob Lanvin. In response to the Soviet obstruction of land and water traffic into Berlin from West Germany, the Western Allies expanded the Gatow, Tempelhof and Tegel airbases in the Western sectors of the city and mounted a massive operation to supply Berlin by air.

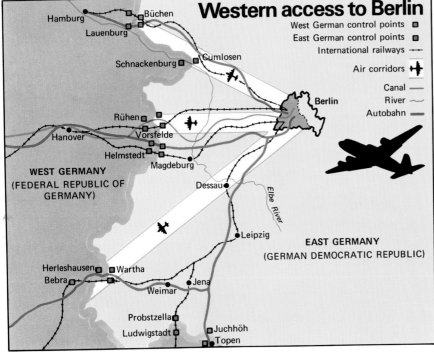

West German control points ▫
East German control points ▫
International railways ↦
Air corridors ✈
Canal ─
River ～
Autobahn ▬

Hamburg
Büchen
Lauenburg
Cumlosen
Schnackenburg
Rühen
Hanover
Vorsfelde
Helmstedt
Magdeburg
**WEST GERMANY
(FEDERAL REPUBLIC OF
GERMANY)**
Dessau
Elbe River
Berlin
Leipzig
**EAST GERMANY
(GERMAN DEMOCRATIC REPUBLIC)**
Herleshausen
Bebra
Wartha
Weimar
Jena
Probstzella
Ludwigstadt
Juchhöh
Topen

Top "Checkpoint Charlie" between the American and Russian sectors of Berlin. The divided city was to remain a potential flashpoint in the Cold War.

could bring in 1,500 tons daily by July 20—a prophecy that nobody credited at all, but which was faithfully met as the four-engined c-54s began to arrive and more RAF aircraft were allocated. The blockade by land was not absolutely complete at this moment. Gaps existed in the Soviet lines of circumvallation through which enterprising German truck drivers managed to infiltrate all manner of illicit goods, especially fresh food. The hot summer months, moreover, placed the lightest demand upon fuel consumption, although it was essential that power should be maintained in order to supply industry. Most of Berlin's electricity was generated in the Soviet sector and this was at once switched off. At the outset there were 201,000 tons of coal in the Western sectors to meet what had been a monthly consumption, in July, 1947, of 123,500 and in December, 1947, of 158,000 tons. First priority of movement was therefore given to coal. Of oil and gas supplies, including some Soviet stocks located in the Western sectors which were duly "borrowed," there were 10,500 tons to meet a monthly consumption of 2,100 tons. Food and fuel for power and heat were inevitably the vital imports required while industrial output was the essential export along with people, above all children who could best be spared the effects of a long siege.

The Allies had executed several large-scale transport projects during World War II, notably in the Far East where the Nationalist Chinese had been supplied, as had whole armies when operating in undeveloped terrain. But never before had a complete civilian economy been maintained by air. Thus, in addition to the enormous problems to be overcome by intensive air-traffic control in the face of a potentially hostile opponent, there arose unprecedented difficulties in handling an almost infinite variety of cargo, some of it volatile, much of it awkwardly shaped and nearly all of it thoroughly uneconomic in terms of normal air-transportation costing. For example, the city needed about thirty-eight tons of salt a day, but loose salt could corrode aircraft controls. Therefore the only way to bring it in at first was in British flying boats, operating from the great Berlin lakes, because in this type of aircraft the controls were carried in the roof instead of the floor. Later special panniers carried externally were employed on conventional aircraft.

Complex base areas had to be created throughout West Germany to support this ever mutliplying air fleet. Civilian contractors began to take a hand alongside the air forces who supplied the major effort. Gatow and Tempelhof airbases, in the British and American sectors of Berlin respectively, had to be extended and a comprehensive ground organization created to handle the vast increase in cargo. Careful planning was needed to reduce wastage in distribution within the city. As time went by and the number of aircraft sorties increased it became vital to develop the Tegel airbase in the French sector. The decision was made in September

view that was not nearly so strongly held on June 25 in Washington but which finally prevailed. That day it was considered feasible to make 400 flights per day to the two major Berlin airports carrying about 700 tons. Next day the airlift began in earnest.

On June 29, the Allies brought in only a little over 500 tons to meet what had been a daily requirement of 12,000 tons. That same day, however, an American staff estimate projected they

The Berlin Wall, built by Walter Ullbricht's East German government in 1961 in order to seal the border between East and West Berlin. This followed a Warsaw Pact communiqué appealing for a halt to the mass flights of refugees to the West.

Left Monument to the Berlin Airlift.

and the work completed before the end of the year. The airfield was opened on December 7, a task contributed to by the French blowing up the Soviet-owned radio mast that obstructed the glide path in the French sector.

With the success of the airlift (it handled 70,000 tons in July from 14,000 flights, 118,000 tons from 18,000 flights in August and 138,000 from 19,500 in September), a bitter Soviet reaction set in. On the one hand the Soviets endeavored to convince the citizens of Berlin that they would surely starve and that the success of the Allies was being achieved by terrorism and oppression. On the other the Allies demonstrated, by maintaining the life of the city, that they were succeeding—and always there was the roar of aircraft to prove their point.

The pressure upon everybody was immense. The political leaders in the city, Mayor Ernst Reuter and his deputy, Luise Schroeder, were subjected, along with senior Allied officers, to all kinds of Communist harassment. Though living on short rations, the people of West Berlin worked diligently as their faith in salvation grew. They felt they might survive because the Allies said so. Improvizations abounded: for example, electricity generating was raised by twenty percent. Morale rose too. The air crews, however, were under terrible strain. The first fatal crash occurred in Berlin on July 24 when a U.S. C-47 plunged into houses on the approach to Tempelhof, killing the crew but injuring only a few civilians. The two dead pilots were exalted as heroes who had merged their interests with those of the Berliners. Their sacrifice was used to spur the air crews to even

greater efforts in what was explained as a prolonged humanitarian mission.

Some of the small private British airlines, which operated on a limited budget, were compelled to fly their aircraft even when servicability was doubtful and when the crew was approaching or past the limits imposed by fatigue. It was not unusual for a crew to make three sorties a night, often carrying, for premium rates, the most dangerous cargoes, such as liquid fuel. And to the hazards of routine flying were added the depredations of Soviet military arms which, from August, began "buzzing" transport aircraft and holding air exercises in the air corridors. These included the firing, at no great distance, of live antiaircraft ammunition. The U.S. authorities alone recorded 733 separate incidents between August, 1948, and August, 1949—anything from buzzing to blinding by searchlights, radio interference and the deployment of balloons. A mere ten to fifteen percent cut in flights was all that was needed to impose failure, but nothing stopped the air convoys from flying through. Records in delivery and the turn around of aircraft became regular. Only by direct action— the actual shooting down of aircraft—could the airlift have been stopped and at that time, in the face of Allied air and nuclear superiority, such a thing went too far in Soviet eyes.

Yet with the onset of winter the plight of the population was bound to give concern. The destruction caused by the war had never been made good. Shelter was at a premium. Food rationing, power shortage, lack of lighting and the apparent oncoming hardships were all utilized for Soviet propaganda. The old, the frail and the undernourished were vulnerable to extreme cold. Inevitably there were deaths from this cause, despite the provision of warming centers in such places as theaters, where two hours were considered sufficient for a "warm-up." Health and morale were under constant review and as many of the infirm as possible were evacuated in returning aircraft whose other cargoes were largely the products from Berlin's ever functioning factories. In November rations in the Western sectors actually increased in calorific value compared with July, serving also as a propaganda response to the Soviets who had increased rations in the Eastern sector.

Yet not all the hardship was borne by the West Berliners. Strain was beginning to be felt by their opponents too. For as the Soviets found ways of tightening the blockade, they imposed a stricter counterblockade upon themselves and their East European allies. Vital rail and road links ran through the Western sector and these were denied automatically to the Soviets as a measure of counterblockade. The already creaking Eastern economy began to suffer breakdowns at a time when it was apparent that the "air bridge" was successfully spanning the gap between the city and West Germany. Toward the end of 1948, when it was apparent that Berlin would hold out, the troubles that the Soviets had hoped to impose upon the Allies recoiled upon them. Instead of discrediting the so-called decadent Western Allies in the eyes of the world, it was they who were losing and, simultaneously, being branded for

Right Berliners watch hopefully as an airplane carrying supplies approaches.

"The airlift goes on." A plane being unloaded at Gatow airport by the lights of a jeep after power, which came from the Russian zone, had been cut off.

their callous inhumanity. Strange concessions sometimes made Soviet propaganda ventures look ingenuous and exposed the weaknesses of their own position. On one occasion in October they left the checkpoints unguarded and a single train got through, unimpeded, from the West; the event coincided with the arrival of an international charitable commission. The Swedish Red Cross was allowed to bring in a trickle of supplies until December, but then even this was stopped.

As New Year's Day came and passed there occurred, despite adverse weather, a marked increase in air deliveries (in December, nearly 142,000 tons; in January, 172,000). The Soviets realized that they had lost and that the project must be abandoned before irreparable harm was done to their condition and cause. Bad weather stopped flying for nearly half of December and coal supplies ran dangerously low in January, but thereafter milder weather prevailed. There was even a noticeable advance in the economic recovery of West Berlin. Moreover, workable coal deposits were actually discovered in the French sector when the situation was most acute. A further currency reform by the West redressed the economic imbalance.

West Berliners now began to take reprisals against their opposite numbers in the East. Attempts at arrest by the East German police were successfully resisted and the West's propaganda war began to play on the nerves of the Communists. People in the Western sector actually were beginning to enjoy a higher quality of life than those in the East.

In January the first peace overtures by the Soviets appeared in the form of requests that the counterblockade be lifted. Not surprisingly these were declined. By April the applications for restarting West to East trade were becoming insistent. The Soviets were searching hard for a face-saving pretext to end the blockade; a desire for trade was as good as any. Peace feelers abounded, many of them intended to be politically divisive. On April 4 there came a further indication of Allied solidarity in their determination to resist Soviet threats: the North Atlantic Treaty was signed in Washington. Twelve days later, to hammer home their strength, the Allies laid on a spectacular operation and flew in nearly 13,000 tons of supplies in one day, thus exceeding the daily minimum requirement of the city as it had stood before the blockade began.

An intensive Soviet peace campaign opened in March as a counter to the provocation of the North Atlantic Treaty and as a means of reducing tension. Simultaneously Soviet diplomats sought closer association with Western delegates. The desire by the Soviets to discuss the currency problem was used as an excuse to hold a council of foreign ministers, while it was suggested by the Americans in March that the raising of the blockade would provide a useful atmosphere for such a step. On May 5 it was finally announced that all restrictions upon the movement of people and goods imposed by both sides would be removed on May 12 and that the foreign ministers would meet on May 23.

It would have been surprising had a condition of normality returned immediately. Time would pass before the land communications were fully working again. There were negotiations to repossess trucks and barges that had been seized, and a few key transport workers staged a strike. Thus the airlift had to continue to tide things over. It was not to be wound up until nearly the end of September. The hundreds of aircraft and crews that had made up the airlift, along with the complex servicing and maintenance organization, began to disperse. The lights on airfields in the West and in Berlin that rarely had gone out at night burned less frequently. The continuous roar of engines fell away, and the waves gave way to a stream and then to individual arrivals and departures following a normal commercial pattern. One estimate of the cost of the airlift has been put at $224 million. The total tonnage flown in was 2,325,809 short tons. The price in lives accredited to the actual airlift personnel was sixty-eight, including nine Germans. In terms of air accidents the U.S.A. suffered seventy-six major and fifty minor out of nearly 190,000 sorties; the RAF one hundred and thirty all-told, of which only forty were due to technical failure.

The Berlin airlift represented the first major defeat of the Soviets in the Cold War. It was a fundamental of success, however, that the war had been kept cold and had been settled in this phase by diplomacy. KENNETH MACKSEY

In their operations room at Frankfurt, members of Transport Squadron Six, one of the two U.S. Navy air squadrons engaged in the Frankfurt–Berlin airlift, receive the announcement that the blockade is lifted.

Latin America

The troubles that afflicted India and Palestine were repeated in many parts of the world during the postwar years. America was the only region to escape the difficulties that came with the beginning of decolonization, and that was because both in North and South America the colonial powers had in general already departed. But in South America there were other troubles. Between 1945 and 1950 there were civil wars in three countries—Colombia, Paraguay and Costa Rica—and coups in two—El Salvador and Panama—while dictatorship remained the normal form of government in most South American countries. Latin America was largely isolated from European and world politics, and none of the South American countries took an active role in World War II. This was mainly due to the attitude of the United States, which remained the dominant force in the continent, and which was determined to prevent the creation of close links between South America and Europe. But, despite the attitude of the United States, the cultural ties between Spain and Portugal and their former colonies in America were noticeable in the fascist sympathies of many of the Latin American states and in the number of dictatorships, similar in many cases to those of Franco in Spain and Salazar in Portugal.

Africa

The ending of colonial power, signaled by the granting of independence to India and the termination of the Middle Eastern mandate, was not confined to Asia. In Africa, too, the colonial powers found themselves under pressure to withdraw. On the whole, they found the pressure easy to resist. South Africa, the only politically and economically developed state south of the Sahara, had been since 1910 a completely self-governing British "dominion." In 1948, the United Party government of General Jan Smuts lost its parliamentary majority in the general election. The new National Party government, many of whose leaders had

The first South African National Party cabinet of 1948. In the front row are D. F. Malan, C. R. Swart, and J. G. Strijdom.

spent World War II in prison because of their anti-British views, represented a triumph for the Afrikaners: for the first time since union, the South African cabinet contained no person of English origin. Moreover, the election had been fought on the "native question." Its outcome set South Africa on a course of racial separation (apartheid). The new government quickly showed its contempt for white liberals and black politicians by changing the constitution. The protests in the United Nations regarding these changes and other issues, such as the ill-treatment of Indians and South Africa's continued occupation of the United Nations trust territory of South West Africa, were ignored.

North of the Sahara, however, the situation was rather different. In Egypt, the British insisted on keeping a garrison, because of the strategic importance of the Suez Canal, but in the Sudan it was only the breakdown of tripartite talks between Egypt, Britain and the Sudanese leaders that prevented the granting of independence in 1947. Libya became an independent country in 1951. The French were under increasing pressure to give up their colonies in Tunisia, Morocco and Algeria; they were, however, able to resist the pressure in the former two countries until 1956 and in Algeria for still longer. In Asia, too, they found themselves increasingly

under fire. The impact of nationalism could be felt everywhere in Asia, not just in British colonies and dependencies.

Indochina

There were three colonial powers which had large territorial interests in Asia after the British had abandoned their Indian Empire. The United States retained the Philippines until 1946; the Dutch reoccupied Indonesia after the war; and the French attempted to regain their former position in Indochina. The French

had been determined to reclaim their lost Asian empire, and had quickly attempted to reoccupy it after the war. But even before their return a democratic Republic of Vietnam had been set up in Hanoi under the leadership of Ho Chi Minh, and the French soon found that they could not reach agreement with the Viet Minh—the nationalist-communist anti-Japanese resistance movement. By 1946 Ho Chi Minh's supporters, who were under the military leadership of Vo Nguyen Giap, were at war with the French, and only after reinforcements had been brought in were the French

Ho Chi Minh, leader of the Viet Minh resistance movement.

the Cold War spreads to Asia

able to reoccupy Hanoi. The Emperor Bao Dai, whom Ho Chi Minh had deposed, was restored to the throne, but the French government made clear that it intended to remain in control of Indochina. But fighting still continued as the Viet Minh had not been destroyed, and from 1950 onward the French found themselves under increasing pressure. The war for Vietnam had begun.

Indonesia

In Indonesia, too, the former colonial power returned, but there the Japanese occupation had had a profound influence on attitudes. Toward the end of their occupation the Japanese had begun to seek the support of wartime nationalist leaders, such as Sukarno. In addition, the Japanese had set up an independent Indonesian army, which opposed the return of the Dutch after the war. As a result, the Dutch found themselves unable to rule effectively. Because of the activity of Communist nationalists in opposition to both the Dutch and to the main nationalist movement of Sukarno, the United States grew worried that the whole of Indonesia might fall to the Communists. The U.S. administration threatened to cut off Marshall Aid to Holland if the Dutch did not withdraw and recognize Sukarno as the head of an independent Indonesia. The Dutch insisted on retaining West Irian (New Guinea) but accepted the need to give up the struggle elsewhere in the colonies.

The Cold War in Asia

The Cold War was not confined to Europe, as had been seen in Indonesia where the American fear of Communism had played such an important role in forcing the Dutch to withdraw. Indeed, in Europe, the neatness of the battle lines served the interest of both the superpowers, who knew the precise extent of their respective spheres of influence. In addition, the possession of nuclear weapons by both America and the Russians (from 1949) meant that both had to compete elsewhere in the world. The situation in Asia was far more fluid, and both Russia and the United States felt that it was important to

Sukarno, first President of Indonesia, making an informal tour of the country.

preserve and expand their interests there in order to establish a border similar to the Iron Curtain. It was with this in mind that Stalin had insisted on retaining Outer Mongolia after World War II.

Conflict in Korea

Germany's fate after the Berlin airlift was to be Korea's as well, for there also Allied occupation forces had found themselves unable to agree on a means of propelling the Koreans toward independence. The ensuing stalemate played havoc with the country's economy, for the north-south division agreed upon at the Potsdam Conference effectively isolated the agricultural south (the U.S. zone) from the industrialized north (the Russian zone). In August, 1948, the South Koreans abandoned hope of uniting the country, and declared all land south of the 38th parallel part of the Republic of South Korea, and elected Syngman Rhee as President. The North Koreans promptly retaliated by proclaiming the lands above the parallel as the People's Democratic Republic of Korea. Inevitably, the two Koreas found themselves in conflict.

On June 25, 1950, North Korean troops swept across the 38th parallel at eleven separate points and invaded South Korea in force. Rhee's government called upon the United Nations for assistance and the United States independently came to the South Koreans' aid at once. At the time, Russia's delegates to the United Nations were boycotting all committees that included representatives of the National Chinese

government-in-exile—and their boycott included the Security Council. For this reason, the Council was able to pass a resolution calling for the United Nations' armed intervention in the Korean conflict without any serious fear of a Russian veto.

In September a counteroffensive launched against the invading North Korean armies pushed them back to the 38th parallel, and in October General Douglas MacArthur, Commander in Chief of the combined U.N.–U.S. forces, crossed the parallel and pressed his attack north to the borders of Manchuria. At this point the war took a dramatic, significant and costly turn; on November 26, the Communist Chinese army intervened on the side of North Korea.

The whole balance of power in Asia was changed; the victory of the Communists in China over their Nationalist opponents during the civil war meant that Western interests were now seriously threatened. By the end of the 1940s China was bursting its seams, for despite the country's immense size, less than fifteen percent of the mainland was arable, and the country's burgeoning population desperately needed new sources of food and raw materials. Excluded from international trade by the Western powers' "containment" policy, Mao Tse-tung's regime turned on its southern, northern and western neighbors. But first it had to complete its defeat of the Nationalist Chinese government.

United Nations troops in Korea.

Red Victory in China 1949

The city of Nanking, longtime capital of Generalissimo Chiang Kai-shek's Nationalist regime, was all but abandoned by the time Mao Tse-tung's troops reached the city's bridges on April 23, 1949. Chiang, his Vice-President Li Tsung-jên and the Kuomintang government had fled, leaving Nanking's terrified populace to face the advancing Communists. The Reds' bloodless "capture" and pacific occupation of the city marked the beginning of the end of the protracted and bitter civil war that had been raging in China for more than two decades. Moreover, it signaled the imminent collapse of the Kuomintang (which had failed to incorporate the Communists in 1923 or 1936—or to eradicate them in 1934). Refusing to capitulate, Chiang and his fugitive government withdrew to Formosa, where they continued to pose an ideological—if not a military— threat to the Communists. From 1949 on, mainland China has belonged to Mao.

The Communists entered Nanking, the Nationalist capital, on April 23, 1949—and to some, Communist hegemony in mainland China begins on that date, although the National Day is celebrated by virtue of an arbitrary decision as October 1, 1949. Canton was not occupied until mid-October of 1949, however, and the large South China Sea island of Hainan was taken still later. On October 1, the Nationalists still had a foothold in Fukien, facing the Formosa Straits. Yunnan, bordering on French Indochina, did not fall until mid-December, and Chengtu, the capital of Szechwan, held out until the twenty-seventh. Actually, in April, 1949, Nanking was a capital in name only. The head of state, Generalissimo Chiang Kai-shek, had resigned on January 21 and both he and the government had departed.

The undefended city did not fall in a military sense, it was merely taken over as a result of a bid that had been made elsewhere and some time before. There had been no fighting, although a few days earlier the Communists, poised on the north bank of the Yangtse River, had indulged in some rather symbolic shelling. Tens of thousands of civilians (who were fleeing an expected massacre that never took place) had been streaming eastward in the direction of Shanghai, only to find themselves already cut off. The armies of Mao Tse-tung were quietly, almost unobtrusively, marching into what had been— except during the Japanese occupation and during the puppet Wang Ching-wei regime—the capital of Kuomintang China for twenty-two years.

No great crowds were about in the streets of Nanking either to curse or to cheer the newcomers. Curiously enough, the Communists were wearing the same uniforms as the Kuomintang troops, although theirs were woven of coarser cotton and were a little greener in shade. The shops had put up their shutters, as had always been the rule in China wherever and whenever the military moved in. Everyone was expecting the worst from the soldiery,

and when the soldiers failed to conform to tradition, the very first reaction of the people was one of puzzlement rather than gratitude. The Communist troops did not loot, rob, ransack, or rape—yet even their decorous behavior, breaking with tradition, was disquieting to the populace. The psychological effect was tremendous. It was, in the fullest sense of the word, revolutionary.

The propaganda machine was immediately set in motion as the Communist army's team of artists, who had arrived with the vanguard, began chalking multicolored pictures on walls. The almost invariable subject was a soldier with a red star on his cap who was freeing the oppressed Chinese people from the imperialists and the "Kuomintang bandits." The drawing was often excellent and the style always typically Russian. The local press resumed publication with new staffs. Less than two hours after the first Communist soldiers had entered Nanking, the radio station was broadcasting again—and even giving the details of programs for the whole week to come. The police, who had for the most part remained at their posts, appeared to have undergone lightning brainwashing. Overnight their surliness and arrogance became smiling politeness to all.

The Chinese Communist Party had come into being on July 1, 1921. It was organized by a Russian Comintern delegate named Gregori Voitinsky, and its early members had all had their political training in Europe: Chou En-lai and Li Li-san in France, Chu Teh in Germany, Ch'ü Ch'iu-pai in Russia. At the time it was essentially a party of intellectuals, one that held little appeal for the proletarian masses. When, for survival's sake, it joined hands with the Kuomintang in 1923, its officially recorded membership did not exceed three hundred.

The Kuomintang, under Sun Yat-sen, the "Father of the Chinese Revolution," was the only organized revolutionary force in the country at the time. No actual merger ever took place, but the Communist Party, Russian-dominated and officially playing

Chiang Kai-shek as a young revolutionary in the Kuomintang.

Opposite A poster commemorating the Communist victory over Chiang Kai-shek in 1949.

The funeral of Dr. Sun Yat-sen, who founded the Kuomintang and pushed China into the twentieth century.

1925 did not palpably affect the situation. What was later to be known as the Northern Expedition—the campaign to capture North China from its ruling warlords—was being feverishly prepared for in South China in that year, and Soviet advice was more than ever required, even though the leaders of the right wing of the Kuomintang, Hu Han-min and Chiang Kai-shek himself, already had their misgivings as to the future of Kuomintang-Communist cooperation. The Chinese Communists were by then efficiently using the Kuomintang machinery for their own ends, and they were successful to such an extent that by 1926 their party membership had risen to some 45,000.

In July of the same year, the Northern Expedition got under way and made rapid progress under the military leadership of Chiang Kai-shek. The Yangtse River—halfway to Peking—was reached the following spring. Almost at once the breach between the Communists and the Kuomintang became an accomplished fact, with the former establishing themselves at Hankow and Chiang setting up his capital at Nanking and dominating the Lower Yangtse Valley.

From then on, the northern drive was forgotten. The warlords, far more frightened by the growing influence of the Communists than by Chiang Kai-shek's nationalism, gradually came to terms with him. At the same time, a new civil war broke out. The tide ran against the Communists, who were forced to retreat southward. The first Chinese Soviet

second fiddle to the Kuomintang, did its best to infiltrate and subvert Sun's party. Sun Yat-sen was willing to welcome Soviet assistance, especially in the fields of party organization and propaganda technique, and the Communists were in a position to provide it. Moreover, the Western democracies, by consistently ignoring Dr. Sun, actually forced him to throw himself into the arms of the Russians.

Indeed, it was with the Russians, not the Chinese Communists, that Sun Yat-sen entered into virtual political partnership early in 1923. His death in

Communist guerrillas overturning a railway line in order to cut enemy supply lines.

Republic was founded in the southeastern province of Kiangsi in 1931. It took the Nationalists no less than five military campaigns to drive out the Communists, and it was not until the fall of 1934 that the Communists' exodus north—known as the Long March—began. By a very roundabout way it brought them to the northwestern province of Shensi, where Yenan became their new capital in December, 1936. For a whole year they had fought their way, not through China, but rather around China, and during that time Mao Tse-tung's political leadership asserted itself.

In these years, other things had been happening in China. There had been the 1931 Japanese aggression, which resulted in the virtual annexation of Manchuria and further encroachments in North China. Another Japanese invasion was imminent in 1936, and everyone in China knew it. It had been widely stated that the Nationalists were then prepared to come to terms with imperialist Japan, but nothing could have been further from the truth. In 1936, Chiang Kai-shek was as acutely aware of the new Japanese threat as everyone else and, it would seem, ready to face it. Still, he made it very plain that he wanted to liquidate the Communists first. A sixth campaign had already been planned against them. The man in charge was the "Young Marshal," Chang Hsueh-liang. His headquarters were at Sian, close to Communist territory. He had all the troops and equipment he needed. Yet he wavered—and so, in December, 1936, Chiang himself flew to Sian,

where Chiang Hsueh-liang promptly arrested him.

The Communist forces had numbered 130,000 when they left their Kiangsi capital late in 1934. A bare 30,000 had reached Yenan after the Long March. The exhausted, if heroic, body of men, hard put to find its feet on new ground, lacking arms and generally unfit, was in no position to resist Chang Hsueh-liang had he obeyed his orders. But Chang hesitated, the Communists captured Yenan, and a few days later the Sian "incident" occurred. It was Communist General Chou En-lai who went to Sian

Students organized by Mao Tse-tung singing anti-Japanese songs. During the Japanese occupation the Red Army became the focus for patriotic resistance.

The Red Army marching into Nanking on April 23, 1949.

Mao Tse-tung, who emerged as leader of the Chinese Communists during the Long March.

The Chinese Communist Revolution 1934-50

U.S.S.R.

MONGOLIA

Controlled by Russians 1945-48

Main areas of Communist activity 1934

Controlled by Chinese Communists

○ by April 1947
○ by July 1948
○ by December 1949
○ by 1950
○ Controlled by Nationalist Chinese Government under Chiang Kai-shek after the fall of mainland China in 1949
○ South Korea (occupied by U.S. and UN 1945-49)
○ North Korea (occupied by Russia 1945-48)
Chinese Communists invaded Korea 1950-53

Yenan — Peking

Area of Communist control 1936-49

The Long March of Communist followers 1934-36

Nanking

Matsu
Quemoy

TAIWAN (FORMOSA)

to negotiate with Chiang, and, indeed, to rescue him. A Kuomintang-Communist truce ensued, and a united anti-Japanese front (later made official and formal) was agreed upon.

The probable truth of the matter is that in 1936, as in 1923, the Communist Party in China could not have survived without entering into some sort of partnership with the Kuomintang.

During the war with Japan, an uneasy truce was maintained, both sides being aware that the struggle for power had merely been postponed. In December, 1941, Pearl Harbor and the simultaneous Japanese

attack on Britain's Far Eastern possessions brought the whole Anglo-Saxon world into the war on the side of China. The events also brought a host of American military and diplomatic personnel to Chungking, China's wartime capital.

The Japanese North China forces had been progressing rapidly southward along the main roads and railways, but they had not advanced along a continuous front, steamroller fashion, and so had left in their rear a vast military, political and administrative vacuum. The Communists began to fill this vacuum, and by the end of World War II in 1945, they had secured for themselves considerable popular support in many provinces.

At Chungking, Chou En-lai, shrewd and brilliant as ever, was concentrating on the Americans, mostly the diplomats, and in so convincing a manner that, years before a pro-Nationalist China lobby had come into being in the U.S. Congress, there existed a pro-Mao faction within the Department of State, where the view prevailed that the Chinese Communists were democratically minded and that their general purpose was to bring about liberal reforms.

Thus when the Japanese capitulated, the position of the Chinese Communists became extremely strong, both nationally and internationally. They were ready for a resumption of the civil war (actually there had been many military clashes between the Communists and the Nationalists during the official truce), but appearances had to be considered and foreign sympathies retained. The Nationalists, on the other hand, were in a difficult situation: they had no illusions about the Reds' plans for total national domination, but they had lost much ground since 1936 when the Communists, although practically at bay, had made their bid to take over China.

In fact, hostilities were resumed immediately after the Japanese capitulation (August 15, 1945) when the Communist commander in chief ordered his troops in North China to disarm the Japanese. Thanks to a prompt American airlift, the Nationalists beat them to it. Nevertheless, the truce had come to a spectacular end, even though both sides continued to proclaim their desire for peace.

By the end of the year, the situation had deteriorated to such an extent that President Truman sent General George C. Marshall to China as a mediator. His efforts resulted in yet another truce agreement, signed on January 10, 1946, and the setting up in Peking of a tripartite commission—Kuomintang, Communist and American—to see that it was properly abided by. It never was. A year later, first the Americans, then the Communists left the commission.

The stage was set for a last act, during which the fortunes of civil war at first seemed to favor the Nationalists, who beat back three Communist offensives led by Lin Piao, and even succeeded in occupying Yenan. The unaccountable capitulation of General Fu Tso-yi, in whom Chiang Kai-shek placed great trust and whose forces in North China greatly outnumbered the Communists, soon turned the tide. All Nationalist resistance then collapsed,

and Nanking fell a short time after Peking.

Relations between Washington and the Nationalist government had been uneasy for a long time. Ever since the war years when General Stilwell, Chiang Kai-shek's American Chief of Staff, was wont to call Chiang "the peanut" in the rather public privacy of his own circle of friends (and even before the press), and when the U.S. embassy was engaged in rather active flirtation with Yenan, there had been considerable mutual distrust. Even before the Japanese collapse of 1945, America and China had been on rather strained terms.

After V-J Day and the almost immediate resumption of civil war in China, the Americans engaged in various efforts at mediation, trying to bring about at least a modus vivendi. But both the Kuomintang and the Communists were playing the game only as far as it suited them and wondering at Yankee political blindness. Washington's diplomacy had come to favor the Reds more and more and continued to do so even after the Marshall truce was broken in 1946, and the Communists, seeing no further reason to placate the Americans, abruptly attacked them in their propaganda. What happened then is reported in a recent edition of Taipei's official *China Year Book* in the following words: "At this juncture, when the Chinese Communists openly launched their anti-American movement, the American Government stopped its supply of arms to the Chinese Government without taking any action against the Chinese Communists despite the latter's violations of the American-mediated truce agreement."

By 1949, after the Communist takeover of the mainland, the Americans were ready to write Nationalist China off. In order to prepare public opinion at home and abroad for such a change in foreign policy, the State Department published a white paper that amounted to a denunciation of the Kuomintang regime and a discreet assurance of American goodwill toward the Communists. This document, the first official hint of an American desire for disengagement in East Asia, was received in Taiwan with much anger. Taiwan would obviously soon stand alone.

On March 1, 1950, Chiang Kai-shek, who had tendered his resignation as President of the Chinese Republic, withdrew it and resumed office. It was at that point an act of courage, for the position of Taiwan looked almost desperate and Chiang could well have taken refuge on the other side of the Pacific Ocean, as many of his friends had done.

On June 25, Communist North Korea invaded the Republic of South Korea. The United States, which promptly came to the embattled South Koreans' aid, eventually extended its military protection to include Chiang's endangered government-in-exile. With the U.S. Seventh Fleet patrolling the Straits of Formosa, the survival of Chiang Kai-shek's regime was no longer in doubt.
JACQUES MARCUSE

The victorious Red Army entering Peking on January 31, 1949.

Georges Clemenceau 1841–1929
French statesman

Paul von Hindenburg 1847–1934
German general, statesman

Paul Gauguin 1848–1903
French painter

Ivan Pavlov 1849–1936
Russian physiologist

Horatio Herbert Kitchener 1850–1916
British soldier

Henry Cabot Lodge 1850–1924
U.S. statesman

Ferdinand Foch 1851–1929
French general

Joseph Joffre 1852–1931
French general

Vincent van Gogh 1853–90
Dutch painter

James Keir Hardie 1856–1915
British socialist statesman

Theobald von Bethmann-Hollweg 1856–1921
German statesman

Woodrow Wilson 1856–1924
U.S. President

Hussein ibn Ali 1856–1931
Grand Sharif of Mecca

Sigmund Freud 1856–1939
Austrian psychoanalyst

George Bernard Shaw 1856–1950
British writer

Theodore Roosevelt 1858–1919
U.S. President

Max Planck 1858–1947
German physicist

Wilhelm II 1859–1941
German Kaiser

Raymond Poincaré 1860–1934
French statesman

Vittorio Emanuele Orlando 1860–1952
Italian statesman

Douglas Haig 1861–1928
British soldier

Franz Ferdinand 1863–1914
Archduke of Austria

Gabriele d'Annunzio 1863–1938
Italian writer and soldier

Edvard Munch 1863–1944
Norwegian painter

David Lloyd George 1863–1945
British statesman

Henry Ford 1863–1947
U.S. industrialist

Erich Ludendorff 1865–1937
German general

Jean Sibelius 1865–1957
Finnish composer

Sun Yat-sen 1866–1925
Chinese statesman

J. Ramsay MacDonald 1866–1937
British statesman

Wilbur Wright 1867–1912
U.S. aircraft inventor

Marie Curie 1867–1934
French physical chemist

Stanley Baldwin 1867–1947
British statesman

Robert Falcon Scott 1868–1912
British Antarctic explorer

Nicholas II 1868–1918
Tsar of Russia

Maxim Gorky 1868–1936
Russian writer

Neville Chamberlain 1869–1940
British statesman

Victor Emmanuel III 1869–1947
King of Italy

Mohandas Gandhi 1869–1948
Indian leader

Henri Matisse 1869–1954
French painter

Frank Lloyd Wright 1869–1959
U.S. architect

Rosa Luxemburg 1870–1919
German socialist

Nikolai Lenin (V.I. Ulyanov) 1870–1924
Russian revolutionary leader

Marcel Proust 1871–1922
French writer

Ernest Rutherford 1871–1937
British physicist

Orville Wright 1871–1948
U.S. aircraft inventor

Grigori Rasputin 1872–1916
Russian monk

Roald Amundsen 1872–1928
Norwegian polar explorer

Bertrand Russell 1872–1970
English philosopher, mathematician

Guglielmo Marconi 1874–1937
Italian inventor

Arnold Schoenberg 1874–1951
Austrian composer

Chaim Weizmann 1874–1952
Russian-British Zionist leader

Herbert Clark Hoover 1874–196◼
U.S. president

Winston Churchill 1874–1965
British statesman

Carl Gustav Jung 1875–1◼
Swiss psychiatrist

Albert Schweitzer 1875–19◼
Alsatian philosopher, missi◼

Mohammed Ali Jin◼
Pakistani statesman

Konrad Adenauer 1◼
German statesman

Leon Trotsky (L. D. Bron◼
Russian revolutionary lea◼

Joseph Stalin (I. V. Dzhugas◼
Russian statesman

tein 1879–1955
rican physicist

Isoroku Yamamoto 1884–1943
Japanese admiral

Papen 1879-1969
sman

Harry S. Truman 1884–1972
U.S. President

glas MacArthur 1880–1964
army officer

David Ben-Gurion 1886–1973
Israeli statesman

Kemal Atatürk 1881–1938
Turkish leader

Chiang Kai-shek 1887–
Chinese general, statesman

Béla Bartók 1881–1945
Hungarian composer

Bernard Law Montgomery 1887–
British soldier

Alexander Fleming 1881–1955
British bacteriologist

John Foster Dulles 1888–1959
U.S. statesman

John XXIII 1881–1963
Pope

Adolf Hitler 1889–1945
German dictator

Kliment Voroshilov 1881–1969
Russian field-marshal

Jawaharlal Nehru 1889–1964
Indian statesman

Alexander Kerensky 1881–1970
Russian statesman

Boris Pasternak 1890–1960
Russian writer

Pablo Picasso 1881–1973
Franco-Spanish painter

Dwight D. Eisenhower 1890–1969
U.S. general, President

James Joyce 1882–1941
Irish writer

Ho Chi Minh 1890–1969
Vietnamese communist leader

Virginia Woolf 1882–1941
British writer

Charles de Gaulle 1890–1970
French general, statesman

Franklin D. Roosevelt 1882–1945
U.S. President

Vyacheslav Mikhailovich Molotov 1890–
Russian statesman

Georges Braque 1882–1963
French painter

Erwin Rommel 1891–1944
German general

Igor Stravinsky 1882–1971
Russian composer

Averell Harriman 1891–
U.S. statesman

Eamon de Valera 1882–
Irish statesman

Haile Selassie 1891–
Emperor of Ethiopia

6–1948

Franz Kafka 1883–1924
Czech writer

Francisco Franco 1892–
Spanish general, dictator

7

Pierre Laval 1883–1945
French statesman

Tito (Josif Broz) 1892–
Yugoslav statesman

9–1940

Benito Mussolini 1883–1945
Italian dictator

9–1953

John Maynard Keynes 1883–1946
British economist

1894 ●
Franco-Russian alliance

1901 ●
Australia a Dominion

1905 ●
First Russian Revolution:
foundation of "soviets"

1910 ●
Union of South Africa
created

1898-1902
Boer War

1902 ●
Discovery of hormones

1905 ●
First moving picture
devised by Edison

● 1908
Austria annexes Bosnia
and Herzegovina

1894–95 ●
Sino-Japanese War in
Korea

1900 ●
Planck's quantum theory

1910 ●
Japan annexes Korea

1904 ●
Entente Cordiale: Anglo-
French alliance

1906 ●
Algeciras Conference:
European hegemony over
Morocco

1910 ●
Mexican Revolution

● 1895
Sino-Japanese Treaty of
Shimonoseki followed by
the "Triple Intervention" of
Russia, France and
Germany

1901 ●
USA: assassination of
President McKinley;
Roosevelt President

1906 ●
Dreadnought launched

●1907
Anglo-Russian Convention
on Persia, Afghanistan
and Tibet; Anglo-French
Entente expanded to
Triple Entente (Britain,
Russia, France)

1903 ●
Pogroms in Russia

● 1896
Russo-Chinese defensive
alliance; railway con-
cession in Manchuria

1904 ●
Building of Panama Canal
under US protection

Hermann Göring 1893–1946
German Nazi leader

J. Robert Oppenheimer 1904–67
U.S. physicist

Jonas Edward Salk 1914–
U.S. physician

Mao Tse-tung 1893–
Chinese statesman

Dag Hammarskjöld 1905–61
U.N. Secretary-General

Moshe Dayan 1915–
Israeli general, statesman

Jomo Kenyatta 1893–
Kenyan statesman

Jean Paul Sartre 1905–
French writer, philosopher

Francis Crick 1916–
British scientist

Nikita Khrushchev 1894–1971
Russian statesman

Samuel Beckett 1906–
Irish-French writer

Harold Wilson 1916–
British statesman

Harold Macmillan 1894–
British statesman

Leonid I. Brezhnev 1906–
Russian statesman

John F. Kennedy 1917–63
U.S. President

Georgi Zhukov 1895–1974
Russian general

Frank Whittle 1907–
British aeronautical expert

Gamal Abdel Nasser 1918–70
Egyptian statesman

Juan Perón 1895–
Argentinian statesman

Joseph McCarthy 1908–1957
U.S. Senator

Pierre Trudeau 1919–
Canadian statesman

F. Scott Fitzgerald 1896–1940
U.S. writer

Lin Piao 1908–71
Chinese statesman

Alexander Dubček 1921–
Czech statesman

Imre Nagy 1896–1958
Hungarian statesman

Salvador Allende 1908–73
Chilean statesman

Henry Kissinger 1923–
U.S. statesman

Trygve Lie 1896–1968
U.N. Secretary-General

Lyndon B. Johnson 1908–73
U.S. President

Robert F. Kennedy 1925–68
U.S. statesman

Bertold Brecht 1898–1956
German writer

John K. Galbraith 1908–
U.S. economist

Fidel Castro 1927–
Cuban revolutionary leader

René Magritte 1898–1967
French painter

Kwame Nkrumah 1909–72
Ghanaian statesman

Ernesto "Che" Guevara 1928–67
Argentinian revolutionary

Chou En-lai 1898–
Chinese statesman

Dean Rusk 1909–
U.S. statesman

Martin Luther King, Jr 1929–
U.S. civil rights leader

Henry Moore 1898–
British sculptor

Andrei Gromyko 1909–
Russian diplomat

Hu

Ernest Hemingway 1899–1961
U.S. writer

U. Thant 1909–
U.N. Secretary-General

Heinrich Himmler 1900–45
German Nazi leader

Georges Pompidou 1911–74
French statesman

Louis Mountbatten 1900–
British admiral

Jackson Pollock 1912–56
U.S. painter

Enrico Fermi 1901–54
Italian physicist

Willy Brandt 1913–
West German statesman

Hirohito 1901–
Emperor of Japan

Richard M. Nixon 1913–
U.S. President

Georgi Malenkov 1902–
Russian statesman

Benjamin Britten 1913–
British composer

1911●
German gunboat at Agadir creates international tension

Votes for women in **1918 ●**
Britain

1921 ● Russia: Kronstadt mutiny; ban on opposition in Party; New Economic Policy

1925 ●
Sun Yat-sen dies; Chiang Kai-shek takes over Kuomintang leadership

1929●
Lateran Treaty: papal recognition of Italy

1935-36 ●
Italy conquers Ethi League of Nations powerless

1915 ●
First U-boat (submarine) attacks: sinking of the *Lusitania*

●1928
A. Fleming discovers penicillin

●1933
Hitler Chancellor of Germany; Germany le Geneva Disarmament Conference and Leag Nations

1911 ●
Revolution in China; imperial rule overthrown and republic proclaimed

1919 ●
Gandhi's civil disobedience campaign in India: troops fire on Indians at Amritsar

1925●
Locarno Pact guarantees Germany's western borders and allows her entry to League of Nations

1929 ●
The Young Plan on German reparations

1916 ●
Battle of Jutland; Gallipoli and Salonika campaigns

Ireland: South gets a **●** republican constitution; **1922** Ulster remains British

First television **1926 ●** transmission

1930 ●
The Allies withdraw troops from the Rhineland

1935 ●
The Saar is restor Germany

Battles of Passchendaele **1917●** and Cambrai

1920 ●
Votes for women in USA; prohibition of alcohol (until 1933)

Washington Naval **1927 ●** Disarmament Conference

1931 ●
Nazi *putsch* in A

●193●

1915 ●
Battles of Neuve Chapelle, Ypres, Aubers Ridge, Loos

1925 ●
Trotsky asserts opposition to Stalin's "Communism in One Country"; exiled 1929

Sino-Japanese War: Japan withdraws from League of Nations

1935 ●
First practical equipment

1919 ●

1932 ●
Geneva Disarmament Conference

1914 ●
Battles of Tannenberg and Masurian Lakes: Germany defeats Russia

League of Nations, World Court, International Labor Organization established

1927 ●
China: massacre of Communists by Nationalists in Shanghai

1923-25 ●
French troops occupy the Ruhr

begins civil war

1931 ●
Financial crisis reaches climax in Europe

●193●
China: "Long Ma north of Commu guerrillas under T Tse-tung

USA enters World War **1917 ●**

General strike in Britain **1926 ●**

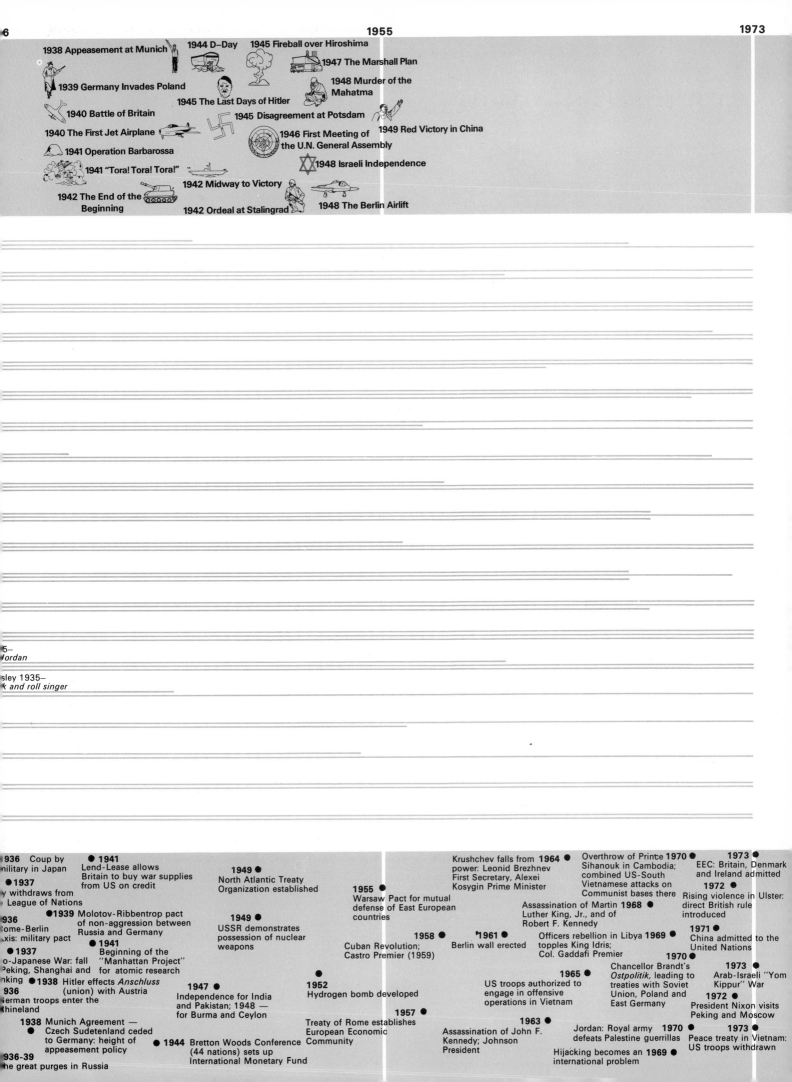

1938 Appeasement at Munich

1939 Germany Invades Poland

1940 Battle of Britain

1940 The First Jet Airplane

1941 Operation Barbarossa

1941 "Tora! Tora! Tora!"

1942 The End of the Beginning

1944 D–Day

1945 The Last Days of Hitler

1945 Disagreement at Potsdam

1946 First Meeting of the U.N. General Assembly

1942 Midway to Victory

1942 Ordeal at Stalingrad

1945 Fireball over Hiroshima

1947 The Marshall Plan

1948 Murder of the Mahatma

1949 Red Victory in China

1948 Israeli Independence

1948 The Berlin Airlift

5–
Jordan

sley 1935–
k and roll singer

1936 Coup by military in Japan

1937
y withdraws from League of Nations

1936
Rome-Berlin Axis: military pact

1937
o-Japanese War: fall Peking, Shanghai and nking

1938 Hitler effects *Anschluss* (union) with Austria

936
German troops enter the Rhineland

1938 Munich Agreement — Czech Sudetenland ceded to Germany: height of appeasement policy

1936-39
he great purges in Russia

1941
Lend-Lease allows Britain to buy war supplies from US on credit

1939 Molotov-Ribbentrop pact of non-aggression between Russia and Germany

1941
Beginning of the "Manhattan Project" for atomic research

1947
Independence for India and Pakistan; 1948 — for Burma and Ceylon

1944 Bretton Woods Conference (44 nations) sets up International Monetary Fund

1949
North Atlantic Treaty Organization established

1949
USSR demonstrates possession of nuclear weapons

1955
Warsaw Pact for mutual defense of East European countries

1952
Hydrogen bomb developed

1957
Treaty of Rome establishes European Economic Community

1958
Cuban Revolution; Castro Premier (1959)

1963
Assassination of John F. Kennedy; Johnson President

Krushchev falls from **1964** power: Leonid Brezhnev First Secretary, Alexei Kosygin Prime Minister

Assassination of Martin **1968** Luther King, Jr., and of Robert F. Kennedy

1961
Berlin wall erected

1965
US troops authorized to engage in offensive operations in Vietnam

Officers rebellion in Libya **1969** topples King Idris; Col. Gaddafi Premier

Overthrow of Prince **1970** Sihanouk in Cambodia; combined US-South Vietnamese attacks on Communist bases there

Chancellor Brandt's *Ostpolitik,* leading to treaties with Soviet Union, Poland and East Germany

Jordan: Royal army **1970** defeats Palestine guerrillas

Hijacking becomes an **1969** international problem

1973
EEC: Britain, Denmark and Ireland admitted

Rising violence in Ulster: direct British rule introduced

1971
China admitted to the United Nations

1973
Arab-Israeli "Yom Kippur" War

1972
President Nixon visits Peking and Moscow

1973
Peace treaty in Vietnam: US troops withdrawn

Acknowledgments

The authors and publishers wish to thank the following museums and collections by whose kind permission the illustrations are reproduced. Page numbers appear in bold, photographic sources in italics.

12 Picturepoint
13 Keystone Press Agency
14 (1, 2) Staatsbibliothek, Berlin
15 Keystone Press Agency
16 Popperfoto
17 Staatsbibliothek
18 (1) Imperial War Museum, London (2) Radio Times Hulton Picture Library
19 (1) Imperial War Museum (2, 3) Camera Press
20 Staatsbibliothek
21 Associated Press
22 Staatsbibliothek
23 (1) Bundesarchiv (2) Staatsbibliothek
24 Staatsbibliothek
25 (1) Popperfoto (2) Staatsbibliothek
26 Imperial War Museum
27 (1) Imperial War Museum (2) Keystone Press Agency (3, 4) Radio Times Hulton Picture Library
28 National Portrait Gallery, London
29 Imperial War Museum
30 (1) Popperfoto (2) Keystone Press Agency
31 (1) Imperial War Museum (2) Keystone Press Agency
32 (1) Search (2) Imperial War Museum
33 (1) Imperial War Museum (2) Search (3) Keystone Press Agency
34 Lockheed Aircraft Corporation
35 Flight International
37 Science Museum, London
38 RAF Museum, Hendon: A. C. Cooper
39 (1) Science Museum (2) Imperial War Museum: A. C. Cooper
40 (1, 2) Bundesarchiv (3) Imperial War Museum
41 (1) Associated Press (2) Popperfoto
42 Robert Hunt Library
43 Robert Hunt Library
44 Staatsbibliothek
45 (1) Bundesarchiv (2) Novosti Press Agency
46 (1) Robert Hunt Library (2) Staatsbibliothek

47 Staatsbibliothek
48 (1) Staatsbibliothek (2) Novosti Press Agency
49 Novosti Press Agency
50 U.S. Navy
51 Weidenfeld and Nicolson Archives
52 Robert Hunt Library
53 U.S. Navy
54 Imperial War Museum: A. C. Cooper
55 (1) Photo Research International (2) U.S. Navy
56 Imperial War Museum
57 Imperial War Museum
58 (1, 2, 3) Imperial War Museum
59 (1, 2) Imperial War Museum
60 U.S. Navy
61 Weidenfeld and Nicolson Archives
63 (1) U.S.I.S. (2) U.S. Navy
64 (1) Keystone Press Agency (2) Putnam and Co. Ltd. (from Japanese Aircraft of the Pacific War by R. J. Francillon) (3) U.S. Navy
65 (1) Imperial War Museum (2) U.S.I.S.
66 Imperial War Museum: A. C. Cooper
67 Imperial War Museum: A. C. Cooper
68 Imperial War Museum
69 (1, 2) Imperial War Museum
70 Imperial War Museum: A. C. Cooper
71 (1) Bildarchiv (2) Imperial War Museum: A. C. Cooper
72 Imperial War Museum
73 Imperial War Museum
74 Novosti Press Agency
75 Novosti Press Agency
76 (1, 2) Novosti Press Agency
77 (1) Novosti Press Agency (2) Imperial War Museum (3) Novosti Press Agency
78 (1, 2, 3) Novosti Press Agency
79 Novosti Press Agency
80 (1) Imperial War Museum (2) Keystone Press Agency
81 (1, 2) Camera Press (3) Imperial War Museum
82 Imperial War Museum: A. C. Cooper
83 Imperial War Museum
84/85 (1, 2) Imperial War Museum
87 (1) Imperial War Museum

(2) Popperfoto
88 (1) Popperfoto (2) Imperial War Museum
89 Imperial War Museum
90 (1) Radio Times Hulton Picture Library (2) Photo Research International
91 (1) Keystone Press Agency (2, 3) Imperial War Museum
92 Popperfoto
93 Ullstein
94 (1) Imperial War Museum: Eileen Tweedy (2) Staatsbibliothek (3) Imperial War Museum: Eileen Tweedy
95 Imperial War Museum: Eileen Tweedy
96 (1) Staatsbibliothek (2) Keystone Press Agency
97 Tretjakow-Galerie, Moscow: Staatsbibliothek
98 Deutsche Presse-Agentur
99 Popperfoto
101 (1) Staatsbibliothek (2) Imperial War Museum: Eileen Tweedy
102 Staatsbibliothek
103 Deutsche Presse-Agentur
104 U.S.I.S.
105 United Press International
106 (1) Culver Pictures (2) U.S. Air Force (3) Brown Brothers
107 Culver Pictures
108 Keystone Press Agency
109 (1) U.S.I.S. (2) Japan Information Center, London
110 (1) Associated Press (2) Radio Times Hulton Picture Library
111 (1) Camera Press (2) Radio Times Hulton Picture Library
112 John Frost World Wide Newspaper Collectors' Club
113 Associated Press
114 Radio Times Hulton Picture Library
115 (1, 2) Radio Times Hulton Picture Library
116 (1) The Times (2) A. C. Cooper
117 A. C. Cooper
118 (1, 2) Keystone Press Agency
119 (1) Library of the Communist Party of Great Britain, James Klugman Collection (2) Radio Times Hulton Picture Library
120 Imperial War Museum: A. C. Cooper
121 National Portrait Gallery,

Smithsonian Institution, Washington, D.C.
122 (1) Keystone Press Agency (2) U.S.I.S.
123 (1, 2) Camera Press
124 Victoria and Albert Museum, London: A. C. Cooper
125 (1) Popperfoto (2) Weidenfeld and Nicolson Archives
126 (1) Keystone Press Agency (2) Radio Times Hulton Picture Library
127 (1) Popperfoto (2) Radio Times Hulton Picture Library
128 Clare Winsten
129 Keystone Press Agency
131 Keystone Press Agency
132 (1) India High Commission, London (3) Keystone Press Agency
133 (1) India High Commission (2) Lord Mountbatten
134 Central Zionist Archives, Jerusalem
135 Jewish National Fund, London
136 (1) Barnaby's Picture Library (2) Israel Defense Department, Jerusalem
137 (1) Barnaby's Picture Library (2) Popperfoto
138 (1) Radio Times Hulton Picture Library (2) Weidenfeld and Nicolson Archives
139 (1, 2) Weidenfeld and Nicolson Archives
140 Department of Defense, U.S. Army
141 Keystone Press Agency
142 Camera Press/G. S. Cubitt
143 (1) Camera Press (2) Keystone Press Agency
144 (1) Keystone Press Agency (2) Deutsche Presse-Agentur
145 Keystone Press Agency
146 (1) Weidenfeld and Nicolson Archives (2) Camera Press
147 (1) Radio Times Hulton Picture Library (2) U.S.I.S.
148 William Sewell
150 (1) Snark International (2) Hsinhua News Agency
151 (1) Hsinhua News Agency (2) Magnum Photos
152 United Press International
153 (1) Hsinhua News Agency (2) United Press International

Managing Editor Adrian Brink
Assistant Editors Geoffrey Chesler, Francesca Ronan
Picture Editor Julia Brown
Consultant Designer Tim Higgins
Art Director Anthony Cohen

Index